Teaching Manual for

The Catholic Church: Our Mission in History

by Carl Koch, FSC

Saint Mary's Press
Christian Brothers Publications
Winona, Minnesota

The project team for this manual included Donnarae Lukitsch,
editor; Mary Duerson Kraemer, production editor; and Therese
Hoskins Gasper, illustrator.

The acknowledgments are continued on page 270.

Printed in the United States of America

Printing: 6 5 4 3 2

Year: 1994 93 92 91 90 89

ISBN 0-88489-162-3

Contents

Introduction to
The Catholic Church: Our Mission in History

Teaching church history in an interesting and relevant manner has to be one of the greatest challenges facing religious educators. Some religious education programs avoid church history entirely. Obviously, we think that this is a terrible mistake. To be ignorant of our history leaves students without a grounding in or sense of the rich traditions of the Church. Thus, their perspective on contemporary problems, events, and persons can be terribly narrow. The Church has been a world-shaping force; civilization as we know it has been profoundly influenced by the message of Jesus and the actions of the Church. Thus, in order to understand the present shape of our world, students must be familiar with church history. In addition, it is important that students become acquainted with the many great women and men who have provided models of lives lived according to Jesus' way. They model the good life to which we are all called, the life offered by Jesus and supported by the People of God.

The Catholic Church: Our Mission in History and this teaching manual have the following goals and objectives:

Goal 1: The student text and teaching manual should help students know and have an appreciation for the major developments of and the key persons in church history.
    Objectives: Therefore, the books will
      a) tell the story of the Church, providing analysis of the major events and insights into the key persons who have shaped the Church
      b) provide maps of especially important places in church history
      c) make the sweep of history more personal and specific by including vignettes about people
      d) be illustrated with pictures of important people and places and of the great achievements of church architecture
      e) provide group activities, questions for discussion, films, supplementary readings, interviews, surveys, research projects, ideas for guest speakers, case studies, role-playing situations and segments of plays to be acted, writing projects, and debates—all designed to deepen students' understanding of the history and theology of the Church
      f) list quiz questions that may be used to check students' knowledge

Goal 2: The student text and teaching manual should help students reflect on their participation in and commitment to the Church.
    Objective: Therefore, the books will
      a) provide students with opportunities—through the review questions, personal reflection exercises, prayer services, writing activities, and group discussions—to consider their stance toward membership in the Church

Goal 3: By using the information and activities in the student text and teaching manual, students should develop a deeper understanding of how God works in human history and in their own lives.
    Objectives: Thus, the books will
      a) help the students encounter people who have been touched by God and have responded in heroic, simple, inspiring, or sometimes dramatic ways

b) emphasize that despite all the seemingly terrible events in history, the Church, because it is the People of God, has continually listened to God and has been capable of reforming itself

c) ask the students to respond—through the prayer services and journal-writing activities especially—to ways in which God is present to them in their own stories

d) illustrate that the Church has always been, is, and will be Servant, Herald, People of God, Sacrament, and Institution

These goals and objectives will be met best if both the student text and the teaching manual are used together. Clearly, you will use your own techniques and materials in your own time and according to your personal teaching style. In fact, your own personhood is an integral part of religious education. However, these books should provide more materials than you will need to meet the goals and objectives of a church history course.

Background Sources for *The Catholic Church: Our Mission in History*

Any history text touches on hundreds of events, persons, problems, and concepts—especially a text trying to cover nearly two thousand years of history. People have spent lifetimes of scholarship in attempting to understand tiny fragments of the story of the Church. Despite the awesome scope of this subject, please do not be daunted by the prospect of teaching church history; you are not expected to know all there is to know, and our aim is not an exhaustive or definitive study. As pointed out in the introduction, our goals and objectives are student-oriented and practical, and the resources you will need are ready at hand in the student text and this manual.

The student text covers the major developments in church history, and this teaching manual should supply plenty of additional material. The emphasis in the student text is on people, concepts, and events that have shaped the Church, civilization, and ultimately us. Some absolutely essential dates are included, but little stress is placed on memorizing dates, names, and places. While this manual and the student text should be quite sufficient to teach a good church history course, the following bibliographies can guide any additional study for which you may have time before or while you teach the course.

General Resources on Church History

I have found the following books especially useful for gaining an overview of church history and ecclesiology. In addition, *The New Catholic Encyclopedia*, several volumes of the Life World Library series and of the Wonders of Man series from *Newsweek* are all very useful for both historical information and pictures.

Bokenkotter, Thomas. *A Concise History of the Catholic Church.* Garden City, NY: Doubleday and Co., 1977.

Catholic Almanac. Edited by Felician A. Foy. Huntington, IN: Our Sunday Visitor. There is a new edition each year.

Dowley, Tim, ed. *Eerdman's Handbook to the History of Christianity.* Grand Rapids, MI: Wm. B. Eerdmans, 1977.

Dulles, Avery. *Models of the Church.* New York: Doubleday and Co., 1978.

Gascoigne, Bamber. *The Christians.* New York: William Morrow, 1977.

Handy, Robert T. *A History of the Churches in the United States and Canada.* New York: Oxford University Press, 1971.

Littell, Franklin H. *Atlas History of Christianity.* New York: Macmillan Publishing Co., 1976.

Marty, Martin. *A Short History of Christianity.* New York: World Publishing Co., 1979.

Noll, Mark et al., eds. *Eerdman's Handbook to Christianity in America.* Grand Rapids, MI: Wm. B. Eerdmans, 1983.

Rice, Edward. *The Church: A Pictorial History.* New York: Farrar, Straus and Cudahy, 1961.

Further Reading

Here are some other very useful sources of information about church history. Many of the stories and portraits of persons that are found in the student text and this manual came from these works.

Ahlstrom, Sydney E. *A Religious History of the American People.* New Haven: Yale University Press, 1972.

Aubert, Roger et al. *The Church in a Secularized Society.* New York: Paulist Press, 1978.

The Augsburg Confession. Translated by Theodore G. Tappert. Philadelphia: Fortress Press, 1980.

Barry, Colman, ed. *Readings in Church History.* Vols. 1–3. Westminster, MD: Newman Press, 1965.

Baus, Karl. *Handbook of Church History: From the Apostolic Community to Constantine.* Vol. 1. New York: Herder and Herder, 1964.

Bausch, William J. *A New Look at the Sacraments.* Notre Dame, IN: Fides/Claretian, 1977.

Brophy, Don and Edythe Westenhaver. *The Story of Catholics in America.* New York: Paulist Press, 1978.

Bruce, F. F. *Paul: Apostle of the Heart Set Free.* Grand Rapids, MI: Wm. B. Eerdmans, 1977.

Casper, Henry. *History of the Catholic Church in Nebraska: The Church on the Northern Plains, 1838–1874.* Milwaukee: Catholic Life Publications, 1960.

Catherine of Siena. *The Dialogue.* Translated by Suzanne Noffke. New York: Paulist Press, 1980.

_____. *Saint Catherine of Siena, as Seen in Her Letters.* Translated by Vida D. Scudder. New York: E. P. Dutton, 1911.

Chadwick, Henry. *The Early Church.* New York: Penguin Books, 1967.

Chadwick, Owen. *The Reformation.* New York: Penguin Books, 1972.

Clark, Kenneth. *Civilisation.* New York: Harper and Row, 1969.

Conzelman, Hans. *History of Primitive Christianity.* Translated by John E. Steely. Nashville: Abingdon Press, 1973.

Daniel-Rops, Henri. *Cathedral and Crusade.* Translated by John Warrington. New York: E. P. Dutton, 1957.

_____. *The Catholic Reformation.* Translated by John Warrington. New York: E. P. Dutton, 1962.

_____. *The Church in the Dark Ages.* Translated by Audrey Butler. New York: E. P. Dutton, 1959.

_____. *Monsieur Vincent.* Translated by Julie Kernan. New York: Hawthorn Books, 1961.

_____. *The Protestant Reformation.* Translated by Audrey Butler. New York: E. P. Dutton, 1961.

Davies, Alan T., ed. *Anti-Semitism and the Foundations of Christianity.* New York: Paulist Press, 1979.

Day, Dorothy. *By Little and Little: The Selected Writings of Dorothy Day.* Edited by Robert Ellsbert. New York: Alfred A. Knopf, 1983.

De La Bedoyere, Michael. *The Greatest Catherine.* Milwaukee: Bruce Publishing Co., 1947.

Delaney, John J. *Dictionary of Saints.* New York: Doubleday and Co., 1980.

_____. *Saints for All Seasons.* New York: Doubleday and Co., 1978.

Dirvin, Joseph I. *Mrs. Seton.* New York: Farrar, Straus and Giroux, 1975.

Doig, Desmond. *Mother Teresa.* New York: Harper and Row, 1976.

Dussel, Enrique. *A History of the Church in Latin America.* Grand Rapids, MI: Wm. B. Eerdmans, 1981.

Ellis, John Tracy. *American Catholicism.* Chicago: University of Chicago Press, 1955.

Ellis, John Tracy, ed. *Documents of American Catholic History.* Milwaukee: Bruce Publishing Co., 1956.

Erasmus. *The Colloquies of Erasmus.* Translated by Craig R. Thompson. Chicago: University of Chicago Press, 1965.

Franklin, Alexander. *Seven Miracle Plays.* London: Oxford University Press, 1963.

Ganshof, F. L. *Feudalism.* New York: Harper and Brothers, 1961.

Graef, Hilda C. *The Scholar and the Cross: The Life and Work of Edith Stein.* Westminster, MD: Newman Press, 1955.

Halecki, Oscar. *The Millennium of Europe.* Notre Dame, IN: University of Notre Dame Press, 1963.

Hamman, A., ed. *Early Christian Prayers.* Translated by Walter Mitchell. Chicago: Henry Regnery Co., 1961.

Hennesey, James. *American Catholics.* New York: Oxford University Press, 1981.

Hilsdale, Paul. *Prayers from Saint Paul.* New York: Sheed and Ward, 1964.

Hughes, Philip. *A History of the Church.* New York: Sheed and Ward, 1949.

Johnson, Paul. *A History of Christianity.* New York: Atheneum, 1977.

McGinley, Phyllis. *Saint-Watching.* New York: Viking Press, 1968.

McSorley, Joseph. *Outline History of the Church by Centuries.* Saint Louis: B. Herder Book Co., 1954.

Miller, William D. *A Harsh and Dreadful Love: Dorothy Day and the Catholic Worker Movement.* New York: Liveright, 1973.

Muggeridge, Malcolm. *Something Beautiful for God: Mother Teresa of Calcutta.* New York: Harper and Row, 1971.

Neill, Stephen. *A History of the Christian Missions.* New York: Penguin Books, 1964.

Nevins, Albert S. *Our American Catholic Heritage.* Huntington, IN: Our Sunday Visitor, 1972.

Ruether, Rosemary. *Faith and Fratricide.* New York: Seabury Press, 1974.

Sanders, E. P. *Paul and Palestinian Judaism.* Philadelphia: Fortress Press, 1977.

Sandmel, Samuel. *Judaism and Christian Beginnings.* New York: Oxford University Press, 1978.

Shannon, James P. *Catholic Colonization on the Western Frontier.* New Haven: Yale University Press, 1957.

Southern, R. W. *Western Society and the Church in the Middle Ages.* New York: Penguin Books, 1970.

Teresia de Spiritu Sancto. *Edith Stein.* Translated by Cecily Hastings and Donald Nicholl. New York: Sheed and Ward, 1952.

Walsh, Michael. *An Illustrated History of the Popes.* New York: Saint Martin's Press, 1980.

Ward, Maisie. *Saints Who Made History: The First Five Centuries.* New York: Sheed and Ward, 1959.

Pedagogical Background: The Learning Process in *The Catholic Church: Our Mission in History*

> . . . the human spirit must be cultivated in such a way that there results a growth in its ability to wonder, to understand, to contemplate, to make personal judgments, and to develop a religious, moral, and social sense. (Vatican Council II, *Pastoral Constitution on the Church in the Modern World,* no. 59)

As the above quotation clearly states, education involves growth. It is a process, a movement from one "place" to another. Educational growth typically involves four elements: a starting point, a significant experience, reflection, and assimilation. The learning process followed in *The Catholic Church* parallels the learning process employed in other texts in the Saint Mary's Press high school series, and it is based on Richard Reichert's *A Learning Process for Religious Education* (Dayton, OH: Pflaum Publishing Co., 1975). Most experts in the catechetical field suggest the same or a similar process.

The Starting Point

The *starting point* in any learning process is basically the sum total of all that one has learned in the past. In that sense, the starting point is our present value system, our conscious behavior patterns, the principles we use in making a decision. A teacher needs to consider the backgrounds, values, concerns, and other life experiences of students. The starting point refers to all that makes up a student at the present time. It is as if a student came to class proclaiming, "This is what I am." To complicate matters, each student has a different starting point. This means that flexibility and adaptability are necessary during the entire learning processes.

There are numerous questions about the starting points of students to consider in relation to *The Catholic Church*. These include concerns such as the following:
- physical and psychological maturity
- levels of faith development
- knowledge about religion, history, and related subjects
- attitudes toward religion
- previous significant experiences
- personal concerns and interests
- relationships in and outside of the classroom

All movement has a starting point. The teacher must begin as much as possible where the students are and must act as a "midwife," helping students to give birth to new personal perspectives. For each topic covered, this course offers various ways of drawing out from the students a sense of their own starting points. It builds on these points in order to nudge the students along in their learning processes.

The Significant Experience

A significant experience is an internal or external event that leads to movement beyond the starting point. The event is called significant because it results in a *meaningful* change in the person. It is an experience in that it ultimately involves the *whole*

10

person—emotions, values, behavior, as well as intellectual awareness. Examples of the type of significant experiences related to this course include the following:

- receiving significant new information
- challenging previously held attitudes
- trying on new behaviors
- examining a fresh perspective on oneself and one's world
- experiencing prayer or a deepening sense of prayer
- questioning personal values
- developing new relationships; seeing old relationships in a new light
- resolving long-held conflicts
- discovering "bridges" where "walls" had existed

The Catholic Church includes readings and activities that offer students a variety of opportunities for significant experiences. Of course, given the variable starting points of individual students, not every lesson will provide significant experiences for each student. Also, the teacher will need to make choices concerning specific activities and the time allotment for each lesson, again based on the students' starting points.

Reflection

When students ask the question, "What does this experience mean?" they are engaging in the reflection stage of the learning process. It involves prayer or quiet individual thinking—sorting things out in writing or in thoughtful discussion with others. Reflection can be described as a slowing down after the speeding up associated with a significant experience. It is not inaction or passivity but "creative quietude." Just as journeying down a road for a significant distance causes a person's view of the surroundings to change, so a significant experience in one area causes a change in perspective in all areas of a person's life. Reflection activities allow students an opportunity to think through the growth that has occurred.

Reflection activities associated with this course include the following:

- journal keeping
- various writing assignments
- creative art activities
- quiet reflection
- prayer activities

Assimilation

If reflection can be described as a question, then assimilation is an affirmation. It is the students' saying yes to the learning process that has moved them from their original starting points.

Education seeks to change a person. Assimilation refers to the change integrated into the life of the students. It is changed perspectives, values, and attitudes. And if these changes are truly integrated into the students' lives, then changed behavior also occurs: real values are lived values.

Assimilation related to this course includes changes similar to the following:

- a changed perspective on certain elements of religion
- a more developed appreciation of one's personal story, of the Christian story, and of the points of connection between the two
- behavioral changes toward others
- an increased sense of participation in one's religion
- making a decision about the importance of God in one's life and acting on that decision
- greater knowledge and appreciation of other people, especially the other students who share in the learning process

A Note on the Learning Process

The four steps of this process describe learning as it often occurs naturally. The purpose of dividing the unified process into four separate parts is to assist the teacher in making directed, conscious, and purposeful contributions to the students' learning. As you plan your lessons for this course and consider the suggestions offered in this manual, it is beneficial to refer back to the four elements of the learning process.

During your lesson planning, ask yourself, Does this lesson reflect consideration of each of the four elements of the learning process? An exciting, meaningful activity can provide a significant experience; but unless there is also an opportunity for reflection, it may not result in the growth described as assimilation. Likewise, if a number of students harbor strong negative feelings about a topic, a well-planned presentation on the subject will be ineffective unless their starting point is addressed.

Since the starting points of your students differ from those of other groups of students, you will need to select activities appropriate for your particular situation. Also, consider your own starting point. One teacher may be more comfortable with quiet reflection, silent prayer, and journal keeping, while another is more at home with lively discussion, movement, and activity. Be sensitive to your own starting point but also be open to the "significant experience" of trying new approaches.

One final but key point to remember about the learning process for this course is that it is a *shared* process. No one is a Christian apart from community; Christian education occurs in a community context. Awareness of other starting points in itself can be a significant experience for students. Experiencing community, sharing reflection, deciding upon group goals, and performing group tasks—all these aspects enhance and reinforce the learning process. They also more clearly distinguish learning as the activity it is meant to be—education of the Christian community.

What the Teacher Offers

What role does the teacher play in aiding the adolescent's faith journey in relation to this course? Primarily, the teacher should assist and direct the journey of the students, and also should join in the journey. The student text and this teaching manual provide numerous suggestions to help the teacher in assisting the students' learning process. However, for personal faith development to occur, the teacher's joining in the process is all-important.

An atmosphere of mutual learning and journeying reflects the spirit of the course. The teacher helps create such an atmosphere by communicating two things to students: (1) that it is a good thing for students to look inquiringly and wonderingly on their world and their religion and (2) that the teacher is also on a faith journey—inquiring, wondering, and seeking new meaning. In this way the activity of personal reflection is encouraged and the risk of responding in faith to God's presence is supported. The atmosphere is one of trust that our God is a living God who can be found in the midst of our world. It is the atmosphere appropriate for the Christian community as well as for Christian education.

One writer describes the role of the teacher in this way: "The role of the catechist is to journey with students and to enable them to keep growing in their relationship with the Lord. Their role is not to 'sell' adolescents the faith, but rather to share, listen, challenge, and affirm" (Michael Carotta, "We're All on the Journey," *Religion Teacher's Journal,* October 1983, p. 29). *Sharing the Light of Faith: National Catechetical Directory* affirms this spirit of mutual journeying when it states: "Catechists not only instruct young adults but learn from them; they will be heard by young adults only if they listen to them" (no. 227).

The teacher who offers new information on church history and who provides an atmosphere where significant experiences, personal reflection, and reintegration can occur sets in motion the spirit of community itself. And when the learning leads to action, then the students will more readily recognize the presence of God in their lives and will accept that their own lives are sacred as well.

Lesson and Session Planning for *The Catholic Church: Our Mission in History*

Let's begin by making a distinction between a *lesson* plan and a *session* plan. (*Note:* Our use of these terms may well differ from your common usage of them. Please read carefully and reflect on the implications involved.) In the sense that we are using the term here, **a *lesson* plan embraces the *full* scope of the learning process.** It has a goal that is based on knowledge of the students' starting point. It provides a significant experience, activities to facilitate reflection, and opportunities for assimilation. As such, a lesson plan can be defined as all those activities designed by the teacher to reach a particular learning goal. On the other hand, **a *session* plan is simply a segment of a lesson plan;** it has a subgoal related to the overall goal of the lesson. For example, a lesson plan may call for one session to provide a significant experience, several more to facilitate reflection, and an additional session to facilitate assimilation.

A lesson plan, therefore, provides an overview that dictates what is to be accomplished in each session. As such, *a lesson plan implies no fixed amount of time; its length is determined by the goal of the lesson.* A session, on the other hand, usually is defined as a prescribed period, say fifty minutes, often determined by circumstances, established schedules, and convenience.

This distinction between lesson plan and session plan is important to religious education. Too often we think only in terms of sessions, not lessons. If the curriculum suggests that we cover twenty topics and we have forty sessions available to us, our answer is two sessions on each topic. That is session planning. Unfortunately, it ignores the learning process. Not all topics are of equal value, and some will require more time to learn than others. Session planning ensures only that we will cover the material, not that any learning is going to take place.

Given the same twenty topics and the same forty available sessions, we would operate much differently using the lesson plan approach. For example, there would be no attempt to think in terms of twenty goals. Rather, four or five goals might be identified as suggested by the students' starting point. Then a plan would be developed to reach each of these goals, using as many sessions for each goal as the nature of the goal warrants. What happens to the twenty topics? They would be dealt with in relation to the goals. One topic might be covered in the process of providing a significant experience. Others could be introduced in the process of reflection. And still other topics might be viewed in terms of possible opportunities for assimilation.

The characteristics, then, of this comprehensive lesson planning are that it is built around goals, not topics, and that it embraces all phases of the learning process sequentially rather than in terms of a fixed number of unrelated sessions.

In this manual, the following information will be provided for each chapter of the student text:

1) **Major concepts** from the chapter, presented in the order in which they appear in the student text
2) **Review questions** from the student text with answers
3) **Personal reflection exercises** from the student text, which are provided in the gray-screened boxes
4) **Other questions and activities** for each major concept
5) **Student handouts,** which are included at the end of the chapter in which their use is described

The Catholic Church: Our Mission in History can be completed in an eighteen-week semester. Eliminating two weeks for snow days, pep rallies, and other events leaves eighty class periods. At the rate of four pages per day, you can complete the student text. Not covering the final chapters would be very unfortunate, but this too often seems to take place in history courses. On pages 27–28 of this manual, I have included a sample outline of a semester course; it may aid your planning.

General Principles for *Lesson* Planning

The following strategy is recommended for planning *lessons,* that is, for determining *in a general way* the strategy you will follow to determine and then achieve your lesson goals—namely, the effective teaching of each major concept.

1) **Read the entire chapter in the student text,** noting specific themes or topics that in your opinion will require special emphasis, topics that may require only brief treatment, and so on.

2) Turn to the section of the teaching manual dealing with that chapter. **Read the major concepts.** For each major concept, **formulate a specific *lesson goal,*** that is, a statement of what you hope to achieve in terms of that concept given your students' starting point. These goals should be written down.

3) **Make an *initial assessment* of the number of *sessions*** (i.e., class periods) you will need to achieve your stated lesson goal. This is your first step toward determining a specific calendar for your course. (*Note:* You will probably have to adjust this schedule periodically, based on the students' response to each class. If your students seem to readily grasp the concept, you simply move ahead; if they take longer than expected to comprehend the concept, you will have to spend more time before moving on to the next concept. To do otherwise would be to ignore the learning process.)

4) **Identify the *purposes* of each session** according to the elements of the learning process. How many sessions or how much time in any given session will be required for significant experiences (direct input, group exercises, films, and so on), how much time for reflection (discussion, prayer), and how much time should be spent on facilitating assimilation?

5) Finally, **read through the remaining material in the teaching manual for the chapter**—review questions, personal reflection exercises, class activities, student handouts, and so on—noting those activities that seem particularly appealing to you.

You are now ready for *session planning.*

General Principles for *Session* Planning

It is suggested that you use a spiral-bound notebook for planning your sessions. This will help organize your initial planning and will also serve as a record of your teaching experience to help you in the future.

The following procedure is recommended for your session planning, that is, for determining your step-by-step, class-by-class strategy for teaching each major concept.

1) **Write down the specific concept and *lesson goal*** that you are pursuing, along with the number of sessions you have initially committed to that concept. This will be based almost entirely on your personal assessment of your students' starting point.

2) In your lesson planning you have already determined the number of sessions or amount of time in any one session that you will set aside for each phase of the learning process. In your *session* planning, you are going to **elaborate on that initial plan**, make concrete decisions on activities, means of reflection, and so on. In colloquial terms, session planning means getting down to basics, to the "nitty-gritty."

You will want to **determine a specific *attitudinal or behavioral objective* for each session.** Remember, in designing sessions you are into very practical and immediate planning, and your statement of objectives should reflect this. Your objective in terms of the attitudes or behavior you want to achieve in any one session should *be one that can be reasonably attained.* To use an exaggerated example, if your lesson goal is "to discuss and increase understanding of the need for personal commitment in living Christian faith," your session objective should not be "that all the students make a public commitment to Jesus." Rather, it might be "that the students can identify three examples of people in their community who have expressed their commitments to Jesus in their daily lives."

3) **Note all of the *preliminary activities*** that you will most likely have to accomplish at the beginning of any session: attendance check, prayer, review of previous session, reports, seating arrangements, announcements, return of assignments, and so on.

4) **Note the discussion questions, class activities, personal reflection exercises, and student handouts that you want to include as all or part of the significant experience for that session.** If these activities are taken directly from the teaching manual, you may only need to note a title for the activity and the page number from the manual on which it can be found. If you alter the activity in some way or create one of your own, you should note this clearly. You will want to retain that information for future use.

5) **Write down the *means of reflection*** that you want to use. At times this will be clearly delineated in the manual, with specific questions for discussion. You may prefer other kinds of reflection: journal keeping, quizzes, essays, and so on.

6) **List the specific and immediate things that you will have to do in order to prepare for each session.** Such a list might include the following preparations: Order the film from the diocesan office; duplicate student handouts; arrange for speakers. You may want to set a particular date by which to accomplish these specific tasks in order to further facilitate planning.

7) Finally, **leave room in your notebook for *evaluation*** after the session is completed. (See "A Special Note on Evaluation" below.)

Upon first reading, this may seem like a rather complex approach to lesson and session planning. But a bit of practice with this method will disprove that first impression. This kind of planning ensures more effective teaching since it reflects the principles of the learning process. It also eliminates that sense of panic and urgency that many teachers experience when they are faced each week with the question, What am I going to do for the next class? The *lesson* plan indicates generally what you want to do and why. The *session* plan provides for immediate preparation and attention to the details not included in the lesson plan. The whole experience of teaching, therefore, becomes more purposeful, calm, intentional. A teacher will have the feeling that he or she is accomplishing objectives insofar as the lesson plan unfolds in the way in which he or she anticipated.

A Special Note on Evaluation

This approach to lesson and session planning greatly facilitates evaluation. Each session has a certain aspect of the learning process that it should fulfill. For example, if a planned significant experience was not successful, you will know it. Rather than go on to the next planned session, you can attempt first to provide another experience. Or if a particular method of reflection has turned students off and you feel they have not achieved the kind of insight you had hoped, you can try again before going on to the next step. Evaluation is not something that takes place only at the end of each complete lesson. If a single session failed, it needs to be repeated in a new format. If it was successful, you can move with confidence to the next activity.

It was mentioned that you should leave space in your notebook for evaluation at the end of each session. It is particularly important to evaluate *successful* sessions. Why especially the successful sessions? Because in evaluating your teaching, it is important not to linger unnecessarily over sessions that did not work out for you. Especially for inexperienced teachers, there is a tendency to be *overly critical of failures* and *uncritical of successful sessions.*

So when a session works well for you, write it up as thoroughly as possible, analyzing its strengths. Was it successful because of your planning? Or was its success accidental? Why? Did the session pivot on certain personalities in the group? Why? How might you otherwise plan the session to assure a successful outcome? Did the session actually meet the objectives you set? How could you improve on the focus of the session?

Of course, if you see clearly how an unsuccessful session might be improved, then do a similar write-up. Each time you teach the course, rewrite this evaluation to create a more effective lesson plan. Remember that developing a successful course takes time and plenty of failures; there is no other way to fashion an effective course.

On the following page you will find a summary table of the learning process and its effect on lesson planning. Refer to the table often as a reminder of this planning procedure. Soon it will become almost second nature to you.

A Model for Effective Lesson Planning

Real learning—as distinct from the simple accumulation of knowledge—seems to take place in a consistent pattern:

A. The potential learner's **starting point** is understood, respected, and taken into account in planning.

B. **Significant experiences** are provided—information or experiences that allow the potential learner to question, reflect upon, evaluate, or become uncomfortable with his or her starting point.

C. Opportunities are provided for **reflection**, for evaluating the import and effects of the new information; here the teacher can be properly defined as a "facilitator of reflection."

D. The new information is assimilated into one's life. **Assimilation** is the responsibility of the learner; at this level the teacher becomes one who supports, encourages, challenges.

The following table shows the effects of this learning process on lesson plan development. For a particular topic or point of information to be effectively shared, that is, truly learned by the student, the effective teacher will do the following:

A.	B.	C.	D.
Attempt to understand and remain continually conscious of the students' **starting point** by	Determine the most **significant experiences** based on the topic, audience, available time, and so on. Possibilities include	Provide opportunities for **reflection** on information. Possibilities include. . . .	Facilitate **assimilation** to whatever degree possible by . . . .
1) understanding basic patterns of psychological development	1) the current life experiences of the students	1) discussion: a) teacher-student b) student-student	1) challenging students to accept responsibility
2) studying the sociocultural environment(s)	2) effective speakers	2) questionnaires and reflectionnaires	2) encouraging, supporting, affirming
3) learning about family and immediate social influences (e.g., peer group, friends)	3) simulation games	3) prayer services	3) following up on students' progress through a) letters b) phone calls c) other personal contact
4) ideally, meeting and developing a personal relationship with each student	4) group dynamics	4) opportunities for private prayer	4) encouraging further study, providing book lists, and so on
	5) field trips	5) journal keeping	5) being available if needed for support
	6) prayer experiences	6) carefully designed quizzes and tests	
	7) case studies	7) interviews	
	8) relevant reading	8) essays, term papers, reports	
	9) films, music, media		
	10) the teacher, who can be a significant experience in himself or herself!		

Suggestions for Effective Teaching of
The Catholic Church: Our Mission in History

If the use of the techniques found in this manual is to be beneficial and effective, it is essential that you develop a real sense for employing them. A sensitivity to detail, a clear perception of intent, an awareness of the need for good timing, and so on, are all necessary elements in the effective use of group exercises. It is also necessary that you remain in touch with the basic techniques for leading effective discussions. Without effective discussion, many group dynamics can degenerate into party games with no purpose or benefit. But with good discussion they can become enjoyable activities that lead to a deepening awareness of a particular topic.

Most teachers will already have a good background in these pedagogical techniques. What is offered here are notes on how the activities suggested in this manual (such as map exercises, reports, interviews, journal keeping, dramatic readings, guest speakers, and so on) can be integrated to enhance the course. In addition, listed below are simple reminders of the more general basics of leading group exercises and discussions. Even the experienced teacher will occasionally forget "the basics," and it is often such simple oversights that make the difference between success and failure in the classroom.

General Principles Regarding Sessions

1) After the students have read a section of the student text, it is important to spend some time doing two things:

a) **Be sure that the students understood the student text.** This can be done simply by asking if anyone has questions about what the author was explaining, whether any words or definitions were not clear, and so on. Obviously, for meaningful discussion to take place, the basic content of the student text must be grasped. For that reason, another and perhaps more effective approach is to begin the session by asking some key questions that would reflect a basic grasp of the main points of the section. Review questions of this kind are found at the end of each chapter in the student text, and suggested answers are provided in the respective chapters of this teaching manual. (Some answers to review questions contain bracketed additional information that is not found in the students' assigned reading. This information is labeled *Teacher's note*.) In situations where a grade is involved, a quiz can provide an incentive both to read and to understand the material. While this practice does not reflect the pedagogical ideal of self-motivation, it may be a prudent measure to encourage the students to read and fully grasp the material.

b) **Spend time initially to determine in what areas and to what extent students disagree with the student text. Remember that voicing such disagreement should not only be allowed but encouraged.** As the teacher you must discover where the problems lie and which topics will need greater attention and discussion. Once the students are convinced such disagreement is allowed, they will usually express it freely.

2) **Discussion should play a greater role in each session than dynamics or experience-related approaches.** Given the maturity of this age-group, students have enough capacity to reflect and to reason to be able to carry on meaningful discussion of the topics presented.

3) Discussion between peers plays a particularly important role. Studies show that this peer interaction, especially when one group disagrees with another, does more to alter or to shape a student's views than similar interaction with authority figures like parents or teachers. For that reason it is a good idea to encourage debate whenever significant differences of opinion are involved. The teacher can both guide and participate but should never dominate such debates.

4) It is always good to keep the focus on the real world of the students and on the life situations they actually face. Theorizing on issues that students seldom if ever face will cause the students to lose interest quickly. However, it is important to distinguish between theorizing on the issues and learning the facts about the issues. As the facts are being studied, most students come to discover how we are all part of these issues—a major discovery that can motivate them to want to learn more and to see how they can be part of a solution.

5) On sensitive issues, no student should be forced to speak if he or she prefers not to do so. The teacher should not hesitate to invite and encourage students to probe more deeply; however, it should be understood that students can simply say they prefer not to comment at this time.

6) Some issues will be raised in discussion that are not dealt with in the student text. One approach to these issues would be to treat each of them as it comes up or as it is raised by a student. This can be unwieldy, however.

A more orderly approach (and often more effective to any discussion of these topics) might be to recognize them when they are raised and then design a later session to deal with them. This can allow you and the students to do some thinking and preparation for discussing the issues involved. It is important, however, that issues raised by the students be dealt with properly. The decision to deal with such issues as they come up or to plan them into the course at a later time should be at the teacher's discretion.

7) On the other hand, **discussion of an issue should not be put off if the majority of the students show a keen interest and if it has relevance to the kinds of situations they face.** Usually in this case, until the topic is discussed, students will show little interest in whatever else is pursued. If a real concern is expressed by only one or two students you can perhaps arrange to discuss it with them privately outside of class.

8) Various passages from the Scriptures are either referred to or paraphrased in the student text. Most can be considered well-known passages, but it is not safe to presume that students know them all. It is usually a good idea to ask a student to retell the episode mentioned or to have a student read the passage out loud for the class.

9) Begin each session with time for review and reports. Include prayer in each session. Conclude each session with a summary, assignments, and dismissal.

10) Finally, it is good to keep in mind that the course should be viewed as one more step toward mature faith. As teacher, all you can hope to do is to explain how the story of our Church relates to the life of the Church. If you can do that, you are successful. The rest is up to God and to the individual.

Effective Use of Group Exercises

1) Make sure you understand thoroughly the purpose of each exercise. Any exercise could be used to bring out any number of points; be sure you know precisely where you want to go with the experience.

2) Toward that end, **experience the exercise yourself before conducting it for others.** At times this may be difficult, as in the case of those exercises that demand a group of some size. However, one can still experience it with some imagination and effort. In cases where a duplicated student handout will be used, go through each part thoroughly, reacting not only as an individual but as you feel the students themselves will react.

3) **Have all materials required for the exercise available and ready for use.** Don't let a broken pencil or some other minor problem ruin the entire experience.

4) **Try to set the appropriate mood for the group** *before* **introducing the dynamic.** For example, if your first exercise is going to be loose and intentionally humorous, set the proper tone with a joke or a more casual welcome. If silence during the exercise is critical, begin setting a quiet tone even before conducting the exercise.

5) **Explain the directions thoroughly and then** *re-explain* **them.** Students can be staring right at you, apparently attentive, and be miles away in their thoughts. When you get the feeling that they are distanced from you, say something like "Does everyone know just what I mean? Dave, do you know? How about you, Beth?" More exercises are wasted because of this lack of real direction and understanding than for any other reason.

6) However, **do not get trapped by** *over*-**explaining.** Too many details can so influence a group's response that nothing will be gained. For example, you may be conducting an exercise on prejudice. If you tell the group what you are doing, they will struggle like mad to prove that they are *not* prejudiced, and the entire exercise will be lost.

7) **Always stress the need for cooperation.** Emphasize that nothing will be gained, nor will the students have any fun, if they fail to go along with the exercise. Normally students will become progressively more cooperative during the course as they realize how enjoyable it can be if they cooperate. At the beginning of the course, however, you might have to emphasize this.

8) **When the purpose of the exercise is to create certain feelings in the group,** *time* **the exercise in such a way that these feelings are heightened.** The key is to do the exercise yourself, when possible, to get a "feel" for this.

9) **Go** *immediately* **into discussion at the close of the exercise.** If you wait too long or allow other conversations to start, you might lose the attention of the group.

10) Finally, **be patient with yourself.** There is a real need to practice "getting a feel" for groups of students, "discerning the spirit" of a group, reading moods. This same kind of practice holds true also for conducting group exercises. You will learn a great deal from your first experience with them; by the time you have conducted a group exercise several times, you will have mastered it, adjusting details to fit your personality, the environment in the room, and so on. Each time you will be more relaxed, you will enjoy the exercise more, and your students will continually gain more from the experience.

Leading Discussions

Discussion as a learning technique may refer to a teacher-centered discussion involving an entire class or to the placement of students in small groups ranging in number from pairs to eights. Naturally, guidelines for effective discussion vary depending on the size of the group.

In this manual, "large-group discussion" refers to the teacher-centered situation involving the entire class, whereas "small-group discussion" refers to groupings of four to eight students unless otherwise specified.

The following are general guidelines applicable to both large- and small-group discussion.

1) **Do not expect discussion to do what it cannot do or is not intended to do.** Discussion must be seen as one part of a much larger learning experience or process.

2) **Discussion is primarily a *reaction to* some other stimulus.** There must be something real and tangible to discuss. This course is designed in such a way that discussions are normally introduced by a group exercise, assigned reading, student handout, or other input. The discussion will only be as effective as the activity that motivates it.

3) **Discussion only works if the group is interested in, excited and knowledgeable about what is to be discussed.** You cannot expect sophomores, for example, to have a good discussion on the commitment required in marriage. Their level of knowledge and experience might only allow a discussion on relating with the opposite sex.

4) **Specific questions are more effective in stimulating discussion than vague ones.** For example, rather than asking, "What do you think of the film we just viewed?" the teacher could say, "What do you think are the three most important points made by this film?"

5) **Discussions should have a definite time limit.** Be stingy—let the students ask for more time if necessary.

6) **Let each student have a chance to talk.** But don't put undue pressure on those who are shy or introspective; you will only make them more reluctant if you do.

7) **Do not mistake silence for disinterest.** At times students will have nothing to say simply because they are thinking through the question at hand. Though silence can be frustrating and can cause tension, it is often just this tension that will spark a response later.

8) **If the students seem particularly mature or demonstrate a real attitude of cooperation, it is often helpful to let them choose their own discussion groups.** In this way initial tensions are dispelled and the groups can get right into the matter at hand. If the class is not cooperative, students might have to be designated for each group, although discussion almost by definition will not work well when such an attitude persists. Some other form of sharing (e.g., a project to work on) might be necessary in such situations.

9) **Each group should have a recorder** (other than the teacher) appointed to take notes and to report to the larger group.

10) **The teacher participates *directly* only at the end of the discussion.** The teacher's role until that time is to stimulate interest, to ask questions, and to request clarification. At the end, the teacher's own ideas and attitudes can be offered by way of summary. If the teacher gives direct input too readily, he or she can become the focus of the discussion, someone to whom the students are always looking for information.

11) **Always close discussions with a summary** of points raised in order to highlight the main issues discussed.

Small-Group Discussion

In addition to the general guidelines for discussion listed above, small groups require other directives. Consider the number involved. Certain activities work best in dyads (pairs). At times triads (threes) are a more appropriate number. Generally speaking, a group larger than eight becomes unwieldy. Group tasks are different from group discussions. A *group task* refers to a specific goal that a small group is to achieve. *Group discussion* is more open-ended. For instance, a group task is "Create a rule to guide a community of religious. List rules governing work, prayer life, study, eating, and so on." A group discussion is "In your group, discuss the pros and cons of allowing priests to marry. After ten minutes, a recorder should report the results to the class."

With a group task, there is a specific project that a teacher expects to result from the time spent in the small group. Completing a worksheet, creating an art project, or doing some other activity often accompanies a group task. The structure of a group task makes the purpose of being in a small group clearer to students.

An open-ended discussion in a small group can be very beneficial to students, especially to those mature enough and interested enough to stay on a topic. Even here, however, establishing a structure and presenting a clear purpose help the experience to be successful. Appointing one student to be a recorder offers a structure that makes it clear that an end product is expected. In addition, stating a time limit provides structure, and making the topic of discussion clear and precise helps. Often group discussion can be combined with a specific group task.

Map Exercises

Many map exercises are suggested in this manual. My observation is that very few students have a good grasp of geography. But, to really understand the implications of many events in history, a grasp of the geography is important. Some maps are included in the student text, but obviously these are not sufficient to cover all the places mentioned. I recommend that you hang a large wall map in the front of the room as a permanent feature. Each chapter's activities in this manual will point out times when reference to this map will be helpful. With frequent references to cities, countries, and other geographical information, your students will learn not only church history but also more about the world in which they live.

If you do not have a good wall map and wish to purchase one, one source is Denoyer-Geppert, 5215 North Ravenswood Avenue, Chicago, IL 60640; phone 800-621-1014. They have a useful, fold-up wall map of the world.

Additional Readings and Stories

For some of the chapters, additional readings are included in this manual in the form of student handouts. Often these readings will simply flesh out some of the ideas in the chapter. You might wish to duplicate just enough copies for your largest class and then use the same copies for all your classes. Since most of these additional stories are short, they could be read in class, collected at the end of the class period after reading and discussion, and reused in the next class. The teaching manual will generally include questions for discussion and/or activities to be used with these additional readings. Clearly, as with all the extra ideas, you must select only the material you need and have time for.

Role-Playing Activities and Short Cuttings from Plays

In some chapters of this manual, short sections from plays are included; in other units, I have taken prose passages and put them into play form. In almost all instances, these playlets can add an interesting dimension to your class presentation—if they are done rather well.

When you decide to have your students produce one of the plays, assign parts to the players, give directions, and set a production date well in advance—even if they simply read their parts as in a readers' theater. Especially for the first few plays, make sure you choose adept speakers for the roles. Instruct them about the background of the play, and encourage the actors to imagine themselves in the assigned roles. (I suggest letting the students use the scripts—doing an interpretative reading—rather than having them memorize the script; this cuts down preparation time and gives them something to do with their hands.) If time permits, have the students read their parts in a practice session with you. The timing of the delivery of their lines is very important; the actors should keep the dialogue snappy so that time does not drag.

Before the actual production in class, be sure to explain the background of the play (or have a student do this). Remind your students that the actors are taking these roles in order to help the class understand a significant event or concept in church history. After the performance, discuss the play—usually there are discussion questions included in this manual.

Research Projects and Class Reports

For almost every major concept in the manual there are research topics listed. Since there are so many subjects, you will have to be judicious about the ones you assign. Select ones that you think will interest your students and for which materials are readily available. Many of the topics can be researched in the *Catholic Almanac* or the *New Catholic Encyclopedia* or a general encyclopedia. For other topics, students may have to dig more deeply.

Most importantly, assign these research projects and the dates of reports well ahead of time. This means that *before* actually covering a unit, you will have to know the topics related to it. At the beginning of the semester you might want to go through the entire teaching manual and mark research projects that you want students to do. Then make out a tentative schedule for the presentation of reports, maybe three or four each week. This way, each student might have to do two or, at most, three reports for the semester.

The reports should be written out in essay format. However, besides being turned in to you, the reports should be delivered orally to the class. The reports should be no more than two or three minutes long. Remind the students that they are to deliver the reports like regular speeches, keeping in mind principles of good public speaking, like speaking loud enough, knowing the material so well that they do not stumble over parts of it, enunciating carefully, maintaining eye contact with the class, and so on. Reports not only will add information to your class, but also will provide good opportunities for public speaking.

Interviews

Scattered throughout the activities in this manual there are exercises in which the students are asked to interview other people. Interviews are included to broaden the students' perspectives about various issues. Most frequently, students are assigned to interview someone older—parents, relatives, teachers, and so on. Again, planning is required in order to use interviews well because students will need time to set up an appointment, formulate questions, and so on. As was the case with research reports, you may want to select only some students to do the interviews for a chapter. For example, the following combination of individual assignments might be made for one chapter: eight students will do interviews, four students will give reports, four students will present a play, and the rest of the class will have a week off (the following week the rest of the class will have to give reports, present plays, or tell about interviews). If every class member does one or two interviews in a semester, they will have learned a lot.

Here are some guidelines about which you may wish to tell your students as they prepare for interviews:

a) Before anything else, make sure you know the main questions for which you want answers. Write down all the questions you wish to ask, and then number the questions from most important to least important. In this way, if you run out of time, you will at least have gotten some of the most important information about the topic.

b) Set up a mutually agreeable time to interview the person. Remember that the interviewee is doing you a favor; so be flexible about a time for meeting.

c) Come prepared for the interview. Have your questions all prepared, a notebook and several pens for writing down responses, and a relaxed disposition.

d) During the interview, ask your questions and listen carefully to the responses. Take brief notes while you listen. Add follow-up questions; sometimes people need a little encouragement to say more.

e) Do not interrupt the speaker, and do not get into an argument with him or her: your job is to report what the speaker thinks—accurately, even if you do disagree. A good interviewer gets people to talk; if you seem to be objecting to what he or she says, your interviewee might clam up.

f) Immediately after the interview, write down everything that you remember the interviewee saying. Use your questions as an outline for your report. The responses are the body of the report itself. At the end of the report, you may wish to add some of your reactions or reflections about the interview.

In some cases, interviews will be the springboards for discussions; in other instances, the interview reports will just be handed in to you. You will probably think up other ways of using interviews too.

Guest Speakers

Guest speakers have always added an enjoyable dimension to my classes—although I was not always as organized as I might have been. The teaching manual suggests all sorts of people who might enliven your students' understanding of history, for example, missionaries, immigrants, refugee resettlement workers, members of religious orders, and permanent deacons. Since guest speakers tend to take up a full period, you probably cannot afford to have very many presentations. Also, you most likely will have to make arrangements with whoever is available. Thus, I suggest that before the course begins you make yourself familiar with all the possible guest speaker topics, choose ones that you think students might appreciate best, and then try to line up two or three guest presenters for each semester. Be sure to prepare your students with some background about the speaker and the topic.

Films

A few movies are recommended in this manual. In fact, there may be many movies that would fit into different chapters, but the ones listed in this manual are films that I previewed and found acceptable. A movie now and again can add some variety to class presentation, as you no doubt know. Again, since there is so much to cover in the course, you will probably only be able to fit two or three movies in a semester.

The TeleKETICS films may be rented directly from the following distributors:

Ideal Pictures
4431 West North Avenue
Milwaukee, WI 53208
414-873-4617

TeleKETICS
1229 South Santee Street
Los Angeles, CA 90015
213-746-2916

Learning Corporation of America films are available through major university libraries around the country, Ideal Pictures, and the address below:

Learning Corporation of America
Distributed by Simon & Schuster Communications
108 Wilmot Road
Deerfield, IL 60015
800-621-2131

Prayer Services

Each chapter of the teaching manual ends with a suggested prayer service. Usually readings, songs, and prayers are selected from the period being studied in the chapter. The themes of the prayers match themes mentioned in the respective chapters of the student text. Assign the roles in the prayer services to the students; by the end of a semester, each student should have had a part in at least one prayer service. Songs are recommended, but I know that singing in a classroom may not work. If you cannot use class singing, maybe you can at least listen to a recording of the contemporary song suggested.

The fact that each chapter ends with a structured prayer service does not mean that you should delete prayer from your other class meetings for the week. The prayer services are simply a way of wrapping up the chapter, reflecting on significant learnings, and asking God's continual help in understanding ourselves and the Church.

Quizzes

Multiple-choice quizzes are included for most of the chapters. I prefer daily quizzes, but you may wish to give these quizzes as unit tests. In either case, the questions should help you check the students' knowledge of each chapter. For essay questions, you could use the review questions at the end of the chapters in the student text.

Writing Assignments

Many writing assignments are offered in this manual. They require that students reason logically, argue convincingly, and refer to the material of the course. The questions raised in a reflective essay do not have a single, right answer, but they do require reflection and speculation. Try to evaluate the students' essays on (1) how clearly they state their positions or theses and (2) how well they defend and develop their positions. Encourage the students to proofread their papers for grammatical correctness. Naturally, you will want to space these essays between the written research reports so that you will not end up with two written assignments being turned in too closely together.

Journal Keeping

A journal is a written record of a person's inner dialogue—the thoughts, feelings, questions, impressions, and connections that come to mind over a period of time. For this course it is suggested that each student keep a journal. Specific directions for the students are given in chapter 1, concept A, activity 1 of this teaching manual.

Generally speaking, the more one writes in a journal, the more effective is the activity. And if students truly give themselves to journal keeping, they will find that it generates as well as records their inner dialogue.

Recommended Grading Procedures

The giving of grades for courses in religion has been a persistent problem. The need for some measure of academic success or failure appears to be evident; most attempts at a pass-fail approach to religion grades have been unsuccessful, many times because of the dissatisfaction of the students themselves. And yet there is a legitimate concern that the academic grades given in religion courses are often interpreted falsely as a measure of one's personal faith-life, an equivalency we certainly want to avoid.

We cannot deal with the complexity of the grading issue in this manual. It is likely that each school has its policy well established and already functioning. What we offer here is a suggested approach for grading this course that respects the sensitivity of the issues involved while offering some means to measure student performance. This approach uses letter grades (A, B, C, D, F), which is the most common practice, and will require some adjustment for those schools using numerical grading procedures.

One possible set of procedures for helping you determine grades in this particular course is as follows:

1) As has already been indicated, each chapter in the teaching manual includes a set of quiz questions. You may select some of these questions for daily quizzes or give a quiz over the entire chapter.

2) At the end of each chapter in the student text you will find review questions. These sections are written to identify clearly the major points raised in each chapter. They can be used as the basic questions for periodic tests; you may find it useful to give brief essay tests after completing every two or three chapters.

3) As will become increasingly clear throughout this manual, the classroom activities recommended for this course significantly expand upon and clarify the student text material. Students should be encouraged to enter fully into classroom experiences and should be rewarded if they do so. Research reports completed, participation in plays, interview reports written, and so on, should all be reflected in the final grades.

One gentle reminder is in order: Teachers must be sensitive to those students who, because of personal shyness or introversion, find it difficult to participate actively in class. These students should not be penalized for this personality trait; in fact, the achievement of a higher grade may help to affirm them and alleviate some of their fears.

4) The students' journals should be read frequently, but assigning a grade to personal reflections is hardly appropriate. What you might wish to do is give everyone who has completed all the entries an "A" for the journal component of the grade; if they have missed two entries, they get a "B"; if they miss four, a "C," six, a "D," eight, an "F."

5) Finally, it should be emphasized throughout the course that the grades are only intended to reflect academic performance in the course and in no way reflect the attempt to judge the level of the student's personal faith-life.

A Sample Schedule for a Semester Course

The schedule that follows is by no means meant to be definitively the best way to go about teaching this course. Ideally, you will focus session planning around each chapter's major concepts. This schedule is given to simply indicate that, indeed, the complete student text can be handled in sixteen weeks—in five, forty-five-minute class periods per week. Granted that more time would be even better, a solid experience of church history is possible in one semester. Where more than a four-page reading assignment is indicated, usually full-page pictures or other illustrations take up considerable space and/or only part of a page is to be read for that day. The division by pages is roughly done; indeed, you may spend more class time on some concepts and simply review information from some pages. But it may be best to keep the reading assignments somewhat equal in length.

In the schedule below, the phrase "assign projects for chapter" indicates that on that day you may wish to designate students to complete research projects, to prepare sections from plays, or to do whatever assignments are due for the following chapter and will take a week to prepare. The days designated for "reflection, prayer, and wrap-up" should provide time for these activities that are essential to the assimilation phase of learning. Naturally, you will have to adapt these suggestions to your time, style, and, most importantly, students.

Assignment to Be Completed for the Day

The page numbers listed below indicate readings from the student text.
Day 1: Introduction
Day 2: Pages 7–10; assign projects for chapter 2
Day 3: Pages 12–18
Day 4: Reflection, prayer, and wrap-up
Day 5: Pages 21–28; assign projects for chapter 3
Day 6: Pages 29–32
Day 7: Reflection, prayer, and wrap-up
Day 8: Pages 35–42; assign projects for chapter 4
Day 9: Pages 42–46
Day 10: Pages 46–48
Day 11: Reflection, prayer, and wrap-up
Day 12: Test: chapters 1–3
Day 13: Pages 51–55; assign projects for chapter 5
Day 14: Pages 55–61
Day 15: Pages 61–65
Day 16: Reflection, prayer, and wrap-up
Day 17: Pages 69–73; assign projects for chapter 6
Day 18: Pages 73–78
Day 19: Pages 78–85
Day 20: Reflection, prayer, and wrap-up
Day 21: Pages 89–93; assign projects for chapter 7
Day 22: Pages 93–97
Day 23: Pages 98–101
Day 24: Pages 102–104
Day 25: Reflection, prayer, and wrap-up
Day 26: Test: chapters 4–6
Day 27: Pages 107–111; assign projects for chapter 8
Day 28: Pages 112–117
Day 29: Pages 117–122
Day 30: Reflection, prayer, and wrap-up
Day 31: Pages 125–131; assign projects for chapter 9
Day 32: Pages 132–138
Day 33: Pages 138–142

Day 34: Reflection, prayer, and wrap-up
Day 35: Pages 145–149; assign projects for chapter 10
Day 36: Pages 150–156
Day 37: Pages 156–160
Day 38: Pages 160–162
Day 39: Reflection, prayer, and wrap-up
Day 40: Test: chapters 7–9
Day 41: Pages 165–170; assign projects for chapter 11
Day 42: Pages 170–177
Day 43: Pages 177–181
Day 44: Pages 182–186
Day 45: Reflection, prayer, and wrap-up
Day 46: Pages 189–193; assign projects for chapter 12
Day 47: Pages 194–199
Day 48: Pages 199–202
Day 49: Reflection, prayer, and wrap-up
Day 50: Pages 205–211; assign projects for chapter 13
Day 51: Pages 211–215
Day 52: Pages 215–219
Day 53: Pages 219–224
Day 54: Pages 225–228
Day 55: Reflection, prayer, and wrap-up
Day 56: Test: chapters 10–12
Day 57: Pages 231–237; assign projects for chapter 14
Day 58: Pages 237–242
Day 59: Pages 242–248
Day 60: Pages 248–254
Day 61: Reflection, prayer, and wrap-up
Day 62: Pages 257–262; assign projects for chapter 15
Day 63: Pages 262–268
Day 64: Pages 268–271
Day 65: Pages 272–276
Day 66: Pages 276–279
Day 67: Pages 280–284
Day 68: Reflection, prayer, and wrap-up
Day 69: Pages 287–292; assign projects for chapter 16
Day 70: Pages 292–296
Day 71: Pages 296–302
Day 72: Pages 302–304
Day 73: Reflection, prayer, and wrap-up
Day 74: Pages 307–314
Day 75: Pages 314–319
Day 76: Pages 320–323
Day 77: Reflection, prayer, and wrap-up
Day 78: Test: chapters 13–16
Day 79: Course summary
Day 80: Class celebration

Lesson Resources, Including Student Handouts, for *The Catholic Church: Our Mission in History*

A Brief Checklist on Lesson and Session Planning

Planning Lessons

1) Read the entire chapter in the student text, noting themes or topics requiring special emphasis given your students' starting point.

2) Read the major concepts for that chapter as provided in this manual. *For each major concept,* formulate a lesson goal, a general statement of what you hope to achieve with that concept given your students' starting point. Write these lesson goals in your planning notebook.

3) Make an initial assessment of the number of sessions that you will need to achieve your stated goal for each concept.

4) Identify the purposes of each session in accord with the components of the learning process: significant experiences, opportunities for reflection, or aids to assimilation.

5) Read through the remaining material for that chapter in this manual, noting those activities and exercises that particularly appeal to you.

Planning Sessions to Achieve Your Lesson Goals

1) In your notebook, write the specific concept and lesson goal you are pursuing in a given session or series of sessions.

2) Note the number of sessions you have initially set aside for the achievement of your goal. For each session, state clearly a *reasonably attainable objective,* a practical step, if you will, that will move you toward your goal.

3) Note all necessary preliminary activities for the session: attendance check, prayer, seating arrangements, return of assignments, review of the previous session, announcements, and so on.

4) Note the discussion questions, class activities, student handouts, and personal reflection exercises that you want to use in the given session, along with an estimate of time to be spent on each. Also note the means of reflection you plan to use.

5) List the immediate things you must do to prepare for the session, for example, arrange for a speaker, duplicate the student handout, and so on.

6) Allow yourself time for evaluation after the session is completed.

CHAPTER 1

Why Study Church History?

Major Concepts

A. Why study history at all? Our identities are formed by our histories. Having a sense of history helps us know who we are.

B. The job of the historian is to help us have a sense of the history of humankind and of specific groups of people so that we can learn from the past—thus building on the great ideas and avoiding the repetition of tragic mistakes. As a consequence of knowing and appreciating history we are more free to create a better future.

C. Knowing church history can give us a much sharper idea of our identities as Christians. Our identification with the Church helps shape us; by knowing the story of the Church, we can help to shape it. Learning history is like building a relationship.

D. The Church began with people like us who were open to Jesus' call; the first person to follow Jesus was Peter.

Activities for Concept A
Why study history at all? Our identities are formed by our histories. Having a sense of history helps us know who we are. (Pages 7–8 of the student text.)

Review Questions and Exercises from the Student Text

Personal Reflection Exercise
The following exercise might best be completed before using review question 1.

In order to get more in touch with your own personal history, to remind you of key events in your own story, you might find this exercise enriching. On a sheet of paper, list in random order as many important events from your life as you can remember. These key events may not seem important to others, but they are to you. Leave several lines between the events on your list. Then, answer the following questions:
- Who was there with you?
- Where did the event take place?
- What exactly happened?
- When did it happen?

After you have answered these questions, try to list and describe the causes for and effects of one very early event that you listed. Usually our lives are marked by these key events, so dig deeply into your memory. From this exercise you could probably write an autobiography—which is a kind of history.

Now, on a different sheet of paper, write the name of one of your closest friends. Then, list five very important times in this relationship: conversations, joint projects, trips, other things done together. After you have made your list, write a brief summary of why each event was so important to your relationship. Consider the effects of the events. Afterward, answer the following question: How important has it been to me to know a lot about my friend?

Question 1: Explain what it would be like for you not to remember your personal history,

Answer: We would not know who we are. We would not be able to do many of the practical things we take for granted. In effect, we would almost have to start our lives over again. We have confidence in ourselves because of the long built-up image of what we can do. In addition, without our memories, we would feel isolated.

Other Questions and Activities for Discussion

1) **A Personal History Journal:** Have your students keep a "Personal History" throughout the course—beginning with the material they wrote for the personal reflection exercise above. This journal could be kept in a notebook or folder. It might contain all of the writing they do as part of the exercises for personal reflection given at the end of each chapter. Also, after chapter 2 has been completed, and at the end of each subsequent week of the course, you might have your students reflect on the week just finished and answer in a paragraph or two one of the following:

- How was I (pick one to write about) a Herald, a Servant, a Sacrament, a part of the People of God, or a participant in the Institutional Church?
- Or, offer a question for reflection that is pertinent to the particular chapter and one about which you want the students to reflect.

The students may want to reflect on the material in the personal history journals during prayer services. But assure your students that all material in the journals is private; the only person with whom they will share the journal is you—that is, unless *they* want to share some of the reflections with the class.

Some suggestions about handling journals: Spiral notebooks are cumbersome—especially if you take them home to read. What might be easier is to have each student buy a folder with pockets and with a three-ring binder. The students can write the journal entries each week on loose-leaf paper; then when you return the papers, they can be inserted in the binders. The folder pockets can be used to save handouts and other materials that you give to the students. Naturally, keeping the notebooks in a safe place in your classroom might solve the problem of lost journals.

What to write in response to the journals: Perhaps the best way to treat the journals is as if they were conversations between you and the students. Writing, in and of itself, pushes the student to reflect, formulate, meditate; thus, even if the quality of writing is doubtful, the process has some positive benefits to the person writing. Since it is almost impossible to fairly grade someone's meditations, it might be best to simply make a few comments on the journals and ask some questions for the student to think about in the future entries. In short, affirm what you can in the journal entry and challenge the student to think further on a point or two. If you judge it necessary, you may dock students for entries missed. In this way everyone begins with an "A" for journal writing; the only way to not get an "A" is to not write entries.

Should journal entries be done in class or at home? If students write their entries in class, there is some assurance that they will be done, but writing in class takes time away from other activities. If students write at home they may occasionally take more time and really say a lot because they have an open-ended time period; on the other hand, there are many temptations not to write at all. Consequently, each teacher has to judge which way is most effective for a particular class. That may sound like a cop-out on my part, but I have tried both ways and have met with equal parts of success and failure.

2) Have the students list some memories that have given them courage or hope. The students' lists of memories of hope and courage may be used in several ways: (*a*) students may share one or two memories with one or two other people, perhaps a friend

or relative; (b) they may write them down to be turned in to you (perhaps they could write a brief essay describing the most important memory and submit it along with the list).

3) Sharing a Story: Depending on how comfortable the class members are with one another, instruct the students to break into groups of three or even to pair up and take turns sharing one of their stories about an important event that they described for the personal reflection exercise for chapter 1. Stories are made to be told. The telling also reinforces the point that our histories are a deep-rooted part of who we are. Remind the students that whatever they share is their personal responsibility. The incident they tell about can be as superficial or deeply personal as they choose. They should feel comfortable in sharing the content of their history.

4) Autobiography: If you have time and really want to stress the point that we all have a history to tell, require that the students write an autobiography. It could consist of a series of stories based on the important happenings listed in the personal reflection exercise. Give the students two weeks or so in which to complete the autobiographies.

5) Building Friendships: After your students have completed the part of the personal reflection exercise in which they are asked to think about their closest friends, ask the students to compose a list of the steps a person goes through in relationship building: What seems to be the process of establishing a friendship? Then discuss the following questions:

- What can happen if you know too little about someone and then trust him or her with something that is very personal to you?
- What can happen in a relationship when two people do not trust each other enough?
- What helps us trust people more?

This preliminary discussion of relationship building will be useful when you come to the section of this chapter that compares getting to know the Church to relationship building. Both processes depend on knowledge gained. Also, we tend to distrust people we do not know. Consequently, if we do not know much about the Church and its history, we will not understand why certain things about the Church are as they are, and we will not trust the Church as much as we might if we knew more.

6) Direct the students to make a list of the individual talents that they have used during the last two or three days. Then have them pick one of the talents and describe how they acquired this talent. What steps did they have to learn and practice over and over before they could really say that they possessed this talent? Then make some comments like the following:

> We develop our talents over a long period of time. We may be good guitar players now, but when we first started there was much we had to learn: reading music, proper strumming technique, correct fingerings for the notes, timing, and so on. To be good now, we had to spend hours and hours practicing. Some people, even after hours and hours, are still not good guitarists. In any case, after a while, playing becomes almost automatic—we are not conscious of all the small steps required to play, all the small steps that we acquired one by one. Just because we have forgotten all these small steps does not mean that they are not essential.

> In a similar way, all of us forget many of the small events in our lives that form our histories—all those events that have made us who we are. Just because we have forgotten them does not mean that they are not still influencing our behavior. Sometimes a guitar player has to go back and review certain techniques if she or he is to learn a new song. In a similar way, sometimes a person has to review some parts of his or her history if he or she is to grow or change. In short,

knowing our history and the forces that shaped us can enable us to reshape our future and not be slaves of our past development.

7) Finally, suggest that your students describe one or two instances when they could not remember some important piece of information or some important date. Inquire as to what happened. Then seek feedback to the following questions:
- Just on the practical level, why is a keen memory very useful?
- What are some of the negative effects of having a poor or undisciplined memory? What are some practical examples?
- What are some ways of improving your memory?

Some practical examples of the benefits of a good memory might be remembering people's names, how to change a tire, relatives' anniversaries and birthdays, or fundamentals in sports.

One of the best ways to remember things is to write them down. Another way of reinforcing our memories is to discuss things with other people. In effect, the journals are a way of aiding the students' memories about themselves—their histories.

Activities for Concept B
The job of the historian is to help us have a sense of the history of humankind and of specific groups of people so that we can learn from the past—thus building on the great ideas and avoiding the repetition of tragic mistakes. As a consequence of knowing and appreciating history we are more free to create a better future. (Pages 8–9 of the student text.)

Review Questions and Exercises from the Student Text

Question 2: Why is it important to have a sense of world history? Can you think of some recent events that have changed our ways of living?
Answer: If we forget historical developments we can repeat tragic mistakes. For example, the students can summarize the fate of Jews under Hitler and the story of Hiroshima. On the other hand, authors such as Shakespeare, having learned the lessons of earlier writers, have been able to create great masterpieces of literature.

Question 3: Why does the author state that knowing history can be liberating? Do you agree?
Answer: The records of history show us more possibilities for action. Thus, we can make better, more informed choices. Ignorance is a type of slavery. The researcher who does not know about experiments already performed is condemned to repeating all sorts of work, some of which may be a complete waste of time, money, and energy. (Ask for other examples of how knowing history can be liberating.)

Other Questions and Activities for Discussion

1) In order to stimulate your students to think of recent events that have changed our ways of living, require them to find some clippings of current events that are going to change the immediate future for many of them. For example, there may be a story about new laws governing entrance into state universities. Another story may be about unemployment of teens during summer vacation periods. All events have effects in some ways. Then, perhaps in their journals, direct them to write a brief summary of how the news event has, will, or can affect history. Volunteers can explain the events they selected and the effects.

If you wish to seek examples closer to home, you might have your students describe the long-range effects of some events that are happening at school. How have these events affected the way the school is run?

2) Remind the students that just knowing history does not ensure that people will not repeat previous errors. But without a historical sense we inevitably repeat past mistakes. To encourage discussion of this point, use the following questions:
- What historical events seem to be repetitions of earlier events?
- What are other examples of times when we have clearly learned from history and so avoided mistakes?

You might wish to list the examples on the chalkboard. Since the students may come up with only a few examples, point out that by the end of the course they will have developed a much better sense of history.

Activities for Concept C
Knowing church history can give us a much sharper idea of our identities as Christians. Our identification with the Church helps shape us; by knowing the story of the Church, we can help to shape it. Learning history is like building a relationship. (Pages 10–13 of the student text.)

Review Questions and Exercises from the Student Text

Question 4: Why is it important for Catholic Christians to study church history?

Answer: Christianity has its roots in history and has developed through history. Without an understanding of its history we cannot fully understand the present-day Church because it has been shaped by that history. If we identify with the Church, it shapes us to some extent: it becomes part of our identity. Therefore, to fully comprehend our own identities we need to understand the Church. Also, we will be less surprised by developments in the Church if we know its history. (Ask the students to explain some of the changes of Vatican Council II that were really not "new" but that shocked some people who did not have a historical sense.) Finally, we shape the future of the Church by who we are.

Question 5: How is learning history somewhat like developing a relationship or friendship?

Answer: Recall with the students the discussion the class had earlier in this chapter about building a relationship with a close friend and all the steps involved (see concept A, activity 5). Then review the steps of relationship building mentioned in the student text. First, we become acquainted with people on a superficial level: we learn their names, some of their interests, where they are from. Then we share more personal information with the other persons; this deeper level of sharing teaches us about how trustworthy the other persons are. Finally, we also have many opportunities to see our friends in action. Learning about the Church follows the same process. If we are to make good decisions about the Church, which is composed of people, we must get to know some aspects of it, then share more personally in its life and see it in action. With all this information we can make a fair decision about our participation in the Church.

Other Questions and Activities for Discussion

1) In order for the students to have a clearer perception of the adaptations required of people by the changes of Vatican Council II, assign them to interview a few

adult members of their families. Some questions they may wish to ask are listed below:

- When Vatican Council II was finished, were there any developments from the council that surprised you?
- What changes have been most significant for you?
- Do you know anyone who was very upset by the changes? If yes, what specific changes upset this person?
- Do you find that the changes have helped people identify more closely with the Church? Do you think that people are more actively involved in the Church because of the changes?

These interview reports may be oral or written—perhaps recorded as entries in the journals. After the interviews, your students may report to the class on their findings. Point out areas of similarity and difference. Remind them that interviewing is an important historical research tool; their interviews are a kind of oral history of the Church.

2) To illustrate in a brief way that the Church is shaping history right now, ask the students to give some instances of contributions that the Church has made to human history. List these on the chalkboard. The examples can range from ancient history to contemporary events. Encourage them to describe the long-range effects of the events.

To get the discussion started on contributions of the Church, you may wish to use the following examples:

a) The classroom method of teaching was designed by Saint John Baptist de La Salle, founder of the Christian Brothers, over three hundred years ago. Before his involvement, only rich children received an education, usually by private tutors.

b) The university was a development begun by the Church, used first to train priests.

c) Spaghetti was brought back from China by merchants who went to the Far East as a result of the Crusades.

Clearly many other contributions made by the Church to the history of the world will be explained in the student text. The influence of Catholic Christianity should not be underestimated.

3) Even at this early stage in your students' lives, they have made contributions to the life of the Church. Invite the students to identify ways in which they have shaped the Church. The most obvious examples will come from their participation in parish life, but seek to illustrate how their attendance at a Catholic school shapes the image of the Church too.

Activities for Concept D
The Church began with people like us who were open to Jesus' call; the first person to follow Jesus was Peter. (Pages 13–18 of the student text.)

Review Questions and Exercises from the Student Text

Question 6: What was Peter's role in the formation of the Church?

Answer: Peter was first among the Apostles—the first followers of Jesus. Clearly, Jesus gave Peter leadership of the group that was forming around him. Jesus said, "You are Peter and on this rock I will build my Church." Later, Peter preached at Pentecost under the influence of the Holy Spirit. From that point on, people identified him as first among the Apostles.

Question 7: Why did Jesus pick Peter to be the "rock" on which to build the Church? Do you agree with the reasons given in the imaginary interview with Peter (see pages 16–17)?

Answer: The reason that Jesus chose Peter is a mystery. Peter certainly did not have the years of theological training, pastoral experience, and so on, that people would associate with popes. It is likely that Peter was illiterate, and he was married. But, the ways of God are not the ways of humans. Jesus must have seen Peter's courage and faith, his integrity and passion. Ultimately, we do not know for sure why Jesus chose Peter, but Jesus did come to save the sinners, to call the ignorant. And if Jesus could call, love, and make Peter first among the Apostles, he can certainly call and love us.

Question 8: Why was Pentecost such a key event for Peter?

Answer: At Pentecost Peter, and the other Apostles too, fully realized that he was not alone, that the Holy Spirit dwelled in him and would give him the power and presence to preach the Good News of salvation that was brought by Jesus. Also, Peter was confirmed as chief among the Apostles; he was the one who spoke to the crowd gathered outside the place of the Apostles' meeting.

Other Questions and Activities for Discussion

1) Explore with the students their images of Saint Peter. Perhaps the most common image is of Peter at the gates of heaven. Maybe some of the students can tell a joke or two (there are hundreds) about Peter at the gates. Then examine the accuracy of the popular images of Peter compared to the image of Peter found in the Scriptures. For additional images of Peter, have the class read some of the following passages from the Bible:

Mark 1:16–18 (Peter and Andrew are called by Jesus.)
Matt. 8:14 (Jesus cures Peter's mother-in-law.)
Matt. 14:28–31 (Peter attempts to walk on the water.)
Matt. 16:21–23 (Peter is scolded by Jesus.)
Mark 14:37 (Peter falls asleep at Gethsemane.)
John 18:10–11 (Peter assaults one of the people who arrests Jesus.)
Acts 1—12 (Peter is seen as clearly the leader of the early Christian community.)

2) Pose this question about Saint Peter to your students:
• If Peter were to walk into your classroom as a guest speaker, what questions would you like to ask him?

Discuss the questions raised by the class. Then, reminding the students to keep in mind what they know about Scripture, ask them to try to answer the questions as they think Peter would.

These questions and answers can be used as the focus of instruction on certain topics as the course progresses. Try to focus on discussing the questions that concerned the early Church; record questions that will be considered later in this church history course. For instance, if students ask Peter about why he could have a wife, but priests cannot now, you might want to note this question and use it as a focus during the chapters leading up to the year 1215 when the Lateran Council finally and firmly forbade priests to marry.

3) If time permits, have the students read the whole account of Pentecost (Acts 2:1–41). This is a wonderfully dramatic reading. Perhaps select a student with some experience in public speaking to deliver Peter's speech.

4) Consider with the students why fire is associated with Pentecost and why a dove is used as a symbol of the Holy Spirit. Here are some questions to discuss with your students:

- Why is fire associated with Pentecost?
- What does fire indicate about the experience the Apostles had at Pentecost?
- Why is a dove used to symbolize the descent of the Holy Spirit?
- How can the Holy Spirit be both flame and dove?

Summary Activity for the Chapter

You may wish to close the study of this chapter by using the prayer on Student Hand-out 1-A, "Prayer Service: A Prayer from Saint Peter" (found at the end of this chapter).

Prayer Service: A Prayer from Saint Peter

Leader: Let us remember that we are in God's hands; God has chosen us and loves us now and at every moment. The Creator has blessed us with people who are important in our lives and gives us a sense of our part in the Church. God wants us to rejoice in our weaknesses like Saint Peter did so that we will listen to the truth and celebrate our talents with which we can do God's work.

Reading from the words of Peter—
A humble fisherman, but a firm rock of faith

The truth I have now come to realise . . . is that God does not have favourites, but that anybody of any nationality who fears God and does what is right is acceptable to him. . . . Jesus Christ is Lord of all. . . . (Acts 10:34–36)

Free your minds, then, of encumbrances; control them, and put your trust in nothing but the grace that will be given you when Jesus Christ is revealed. . . . Let your love for each other be real and from the heart— your new birth was not from any mortal seed but from the everlasting word of the living and eternal God. (1 Peter 1:13,22–23)

Prayers

Leader: For the gifts of our memories . . .

All: We thank you, Lord.

Leader: For all the people who have affirmed us, given us knowledge and care . . .

All: We thank you, Lord.

Leader: For helping us understand the importance of our story and the story of the Church . . .

All: We thank you, Lord.

(Other prayers of thanks may be added here. Respond to each prayer.)

All: We thank you, Lord.

CHAPTER 2

Five Ways of Seeing the Church

Major Concepts

A. *The Church as Mystery:* Just as people are mysteries, so the Church is a mystery too. While we can never totally understand the Church, using models can help us know it better.

B. *Model 1: The Body of Christ, or the People of God:* The community of believers becomes the physical expression of Jesus on earth. Each person has a role to play in making Jesus visible to others.

C. *Model 2: The Institution:* As a group of persons organized for a similar purpose, the Church is an institution that has structures through which it serves all its members and the larger community.

D. *Model 3: The Sacrament:* When the people of the Church worship, serve, and preach, God's saving power is revealed as present in these physical signs; thus, the Church is a Sacrament.

E. *Model 4: The Herald of God's Word:* The Church is the messenger sent to proclaim the Word of God to all people everywhere.

F. *Model 5: The Servant:* The Church not only makes Jesus present to people through the community of believers and through worship and preaching, but also through service.

Activities for Concept A

The Church as Mystery: **Just as people are mysteries, so the Church is a mystery too. While we can never totally understand the Church, using models can help us know it better. (Pages 21–22 of the student text.)**

Review Questions and Exercises from the Student Text

Question 1: Why do we say that the Church is ultimately a mystery?

Answer: People are mysteries because they are always changing. Because the Church is the manifestation of Jesus and since we cannot know Jesus fully, the Church is finally a mystery.

Question 2: What are the benefits of using models to discuss the Church?

Answer: Although a model is not the reality, a model can give us a clearer picture of something. For example, a model plane can be used to show what the real plane would or does look like. Thus, in studying the Church, models can give us various perspectives on what is ultimately a mystery.

Other Questions and Activities for Discussion

1) Frequently we do not like to admit that there is much that is mysterious in our lives. To admit this is like admitting that we are not in control of things. To reinforce the idea that people are mysteries, you might wish to use the following exercise:

Tell your students to list in their journals or on loose-leaf paper five people who are important in the students' lives; remind them to leave several spaces for writing between each name. Then say something like the following:

The people you listed are important to you. That implies that you must know a fair amount about them. But do you know everything there is to know about them? Probably not. For a few minutes, reflect on each of these people, and then next to each name, write questions you wish you could ask each person or statements describing some aspect of each person that you find mysterious—something you just do not understand about the person.

After these instructions, give the students some time to complete their writing. When they are finished, comment:

Some of the questions you wish to ask may have answers that you will eventually find out. Other questions or mysteries may have no answers that you will ever know. Underline the questions or mysteries that have no complete answers and probably never will.

Then ask the following questions:
- How do you feel about these mysteries?
- Why are people mysterious?
- Would we be better off if there were no mysteries about people?
- Would you like it if someone thought they knew everything about you?

Most of us do not like the idea that people think they know all about us—especially because we know that only God really knows everything about us. Reiterate to your students that the Church is composed of people in union with God and Jesus. People are mysterious, and to our limited human minds, God and Jesus are certainly mysterious too. Thus, the Church is a mystery. But just as we make friends with people and keep learning more and more about them—even if they are mysteries—so we can become closer to God, Jesus, and the Church by learning more and more about them.

2) In order to discuss the role of models in learning, bring in a model airplane, a model of the human body (perhaps your biology teacher has one), a model essay used in a composition book, a model of Shakespeare's stage, or a model of a DNA molecule—some kind of visual model. Discuss why these models are helpful in visualizing the reality modeled. Remind your students that we learn through our senses and that models can help us see what we cannot experience directly. For instance, a live human brain pulsing with blood, sending messages to all the organs of the body is certainly different from the plastic model, but it is just not practical to bring in a living brain. Consequently, the model at least gives us some idea of what the brain looks like in all its parts.

3) Before actually reading about and discussing the models of the Church, your students can probably put together a "job description" of the Church based on their experiences. Thus, when you begin studying the models, the students can see that they have already experienced the Church as Herald, Institution, Servant, Sacrament, and People of God. To get the discussion going, these questions can be used:
- You have been experiencing the Church for over ten years now. If you were to write a "job description"—an outline of the duties of someone's job—what would be included in a job description of the Church?
- Based on your experiences, what functions, jobs, and roles does the Church undertake?
- How could we group or categorize the different jobs into a few main groups?
- Would you say that any of these functions, jobs, or roles are more important than the others? Why?

Most likely the functions that the students list can be grouped into the roles of the Church as Institution, Servant, Sacrament, and Herald. They may have a harder time seeing how their parishes are the Body of Christ or the People of God. Point out though that they have identified the main roles of the Church—the models. The focus of the rest of the course in church history is to show how the Church has always lived up to its mission as People of God, Herald, Sacrament, Servant, and Institution. What they experience today as the roles of the Church have been basically the same for nearly two thousand years.

Activities for Concept B

Model 1: The Body of Christ, or the People of God: The community of believers becomes the physical expression of Jesus on earth. Each person has a role to play in making Jesus visible to others. (Pages 22–23 of the student text.)

Review Questions and Exercises from the Student Text

Question 3: Why does Saint Paul compare the Church to the human body? What unifies the Body of Christ? What must we do to help the Body of Christ survive and grow?

Answer: To help people understand the nature of community in the Church, Paul compares the Church to the ways in which the parts of the body work together. To be really healthy the body parts must work together—each having its unique role in the total organism. The parts are all different, but this does not mean that any are less important. The community of the Church should be like that, everyone working in harmony, doing his or her part to build up the community of faith. What holds the Body of Christ together is shared faith, blessed and supported by the power of the Holy Spirit. To help the Body grow, each Christian must care for others and for himself or herself; in short, one must help love grow.

Personal Reflection Exercise

> **1) Complete the following statements:**
> Today, in my activities,
> **I can be the mouth of Christ by** . . .
> **I can be the hands of Christ by** . . .
> **I can be the eyes of Jesus when I** . . .
> **I can be the ears of the Lord by** . . .

Other Questions and Activities for Discussion

1) Read these instructions to your students:

What would the world be like if it became completely the Body of Christ or the People of God? Imagine what sort of behaviors you would expect from a group called "the People of God," and make a list of your expectations. Do your expectations match those of your classmates? Compile a list of common expectations and then describe a world community called "the People of God."

This activity might best be done in small groups of three or four. First, instruct all of your students to make individual lists of behaviors and expectations. Once these lists are ready, divide the class into groups. Their job is to come up with composite lists of expectations of what the world would be like if it was the People of God. Then one spokesperson from each group can add his or her group's expectations to a class list that should be written on the chalkboard. To conclude your reflections on this Kingdom of God, you might use the following remarks and queries:

- Obviously we have not yet transformed this world into the Body of Christ. Why not?
- What would we have to do to have the world as we know it meet our expectations as the Kingdom of God?

Conclude with a remark like this:

Just as in our own bodies, we experience illnesses in the Body of Christ. Nevertheless we do have the means to build up the Body of Christ: the help of the Holy Spirit, prayer, the love of others, the sacraments, and the Word of God. As human beings we cannot expect perfection, but anything is possible with God. Each person's job is to fulfill his or her own unique part in the community.

2) Different communities have different ways of establishing their unique identities as communities united for a common purpose. Catholic schools, parishes, clubs, or organizations have ways of identifying themselves to the public and among other Catholics. Discuss with your students some of the things that signify various groups in the Catholic Church:

- What are some ways in which the school and/or parish establishes its identity and demonstrates that identity to others? (for instance, school or athletic uniforms, stickers on cars, publicized annual picnics, etc.)
- How are these demonstrations of Catholic identity really connected to the idea of the Church as the People of God and the Body of Christ?
- Are any of these means of identification actually poor or inconsistent with the identity of the Church as a People of God?
- Would Jesus be able to feel comfortable with these practices or symbols? (For instance, would Jesus play linebacker for a high school football team and see it as being a fitting symbol of building the Body of Christ?)

The main thrust of this discussion is not to criticize high school football, for example, but to point out in specific ways that much of what can be identified with Catholic schools and parishes may have little to do with building the Body of Christ. Consequently, we must consciously analyze what we are saying as Church through some of the practices that we sometimes take for granted.

Activities for Concept C

Model 2: The Institution: As a group of persons organized for a similar purpose, the Church is an institution that has structures through which it serves all its members and the larger community. (Pages 23–24, 26–28 of the student text.)

Review Questions and Exercises from the Student Text

Question 4: What are the advantages of having structures in the Church?

Answer: The leadership within an organization, its rules, and its committees all provide a means for fulfilling the basic purpose of the group and ways for services to be performed for members. Without some structure any human organization will collapse.

Question 5: Write a brief essay on the ways in which your school helps build the Church.

Answer: Certainly there is no one answer for this question, but what should evolve here is a discussion about why Catholic schools were begun and why they are important. Millions of dollars are spent on Catholic education each year. The Church believes that schools are important as a source of religious instruction and in maintaining the faith. Do your students really see these as the goals of Catholic education?

Other Questions and Activities for Discussion

1) Direct the students to find out what committees or organizations function in their parishes. If there are several members of the same parish in the class, you might form them into a group. Encourage them to talk with the heads of the parish committees to get a clearer idea of what the committees do.

Clearly this activity may take up a considerable amount of time. However, it is included because students may be unaware of what sort of services and opportunities are available in their local churches. When they have finished doing this exercise, they may report their findings in oral reports or in essays. I would recommend that you spend some time talking about the various structures and their purposes so that students have a clear idea that much is happening on the local level of the Church.

2) You might wish to have your students accomplish this exercise in small groups and then report their findings to the class. Give the following instructions to the students:

Using your personal experiences with people in each of these roles, write a "job description" of one of the following roles in the Church: pope, lay ministers, deacons, cardinals, bishops, religious sisters, brothers, chairpersons of parish councils.

One purpose of this activity is to tell you how much the students really know. In addition, they will have time to reflect on their perceptions of these people and their important roles in the Church. Ask the students if their perceptions match the roles these people *should* play in the Church. The development of each of these roles will be described in the student text as the history of the Church unfolds.

3) Brainstorm with your students about these questions:
- What would your growing up have been like if you did not have available some of the institutions sponsored by the Church?
- Imagine your city without church buildings and organizations. What would it look like? Would it be a better or worse place to live?
- Do any of these church-related institutions seem unnecessary? Could they be eliminated? Why or why not?

4) By referring to your diocesan directory, you or the students should be able to draw up a chart of the church institutions present in the diocese and of the different offices that serve under the bishop. Students might be assigned to interview some of the diocesan officers to find out what they do.

Activities for Concept D
Model 3: The Sacrament: When the people of the Church worship, serve, and preach, God's saving power is revealed as present in these physical signs; thus, the Church is a Sacrament. (Pages 24–25 in the student text.)

Review Questions and Exercises from the Student Text

Question 6: Explain how the Church is a Sacrament. What activities of the Church show that it is a Sacrament? Why is unity so important in making the Church a Sacrament?

Answer: When the members of the Church worship, serve, and preach, God's saving power is revealed as present. People remember who Jesus was and what he did; consequently, Jesus is made present. If one considers even the traditional definition of sacrament, "an outward sign instituted by Christ to give grace," it is apparent that this description fits the Church: it is an outward sign begun by Jesus to nurture the People of God. In a simpler way, the very existence of people who proclaim faith in Jesus reminds others of Jesus' presence. The most obvious time when Christians explicitly show that the Church is a Sacrament occurs when they are joined together in faith to partake of the Eucharist. All partake of one body and blood of Jesus and are publicly joined in unity with him. The Eucharist is the community celebrating its salvation together. When the community is split apart, people cannot see Jesus in the division and strife.

Other Questions and Activities for Discussion

1) The eucharistic celebration should be a sign of the unity within the community of believers. Built into the Mass are expressions of community—ways of making contact with one another. For most of us the effectiveness of these expressions of unity depends on many factors: the style of the presiding celebrant, how well we know the people of the community, and so on. Nevertheless, in the liturgy there are ways of showing the communal nature of the celebration. Ask your students to list as many instances of communal action in the Mass as they can think of; this list should not include optional communal activities (e.g., singing hymns). Then, have your students list activities that the worshiping community may do as part of the Mass that are optional but very helpful in creating a sense of sharing (e.g., singing hymns, passing the cup at Communion, bringing up the gifts by members of the congregation, holding hands during the Lord's Prayer). After this discussion, ask the students to consider the following question:

- If someone from a non-Christian faith came with you to Sunday Mass, what sort of remark do you think he or she would make about the experience? Write a brief remark that you think might be made—ten words or less—through which he or she would characterize your parish community.

Once your students are finished writing their statements, ask them to read aloud the statements. The other students should be listening for similarities in the phrases. After all the students have finished, through class discussion try to summarize the most commonly heard reactions of our imaginary non-Christian to Mass. Once the summary is done, try to choose one student's sentence that best typifies the class discussion. Then ask the students the following questions:

- Would this reaction of our non-Christian visitor imply that he or she saw the Church as a Sacrament?
- Would you change anything in the worship of your community in order to make Sacrament a more obvious model of your community?
- What elements would you want to remain the same?

This exercise reflects on the well-known statement of the non-Christians who remarked about the early Church: "Look how these Christians love one another." Would non-Christians see this love as an obvious trait of parishes today?

Activities for Concept E
Model 4: The Herald of God's Word: **The Church is the messenger sent to proclaim the Word of God to all people everywhere. (Pages 29–30 of the student text.)**

Review Questions and Exercises from the Student Text

Question 7: Why is the model of Church as Herald so important? What church activities illustrate this role?

Answer: Faith comes from hearing the Word of God. We cannot believe in something of which we have never heard. Students can list many ways in which the

Church is Herald, but, if they miss some, you might add the following: translations of the Bible, demonstrations and public devotions in which Catholics participate, diocesan newspapers, publishing houses, Catholic schools and parish religious education programs, and so on.

Personal Reflection Exercise

2) The more we are familiar with the Gospels and Epistles, the more we can participate in the Church as Herald of the Word of God. Find a short passage from the Christian Scriptures that interests or touches you. Spend some time reflecting on the passage you chose. What is God telling you about your life? After some close reflection, write a response to God that discusses two topics: (*a*) what the passage seems to be telling you about yourself, (*b*) how you will change in light of the passage. You may wish to write your reflections in the form of an imaginary dialogue with God (see the interview with Peter in chapter 1, pages 16–17, as an example).

Other Questions and Activities for Discussion

1) Tell the students to list some words that have real power, that is, real impact or effect when used. They should list some words whose impact is constructive and some whose impact is destructive. Discuss what these words suggest beyond their dictionary meanings.

The words listed will vary from class to class. The main idea of this process is to help students understand that words do have literal meanings and connotative meanings. Words have power to heal differences or create strife, to encourage or hurt. The Word of God is the person of Jesus Christ as experienced in the Christian Scriptures. If ordinary words have power, how much more power can come from the Word of God? If ordinary words have literal and connotative meanings, how much more does the Bible offer us?

2) Television is certainly the most powerful medium today. Its programs have influenced our values in profound ways. The focus of this activity is to study in an objective way just how much emphasis is given to specifically religious programs, especially on the major networks. Are religious programs any match for the other programs? The following steps can be used to complete this activity:

Form study groups of three or four students. You may want each group to examine several of the networks or just one, depending on the amount of time you have available for this activity. Assign one day of the week to each study group. Then read the following instructions to the students (or make up your own):

The goal of our research is to find out just how much time the major networks actually spend on religious programs and whether religious programs are given much emphasis in comparison with nonreligious shows.

Your group has been assigned a day of programming to study. The next step is to list all shows that are specifically religious. Alongside of each title, note the number of minutes the show runs, on which network the show appears, at what time of day the show runs, and which denomination sponsors the program—if this can be determined. And finally, add up the total number of minutes spent on religious programs for the day studied by your group.

Each group will be asked to put its list on the chalkboard, including the total amount of time spent on religious programs.

When the groups have finished studying their assigned days, ask for their reports. Then continue the discussion about using television to herald the Word of God by asking these questions:

- What conclusions can be drawn about the use of television to spread the Word of God?
- Figure out what percentage of total TV network time in one week is spent on religious programs. Is this a significant percentage?
- Are religious shows aired during prime-time television? What conclusions can you draw about the stress given religious programs in relation to the times of day when they are shown?
- Does the Catholic Church use television as much as and as effectively as other denominations? What would the Church have to do to have more TV time? Would it be worth it to have more TV time?

To carry this activity even further, ask the students to watch at least fifteen minutes of one of the programs listed as religious—some may be assigned to look at Catholic programs and others at non-Catholic programs. They should seek to identify the methods used in presenting the religious message: sermons, hymns, panel discussions, personal testimonies, dramatic stories acted out, documentaries, and so on. Ask your students how they felt about the shows they watched; in short, were the shows effective?

- How do religious programs compare to regular shows in terms of audience appeal and technical competence?
- If you were to be asked to suggest effective ways to spread the Word of God on television, what would you recommend?

3) Some of your students may have had experience as lectors in their parish churches. Seek some reactions from them about the experience of lectoring: what it means or meant to them. This is one way of participating in the Church as Herald.

4) An old adage says that "a picture is worth a thousand words." Jesus is, in his person, the Word of God. Explore with your students how our actions are heralds too: how actions speak the Word of God.

Activities for Concept F

Model 5: The Servant: **The Church not only makes Jesus present to people through the community of believers and through worship and preaching, but also through service. (Pages 30–32 of the student text.)**

Review Questions and Exercises from the Student Text

Question 8: What are the origins of the model of the Church as Servant?

Answer: Jesus taught us how to serve. Through parables such as the one about the Good Shepherd, through his actions like washing the feet of the Apostles, and through his words as in the Sermon on the Mount, Jesus made it clear how we are to serve. And Jesus was portrayed as the Suffering Servant in the prophesies of Isaiah.

Question 9: Some examples are given in this chapter about Jesus as Servant. Find some other examples of Jesus as Servant in the Christian Scriptures.

Answer: Students may pick out the miracles as very direct types of service. Here are some other passages that might be referred to in order to expand the notion of Jesus as Servant: 1 John 2:2; 4:10; 1 Cor. 15:3–5; Acts 3:13,26. Clearly, the greatest service of Jesus was this sacrifice—his death on the cross—and his Resurrection. Sending the Holy Spirit and instituting the Eucharist are ongoing services of Jesus.

Other Questions and Activities for Discussion

1) In order to fully understand the meaning of Servant, have your students find the dictionary meaning of the word *servant*. Then, they should list what meanings, feelings, and ideas they connect to the word. They can do the same thing for the verb *to serve* and for the noun *service*. Ask if most of the meanings connected with these words are positive or negative.

The word *servant* means one that serves others; especially, one who performs duties for a master or personal employer. There are many definitions of *serve*: to be a servant, to be of use, to discharge a duty, to give the respect due to a superior, and so on. *Service* is defined as the work of one who serves: contribution to the welfare of others, useful labor that does not produce a tangible commodity, and so on. The connotative meanings of these words are often seen as negative: to be subservient, to be under someone's command. (After discussing these meanings, suggest to your students that when "Servant" is used for Church, it means work done for the welfare of others that is freely chosen by the one serving.)

2) Review the organizational chart for the offices in the Vatican (see pp. 26-28 of the student text). Ask the students to identify the offices that are of direct service to the poor, to the cause of justice, to the sacramental life of the Church, to learning, and to families. Then encourage them to draw some comparisons between the Vatican services and the services offered by the local diocese; there should be some common services.

3) The daily newspapers have articles that show the Church acting as Servant. (*a*) Ask the students to bring in articles that show the Church as Servant. The articles could be pasted to a sheet of loose-leaf paper, and underneath the articles your students might write a report on a brief interview with someone who made use of the service offered. (*b*) After this, have the students bring in articles that show areas where the Church could act as Servant (peacemaking, feeding the hungry, visiting prisoners, etc.). You might talk with them about ways in which the local church is or could be responding to the problems presented.

4) Invite someone from the Catholic Charities Office, Catholic Relief Service, Refugee Resettlement Office of the diocese, a Catholic hospital, Saint Vincent de Paul Society, Catholic Worker House, or some other service agency of the Church to give a talk to your students about the Servant Church.

5) Raise the issue of how Catholic schools serve the Church and the local community. Do Catholic schools really serve the larger community too? If so, how?

Summary Activities for the Chapter

1) Using Student Handout 2-A, "The Mission of the Church" (found at the end of this chapter), might be a fine way of wrapping up this chapter on the models of the Church. First, distribute the handouts and have the students fill them out individually. When they are done, the class can be divided into groups of four members. The groups are to select one of the five options to act on first; they should pretend that they are an early church action group. When all the groups have finished they can share their rationales for selecting the option they did. This can lead into a reflection on the fact that all the models are important to the fullness of the Church.

2) In preparation for the closing prayer service, your students may need to review their journal entries—especially their responses to personal reflection exercise 1. This may be the subject matter for the reflection section of Student Handout 2-B, "Prayer Service: Becoming the People of God" (found at the end of this chapter).

The Mission of the Church

Jesus has risen from the tomb. Although you and all the other Christians are overjoyed, you now have to decide what to do. You are one of the followers who have been with Jesus more than two years. The events of the past week seem to erase the plans you had made for the rest of your life. You now realize that the Resurrection is a reality. But what are you going to do now? Below are some alternatives that come to your mind. There is pressure on you to decide right away (within the next few moments) which option seems right for you. Under each option list reasons for selecting it. Then select the one option that seems of most immediate importance. Be prepared to explain why this option is most important.

1) Proclaim on the streets and in the synagogues that Jesus is the Christ; encourage others to repent, believe in him, and be baptized.

2) Go to those who are afflicted and to the poor, and comfort and care for them.

3) Organize people who share your belief in Jesus into communities to consider action.

4) Go to an isolated place to pray and to sort out the meaning of the last two years.

5) Record immediately as much detail about the life of Jesus and his followers as you can.

6) Organize classes to teach about the lessons you have learned from Jesus.

Prayer Service: Becoming the People of God

Leader: Let us remember that the Creator is present in this place with us. We are held in the palm of the Lord's hand.

Reading from John 15

Left: I am the true vine, and my Father is the vinedresser.

Right: Every branch in me that bears no fruit he cuts away; and every branch that does bear fruit he prunes to make it bear even more.

Left: You are pruned already, by means of the word that I have spoken to you.

Right: Make your home in me, as I make mine in you.

Left: As the branch cannot bear fruit all by itself, but must remain part of the vine, neither can you unless you remain in me.

Right: I am the vine, you are the branches.

Left: Whoever remains in me, with me in him, bears fruit in plenty. . . .

Right: If you remain in me and my words remain in you, you may ask what you will and you shall get it. . . .

Left: As the Father has loved me, so I have loved you. Remain in my love.

All: Glory to God who is and ever shall be. Amen.

Reading of Colossians 3:10–17

Leader: Let us review the ways in which we are God's hands, mouth, eyes, and ears. How can we be of more service?

(Pause for silent reflection.)

In Praise and Thanksgiving (Adapted from the Gospels)

Leader: The harvest is plentiful but the laborers are few.

All: Pray to the Lord of the harvest that he will send out laborers to his harvest.

Leader: And preach as you go, saying, "The kingdom of God is at hand."

All: Do not fear those who kill the body but cannot kill the soul; rather fear him who can destroy both soul and body in hell.

Leader: Are not two sparrows sold for a penny? And not one of them will fall to the ground without your Father's will.

All: Every one who acknowledges me before men, I also will acknowledge before my Father who is in heaven.

Leader: He who receives you receives me, and he who receives me receives him who sent me.

All: And whoever gives even a cup of cold water because he is a disciple, truly, I say to you he shall not lose his reward.

Leader: Glory to God who is here and loves us.

All: Glory to God now and forever. Amen.

CHAPTER 3

A Church of Conversion: The Case of Saul

Major Concepts

A. As a devout Jew, Saul was devoted to the Jewish Law. He studied it and held firmly to Jewish traditions in a world dominated by Greek culture and Roman rule.

B. Saul saw the close-knit Christian community growing in influence and wanted to suppress it. He believed that Jesus was a blasphemer and that his followers were attacking God and Judaism by claiming Jesus as the Messiah.

C. Saul's dramatic conversion changed him from an ardent opponent of the Christians to an even more ardent follower of Jesus.

D. The Good News of Jesus spread even to the Gentiles, but this caused problems because some Jewish Christians thought that Jesus came to save only them. Peter believed that Gentiles should be accepted into the Christian community.

Activities for Concept A
As a devout Jew, Saul was devoted to the Jewish Law. He studied it and held firmly to Jewish traditions in a world dominated by Greek culture and Roman rule. (Pages 36–42 of the student text.)

Review Questions and Exercises from the Student Text

Question 1: Describe what it was like for Saul to grow up in Tarsus—that is, as a Jew in a pagan city.

Answer: Tarsus was a crossroads for trade, and so, Saul was exposed to all sorts of people. Nevertheless, his Jewish identity was maintained through attendance at the synagogue. Judaism also forbade Saul from participating in Greek and Roman education and religious rituals. He learned Greek and much about pagan culture, but he was guarded from its influence by his family and by Jewish Law.

Question 2: Trace on the map (see page 37) Saul's trip to Jerusalem and home, and from Jerusalem to Damascus.

Answer: Your students should have little trouble doing this. Tarsus is now part of Turkey, and Saul's trip took him through what is now Lebanon. You might want to point out that Damascus is the capital of Syria.

Question 3: Why was Jerusalem so important to Saul?

Answer: Jerusalem was the center of Judaism. The teachers who would instruct him in the Law were there. Most importantly, the Temple was in Jerusalem. It contained the holy of holies, the most sacred place in Judaism.

Question 4: What is meant by the Law? Why did the Jews think that the study of the Law was so important?

Answer: The Law was the covenant in which God made a promise to be faithful to the Jews. The Jews were the "Chosen People." On their part, the Jews committed

themselves to live a prescribed lifestyle that showed love and respect to the God who saved Israel. Studying the Law gave Jews a sense of God's saving power in their history. The Jews had both written and oral laws. The written Law contained the history of Israel and many moral teachings. The oral Law described in more detail the obligations required in the written Law.

Question 5: Like any human organization, Judaism was split into religious and political parties. What were these groups? How did they differ?

Answer: The scribes studied and taught both the written and oral Law. The Sanhedrin was the supreme council of the Jews; in it were two factions. One faction, the Sadducees, included many of the Temple priests and those who collaborated with the Romans. They believed that it was sufficient to keep just the written laws found in Scripture. The other faction, the Pharisees, was opposed to Roman rule and tried to follow both the written and oral Law; many scribes were members of the Pharisees' faction.

Question 6: What was life like for Jews of the Diaspora?

Answer: Jews were living outside of Palestine—dispersed because of famines in Palestine or deportation by various conquering armies. Wherever they settled, the Jews built synagogues. In many places the non-Jews respected Jewish customs; in fact, the Romans exempted Jews from serving in the regular army. In other places, Jews of the Diaspora were victims of persecution because they did not conform to the local customs.

Other Questions and Activities for Discussion

1) The goal of this activity is to help students understand what it was like for Saul to live in Tarsus, a Jew in a Gentile world. Here is a case that students can analyze:

> Mark is a junior at Saint _____ High School. He studies fairly hard and participates in two school organizations: the newspaper and the student council. The neighborhood he lives in is heavily Catholic, and most of his best friends are Catholic too. One day his father and mother tell him that because of a promotion and the extra income and because they can be closer to his grandmother who is elderly, they are going to move to another area of the city. Mark is told that he can finish high school at Saint _____ , but the trip will take an hour each way. They think that he would like the public high school in the suburb where they will live, but the choice is his.
> * If you were Mark, what thoughts would cross your mind about the move? What adjustments would you have to make if you moved but stayed at Saint _____? What adjustments would you have to make if you changed to the public school?

Here is a further variation of the case:

> Now imagine that instead of moving to a suburb, Mark's family was to be transferred to Hong Kong. While he will be attending an international school there, most of the people where he will live are ethnic Chinese who ordinarily speak one of the Chinese languages and are Buddhists.
> * If you were Mark, what adjustments would you have to make? What would be exciting about such a move? What would you dislike about the move?

Finish the discussion with a comment like the following:

> From our discussion it is clear that living in another culture has some difficulties and some interesting aspects too. Perhaps it is easier now to understand what it was like for Saul to live in Tarsus. While he learned to cope with Greek and Roman ways, he always felt different.

2) Many of us may have a less positive attitude about law(s) than Saul and the Jews of his day would. To illustrate that the Jews viewed the Law as the source of their identity, their covenant with God, and the source of goodness, passages from Psalm 19 or 119 would be helpful. In fact you might want your students to do a choral reading of Psalm 19.

3) Sometimes it sounds critical to point out that there were factions in Judaism during Saul's life; but this is not an uncommon situation. Address the following issues with your students:
- Are there any "parties" in the Catholic Church today?
- Are there any factions that disagree and dispute with one another?
- How would these factions be described?
- What are causes for and effects of having different religious and political groups belonging to the same Church?

The students may be directed to some contemporary examples. For example, recently the pope made several speeches in which he was critical of capitalism. This caused some alarm and indignation among businesspeople. There are pacifist Catholics and Catholics belonging to the military who believe that the "just-war" theory is a responsible Christian principle.

4) Lest your students think that Jewish religious laws were the only ones that conflicted with civilian authority, ask your students to list some of the Church's moral teachings that are in opposition to government policies. One very obvious disagreement between church law and civil law concerns abortion. Are there others?

Activities for Concept B
Saul saw the close-knit Christian community growing in influence and wanted to suppress it. He believed that Jesus was a blasphemer and that his followers were attacking God and Judaism by claiming Jesus as the Messiah. (Pages 42–46 of the student text.)

Review Questions and Exercises from the Student Text

Question 7: Why did the early Christians seem to pose such a threat to a devout Jew like Saul?
Answer: Saul and other devoted Jews thought that Christians were blasphemers. Christians preached that Jesus was the Messiah, the Son of God. For many Jews, talking about Jesus as the Son of God implied that there was more than one God. The people of Israel had been fighting polytheism for generations, and for other Jews to seem to say that there was a Son of God was onerous, heretical, and blasphemous. In addition, Christians made what to Jews was an outlandish claim, that Jesus had risen from the tomb. And since the Apostles were curing the sick and preaching publicly, Jews could not ignore them.

Question 8: What was life like for the early Christians in Jerusalem?
Answer: The early Christians continued to follow the Jewish laws. Also, they met for prayer and "the breaking of the bread." The Apostles and other Christians worshiped in the Temple, but preached the Good News too. From the many passages describing the early community, we can see that they were held together in love and unity by the common faith they shared. The deacons were appointed to pay special attention to the material welfare of the community, especially the widows, orphans, sick, and poor. On the other hand, Christians were sometimes persecuted because they held beliefs that seemed blasphemous to devout Jews.

Question 9: Why was Stephen considered a blasphemer?

Answer: In addition to claiming that Jesus was the Messiah, Stephen preached that the Temple was no longer necessary for the worship of God. He went further by telling the Sanhedrin that they had pagan hearts and ears because they were resisting the Holy Spirit.

Personal Reflection Exercise

Reflect on the following two cases. While the names have been changed, the events are real. Try to put yourself in each situation described. Keep in mind what you know of the early Christian community. Outline your response to the problems posed.

a) "Fire Destroys Tenement Block"

Bridgetown is a very poor neighborhood, consisting mostly of old houses that were converted into numerous apartments. Some have been condemned, and the rest probably should have been. Two factories have moved out of the area, so conditions are worse than ever. Unemployment is very high. A small parish, Saint Angela's, has managed to stay open, but has only one priest. One very cold night a raging fire sweeps through a block of tenement apartments. Quickly fifteen families are made homeless, and most have lost their few possessions. You are one of a group of parish lay leaders. You meet late at night to decide what the parish should do to help. Since the need is immediate, you must draw up a plan of action very swiftly—if you are going to help at all. What will you do? If you decide to help, draw up very specific plans. Try to outline the reasons for your decision.

b) "The Murdered Missionary"

Your high school is run by a religious order. You like your school and admire the religious who teach there. One day, your religion teacher tells the class that a member of the order was shot down in cold blood in a small Latin American village in which the order ran a school for poor children. The class is asked to pray for the souls of the slain religious and the two students who were also killed. In your social studies class you read that the government of your country supports the Latin American regime that was responsible for the death of the religious, who that regime claimed was a guerrilla sympathizer. Finally, after several days have passed, the religion department asks for donations of money to send down to the mission school to support the work of the religious. You wonder what to do and whom to believe. What would you do—contribute or not? Outline the issues involved.

Other Questions and Activities for Discussion

1) To add to your students' knowledge about the early Christian community (covered in review question 8), these passages from the Acts of the Apostles can be helpful:

Acts 3:1-10 (Peter's cure of a lame man)
Acts 4:23-31 (praying together under persecution)
Acts 5:1-11 (the selfishness of Ananias and Sapphira)
Acts 5:12-16 (the meetings in Solomon's portico)

To continue the discussion, ask the following question:

• How does the life of the early Christian community compare or contrast with contemporary parish life as you know it?

2) If you have a student who can do dramatic readings well, your students may get a lot out of hearing Stephen's entire speech before the Sanhedrin. Ask most of the

students to put themselves in the place of the Sanhedrin; a small group can act as fellow Christians there to witness Stephen's speech. After the student has delivered Stephen's speech, the Sanhedrin members can list why they want to stone Stephen, and the Christians can try to defend him. See Acts 6:8–15 to explain the background to Stephen's arrest. His speech is contained in Acts 7:1–53 (you may wish to cut out some of it).

3) In order to have students reflect on why Stephen was stoned, have them write an imaginary interview with someone who stoned Stephen. They can write the interview in a question-answer format. Encourage the students to examine the interviewee's feelings too. Then, perhaps one or two students could read their interviews to the class.

4) We may not understand the motivations of the Jews very well, but the Jewish Christians probably did. Invite your students to discuss this query:
- Would the Jewish Christians in the Jerusalem community understand why the Jews stoned Stephen?

Taking your investigation further, here is another line of inquiry to take up with the students:
- Would people execute someone today for blasphemy? Why or why not?
- What does the fact that we do not execute people for blasphemy say about our society?
- Are there any examples that you can think of where people are persecuted for not following the majority's religion? Are people actually punished physically for actions such as blasphemy?
- Would we be better or worse off if we treated blasphemers as the Judaic Law did?

5) Persecution of zealous Christians continues even now. There are many stories published about contemporary persecution. In order for students to update the examples of people suffering for the faith that are given in the student text (see p. 44), have them complete the following assignment:

Using recent periodicals or newspapers, research instances of people being persecuted for being Christians: for serving the poor, for praying in public, for preaching, and so on.

Clippings might be displayed on the bulletin board in your classroom as a reminder to all that the faith is alive in the world and that people are still willing to suffer for it.

6) There are numerous new cults flourishing today. Most are offshoots of mainstream religions. Many people fear the powerful influence that these cults have, especially on young people who are looking for meaning in their lives and have not found it with traditional churches. In order for your students to appreciate the position of the Jews toward the early Christian community, they may be directed to discuss these questions:
- List some of the new religious cults that you have heard about.
- What do most people think about groups like these—for example, the "Moonies"? What kind of comments do people make about them?
- How would your parents and friends treat you if you joined one of these cults?
- Most cults come and go rather rapidly, and this will be the fate of most of the contemporary cults. However, what is similar about the reaction of the Jews to the Christians and about our reaction to members of cults?
- Saul's teacher, the Pharisee Gamaliel, told the Sanhedrin to leave the Christians alone. He reasoned that if the Christians were following the directives of God, the Sanhedrin would be opposing God if they fought the Christians. On the other hand, if Jesus was not the Messiah, his followers would sooner

or later disband and die out. How would you evaluate this approach to dealing with contemporary cults? Why don't most members of the established churches follow Gamaliel's line of reasoning?

The topic of cults has many complexities. If you think that your students would profit from a continuation of this discussion, here is an additional approach. The University Religious Council of the University of California at Berkeley developed this list of *characteristics* of cults:

a) a leader who claims divinity or a special relationship with God
b) a leader who is the sole judge of a member's actions or faith
c) totalitarian governance
d) total control over the daily lives of members
e) exclusivity and isolation
f) development of deep emotional dependence
g) prohibition of critical analysis and independent thinking
h) utilization of methods of ego destruction and mind control
i) exploitation of a member's finances
j) underemployment and exploitative working conditions

Using this list with your students, you can illustrate in discussion how different Christianity is from cults. Jesus taught us to judge our own actions and to be responsible. The governance of Jesus was nonexistent; Jesus wanted his disciples to be free to choose. Rather than being exclusive and isolated, Jesus and his followers welcomed everyone. While the Holy Spirit is with us always, our uniqueness is never suppressed; the disciples and Apostles were not emotional dependents. In short, you can analyze this list to show that Jesus' way did not fit the characteristics of a modern cult. Nevertheless, from the Jewish viewpoint, early Christians were treated as we treat members of cults today.

7) Invite a permanent deacon to discuss his role in the Church today. Ask him to describe how his function is historically distinct from that of priests or bishops. Other subjects for the talk include the following:

• Why was the permanent diaconate restored now?
• Why did you want to become a deacon?
• What has being a deacon meant for your life as a husband and a professional?

Your students will probably have many questions too.

Activities for Concept C
Saul's dramatic conversion changed him from an ardent opponent of the Christians to an even more ardent follower of Jesus. (Pages 46–47 of the student text.)

Review Questions and Exercises from the Student Text

Question 10: In Scripture, we are often reminded that God's ways are not the ways of humans. How is this made obvious in Saul's conversion?

Answer: In the ordinary course of things, Saul seems an unlikely candidate for conversion. He had set out on a journey to persecute Christians. In any case, God must have seen in Saul the makings of the great Apostle he was to become. All the passion he put into opposing Christians was now put into preaching the Good News.

Other Questions and Activities for Discussion

1) The reflections from the following exercise on conversion might best be recorded in the students' journals:

Few, if any, of us have been knocked off our feet by God; probably none of us have heard voices like Saul did. However, the true Christian must convert his or her life more and more to become loving, faithful, hope-filled.

- If the Lord knocked you off your feet and told you to reform your ways, what facets of yourself would you need to convert?
- What aspects of who you are would you want to keep and develop further?

2) Students would most likely find it interesting to interview a recent convert to Catholicism. Contacts might be made through catechumenate programs in their parishes. The intent of the interview would be to find out what the process of conversion was like and what motivated the person to consider conversion. Questions could be developed in class before the students do the interviews. If there are few contacts, the interviews could be done by groups of students, or maybe a recent convert could visit your class.

3) A common expression used to describe a conversion experience is "born again." Often the definition of this expression is very subjective and very vague. Ask the students to do some research in magazines and newspapers, and through interviews and discussions to find out what people mean when they say that they are "born again." Ask your students to consider these issues:

- What characteristics would you expect someone who is "born again" to have?
- How would this person be different after the experience?
- If someone told you that he or she was "born again" in Jesus, how would you expect them to act?

As points of reference, consider the following characteristics that are commonly used to determine the validity of someone's conversion: First, the moment of conversion is preceded by much serious thinking. The decision to convert is made freely; in short, no coercion is applied, neither overt nor subtle. After conversion there is a noticeable change of heart that makes converts more open to loving other persons, God, and themselves. All of this leads to a new identity. Christians appreciate that humans are made in God's image; thus, they promote and preserve what is most life-giving. Finally, converts build new loving relationships, even with those who are hard to love.

Surely conversion is a lifelong process for almost all of us. Saul's conversion was very dramatic. Few people are really converted just because they claim to be "born again." The process is more complicated and more gradual for almost all of us.

4) Sometimes part of conversion is the realization of not only our sinfulness but also our giftedness. After all, when we come to a new appreciation of how good we are, we are called to use and develop that goodness. To add a bit to activity 1 above, students might want to write in their journals about times when the "lights went on"—times when they suddenly realized good aspects about themselves, times when they could affirm that truly they were children of a good God.

Activities for Concept D
The Good News of Jesus spread even to the Gentiles, but this caused problems because some Jewish Christians thought that Jesus came to save only them. Peter believed that Gentiles should be accepted into the Christian community. (Pages 47–48 of the student text.)

Review Questions and Exercises from the Student Text

Question 11: Why did the Christian converts from Judaism object to Gentiles' being converted? How did Peter handle their objections?

Answer: Gentiles were not the Chosen People. Many Jewish Christians thought that the Messiah came just for them. Also, since Peter ate with Gentiles, he was breaking Jewish Law. In effect, many of the early Christians in Jerusalem thought of themselves as still subject to Judaic Law. Peter was convinced that Jesus came to save all of humankind. His conviction came from a vision he had. Peter pointed out that Jesus also ate with sinners, tax collectors, and non-Jews.

Question 12: How were the models of the Church reflected in the events of this chapter?

Answer: The church community reminded everyone of Jesus' presence (Sacrament). Peter, Stephen, Philip, and the other disciples preached the Word (Herald). Deacons were confirmed in order to serve the needs of the community, a community that shared so that every person had enough (Servant). As an identifiable group meeting regularly at the Temple, the early Christians were the People of God. The start of an Institution is seen in the prominence given to Peter.

Other Questions and Activities for Discussion

1) We presume today that all people are welcome into the Church. Consequently, students might have a hard time understanding the Jewish Christians' objection to Gentiles' becoming part of the Way. Remind them that for centuries Jews had been taught that they were the only Chosen People. No wonder they felt upset when Peter began accepting non-Jews into their community. To explore your students' reactions to this, here are some queries to pose:

- Why do clubs and other groups have rules governing who can join them—membership regulations?
- Name some clubs that have restrictions on membership. What sort of restriction does each club impose?
- Should clubs restrict their memberships in any way?
- What are the positive and negative effects of exclusivity in club memberships?
- *Optional:* Recently the courts decreed that the Jaycees had to open up their membership to include women. Do you agree that they should have to include women?
- If clubs and organizations that are civic and have little to do with something so personal as religious lifestyle have restrictions on membership, is it understandable why Jewish Christians objected to the inclusion of Gentiles?

The main point of this dialogue is that there are positive benefits to exclusivity, which allows the members to create a sense of identity with the group. And since the Jews were a conquered people—surrounded by Roman legions, hostile neighbors, and heavily influenced by Greek culture—it is clear why even Jewish Christians would balk at accepting outsiders into their community.

2) Peter had a vision that compelled him to accept Gentiles, but in the Gospels, which were written years after the events described in this chapter, the Evangelists tell of Jesus commanding that the Apostles go out and preach to the whole world. If you wish to review Jesus' words, here are pertinent passages: Matt. 28:18–20; Mark 16:15–18.

3) Another way of comprehending the desire for exclusivity is to see it in terms of nationalism. Point out to the students that many of the early encounters with preaching the Good News to non-Jews occurred outside Judaea. In Jaffa, Peter brought Tabitha back to life, and in Caesarea he baptized Roman Gentiles. Philip preached to the Samaritans. Have the students locate these places on the map (see p. 37 of the student text).

The case that follows might be distributed for analysis by groups of your students (four or five students per group):

Congresswoman Hernandez is caught in an agonizing dilemma. In two days she will have to vote on a new immigration law that will severely restrict immigration from other countries. Part of the problem is that if this law had been in effect thirty years ago, her own parents would have been refused admission into the country. Also, she believes in the ideals of this country and in the tradition of openness for immigrants trying to find a better life here. On the other hand, many of her constituents want to stop the flow of immigrants because, at least initially, some immigrants live on welfare, populate the poor areas of cities, and challenge the ethnic balance of some cities. Ms. Hernandez knows that the law cannot accept everyone, but wonders if such a restrictive law is right.

- If you were Congresswoman Hernandez, how would you vote, and why would you vote that way?

After the groups have had enough time to come to a consensus position about the case, ask each group to report its stand and the reasons to support it. Again this discussion should point out the strong pull toward exclusivity that we have, but also the values of openness and inclusion. The decision about including Gentiles in the Christian communities comes up again in chapter 4. The Jews did not have a tradition of including new people in their religion. Thus, if people in a nation with a tradition of including immigrants want to make exclusivity laws, how much more would a people who were the Chosen Race want to maintain their special identity? This conflict was central to the development of the Church. *After all, imagine what might have happened if Peter had not had his vision and the Gentiles had been excluded from membership. Would most of us be Christians today?*

Summary Activities for the Chapter

1) Encourage your students to write their reflections in their journals on these questions:
- As a member of the Church, how were you a Herald of the Word this week? a Servant of humankind? a Sacrament?

2) A closing prayer is offered on Student Handout 3–A, "Prayer Service: Building Community" (found at the end of this chapter).

Prayer Service: Building Community

An Early Prayer by an Anonymous Christian

Leader: Let us join in praying one of the earliest of all Christian prayers, written in Jerusalem by an anonymous Christian in thanksgiving for the release of the Apostles from prison after one of their arrests:

All: Ruler of all, you are the maker of heaven and earth and the sea, and all that is in them. You have said through the Holy Spirit, by the lips of your servant David, our father:

Left: What means this turmoil among the nations?
Why do the pagans cherish vain dreams?
See how the kings of the earth stand in array,
how its rulers make common cause,
against the Lord and his Christ.

Right: True enough, in this city of ours, Herod and Pontius Pilate, with the Gentiles, and the people of Israel to aid them, made common cause against your holy servant Jesus, whom you anointed, and so they accomplished all that your power and wisdom had decreed.

All: Look down upon their threats, Lord, now as of old; enable your servants to preach your word confidently, by stretching out your hand to heal; and let signs and miracles be performed in the name of Jesus, your holy Son.

Reading of Ephesians 4:1–6

Leader: One of the miracles that occurred through the name of Jesus was the formation of the Christian community in Jerusalem, and now all over the world. Listen to Saint Paul's call for unity from Ephesians.

Reflection

Leader: Let us join in silently reflecting on the many good ways in which we can build community.

Closing Prayer Adapted from 1 Thessalonians 5:11–24

Left: Let us give encouragement to one another and strengthen one another as Jesus has already done for us.

Right: Lord, may we be considerate to those teaching us and serving us in our parishes.

Left: Help us to be at peace among ourselves.

Right: May we give courage to those of us who are apprehensive in a world full of dangers, but also full of goodness.

Left: Help us to care for the weak and to be patient with everyone.

Right: May we never take revenge, rather may we think of what is best for each other and for the community.

Left: Help us to search for the Spirit in ourselves and to listen to those who are prophets today.

Right: May we hold on to what is good.

All: For all the good things given freely by God, we say thank you.

CHAPTER 4
Paul's New Community

Major Concepts

A. The Church began to spread out to different cities, yet ties of community bonded the young Church together. At the request of Barnabas, Paul began his mission at Antioch. Then both men brought money to relieve the Christians in Jerusalem. Peter miraculously escaped from prison.

B. Paul began preaching in more distant lands where he was sometimes successful but always in peril. Nevertheless, he established his standard approach of first preaching to the Jews in the synagogues and then spreading the Word to the Gentiles.

C. Jewish Christians objected to Gentile converts' ignoring Judaic Law; this precipitated a crisis. The Council of Jerusalem decided that Gentiles were free from the Judaic Law but that they should be sensitive to their Jewish brothers and sisters. The council became the established means for the People of God to listen to the Holy Spirit and guide the Church accordingly.

D. During Paul's second journey, he spread the Good News in Europe: Philippi, Thessalonika, Athens, and Corinth. Despite more hardships, vibrant Christian communities were founded.

Activities for Concept A
The Church began to spread out to different cities, yet ties of community bonded the young Church together. At the request of Barnabas, Paul began his mission at Antioch. Then both men brought money to relieve the Christians in Jerusalem. Peter miraculously escaped from prison. (Pages 52–54 of the student text.)

Review Questions and Exercises from the Student Text

Question 1: Why was Antioch such an important city in the Roman Empire?

Answer: Antioch was the third largest city in the Roman Empire, and it was an important crossroads for trade. Thus, any idea or movement that caught on here would soon be heard about all over the empire. There was a large community of Jews here too, and thus it was a good place to spread the Word of God. The followers of Jesus were first called Christians here.

Question 2: Why did Paul and Barnabas make the trip to Jerusalem from Antioch? Why would this act be so significant in light of later events with the Antioch community?

Answer: Paul and Barnabas brought money from the Christians in Antioch to aid the community in Jerusalem which was suffering from shortages of food due to a famine. [*Teacher's note:* Later, Jewish Christians caused conflict in Antioch by raising the issue of Gentiles' needing to obey Judaic Law. The community in Jerusalem was the leading force in Christianity at this time, and even though they appreciated the help from Antioch, they assumed some authority in the formation of other Christian communities around the empire.]

Personal Reflection Exercise

> 1) How do you really feel about collections at Mass? Do you feel that people support and encourage you to give money in the collections? Write a list of names of people who encourage you to give. Then, formulate a prayer of thanksgiving for them.

Other Questions and Activities for Discussion

1) There is little comment in Paul's Epistles about the time between his conversion and his active ministry. And, he does not say a lot about his fears of preaching. To reflect on his courage, here are some questions to pose with your students:
- What feelings pass through someone's mind when he or she is attempting something new like trying out for a team, auditioning for a play, applying for a job? Try to describe what is going on inside the person in this position.
- What are some sources of courage for people when they try new things?
- What do you think it was like for Paul when he stood up to give his first speech about Jesus?
- Where did he find his strength?

2) Paul had to flee from those who would have thrown him in jail or maybe even killed him. Peter escaped from prison with the help of an angel. We assume that people are in prison because they did something wrong, and of course, this is generally true. However, the plight of prisoners of conscience has been documented quite often in recent years. In order to raise the consciousness of your students to the fact that there are many people in prisons around the world not for doing wrong but for fighting for justice, assign them to research the status of prisoners of conscience in the following countries: South Africa, the Philippines, Guatemala, the Soviet Union, China, Israel, Poland, Iran, Chile, Argentina. Clearly, prisoners of conscience languish in jails in other countries and could be subjects of research too. When the research is finished, have the students give reports on their findings. Perhaps a special "Prisoners of Conscience" bulletin board could become a regular feature of your classroom. Some useful sources for this sort of information are *The Catholic Almanac, The National Catholic Reporter, Sojourners.*

Then raise these questions with your students:
- Are there prisoners of conscience in the United States or Canada?
- Are there any people whose stance on nuclear arms, the environment, human rights, and so on, has led them to commit illegal actions for the cause of peace, a better earth, or justice?

It is important that the students understand that sometimes it is a moral imperative to confront immoral practices.

3) Some students might be assigned to do research on collections taken up by church groups. They should be urged to find answers to the following questions:
- What is the goal of the collection?
- How much is collected yearly by this group?
- How much of what is collected is spent on administrative costs instead of on direct benefits to the target group?
- What methods are used to raise the money or collect the goods?
- Who has officially approved the collection?

Once the reports have been formulated, each research group should present its findings to the class. A list of worthy causes could be posted in your classroom after the reports have been completed.

Here are some collections that could be researched: local Thanksgiving and/or Christmas drives, school mission collections, diocesan mission collections, Peter's Pence,

Catholic Relief Services, the Campaign for Human Development. Naturally, you will be able to add to this list. One way of adding to the list is to have the students find out from their parents what groups have sent them direct-mail appeals. Also encourage the students to share the results of their research with their parents; this can help families decide which charities are most effective.

4) Here is another assignment about contributing to the welfare of others:

Using at least two passages from Paul's Epistles, write a homily he might have given the people of Antioch in order to encourage them to contribute to the collection for Jerusalem.

Activities for Concept B

Paul began preaching in more distant lands where he was sometimes successful but always in peril. Nevertheless, he established his standard approach of first preaching to the Jews in the synagogues and then spreading the Word to the Gentiles. (Pages 54–55 of the student text.)

Review Questions and Exercises from the Student Text

Question 3: Describe Paul's first missionary journey with Barnabas.

Answer: Their trip took them to Cyprus and Asia Minor where they preached to more Greeks and Romans than they had before. Paul and Barnabas were taking the message of Jesus further from Israel than ever.

Question 4: What was the overall strategy that Paul used in preaching the Word of God? Why did he adopt this approach?

Answer: Paul first went to the Jews, preaching in synagogues and staying in Jewish homes. Jews knew of the Messianic prophecies and shared Paul's religious heritage; they were more likely to understand him. If he was successful in his preaching to the Jews, he would have a base of support as he moved on to spreading the Word to the Gentiles.

Other Questions and Activities for Discussion

1) Have the students find Cyprus and Asia Minor on a map. Then divide the class into three teams and ask them to prepare reports on one of the following projects:

Team A: Paul's Travels
- Estimate the approximate distance covered by Paul and Barnabas on their missionary trip.
- Find pictures of boats used during Roman times, ones like Paul probably traveled in. How were the boats powered? How safe were they?
- Find pictures of the roads that the Romans built throughout the empire. How were the roads constructed?
- What sort of tents would Paul have made? Why were they so necessary at this time?

Team B: Cyprus
- Prepare a report on the island of Cyprus today. What is the ethnic makeup? the population? the principal source of income? What are the main cities today?
- What sort of terrain did Paul have to cover to get across the island of Cyprus on foot?

Team C: Turkey
- Prepare a report on Turkey. What is the ethnic makeup? the population? the principal source of income? What are the main cities today?
- What sort of terrain did Paul have to cover as he traveled through Turkey on foot?

When the teams have completed their research, invite them to report to the class.

2) Paul's attempt to first spread the Good News to the Jews may seem unimportant, but actually, it follows a very human approach. Students will understand this method readily if they consider these questions:
- When you first arrive at a meeting, class, or party, with whom do you associate?
- Why do you first hang around people you know?
- How do you feel if you go to a party and don't know anyone?
- Why was it only natural for Paul to preach to the Jews first?

Activities for Concept C

Jewish Christians objected to Gentile converts' ignoring Judaic Law; this precipitated a crisis. The Council of Jerusalem decided that Gentiles were free from the Judaic Law but that they should be sensitive to their Jewish brothers and sisters. The council became the established means for the People of God to listen to the Holy Spirit and guide the Church accordingly. (Pages 55–61 of the student text.)

Review Questions and Exercises from the Student Text

Question 5: Why did the Gentiles object to the Jewish laws? Were their objections justified? Why did the Jewish Christians insist on following the Law? What did it mean to them?

Answer: The written and oral Jewish Law was passed on to Jews through rich cultural practices supported by familial and religious structures. Most Gentiles, who came from non-Jewish cultures, would find the Judaic laws perplexing and even incomprehensible. More importantly, the Gentiles could not understand *why* they had to obey Jewish laws. Jesus had come to save all people, and he had broken the laws himself; after all, he had eaten with Gentiles. Furthermore, Jesus never said that Gentiles had to follow the Judaic Law.

On the other hand, Jewish Christians thought that although Jesus was the fulfillment of all the prophecies and was indeed the Messiah, he came to the people of Israel, the Chosen Ones. If the Judaic Law was part of being a Chosen One, then all followers of Jesus should obey the Judaic Law. The Law was part of the covenant that the people of Israel made with God. If a Jew broke the Law, he or she broke with God. Thus, to devout Jewish Christians, the Law remained an affirmation of their faith in the one God.

Question 6: Why did the conversion of Gentiles pose such a critical problem for the early Church? What were the motives of the Jewish Christians? How was the controversy finally solved?

Answer: Many Gentiles had accepted Jesus and were part of active Christian communities. If Jewish Christians were going to insist that Gentiles follow the Law, the Church would be split into factions, thus weakening the already threatened group. Both Gentiles and Jewish Christians agreed that Jesus offered salvation to all humankind, but a major theological issue developed: Is the only requirement for salvation that one have faith in Jesus? Or must one also keep all the Judaic laws in order to be worthy of salvation?

The motives of the Jewish Christians were genuine: they really believed that since Jesus was a Jew and had come to the Jews, all people who wanted to be followers of Jesus had to be Jews too. The final resolution was made at the Council of Jerusalem. Gentiles did not have to follow Jewish Law, but they should abstain from food sacrificed to idols, from blood, from the meat of strangled animals, and from fornication.

Question 7: What was Peter's position in the controversy that arose in Antioch? What did he do to bring the matter to a peaceful settlement? What pattern did his actions set for the Church that lasts up until today?

Answer: Peter believed that Gentiles need not practice Jewish laws, but at the same time he was the leader of all Christians and did not want to scandalize Jewish Christians either. The matter was brought before the entire community of Christians in Jerusalem for consideration under the guidance of the Holy Spirit. This first council settled the matter, just as councils since then have done. Whenever crises arise in the Church, councils are called. They are a recognition of the fact that the Church is the People of God.

Question 8: Did Jesus really reject the Jewish Law? What was his attitude toward it?

Answer: Jesus made love of God and neighbor central to his teaching; this love was also central to the Hebrew Scriptures. What Jesus rejected was the slavish following of laws that were unimportant; people sometimes overlooked love in order to fulfill a scrupulous observance. Jesus cured on the Sabbath, showing that the welfare of people was more important than laws forbidding work. In effect, Jesus accepted the important aspects of Jewish Law that were far too often lost in the midst of trivial laws.

Personal Reflection Exercises

> **2) Read again and reflect on Paul's thoughts about the Antioch situation. Realizing that what he says about Jesus is as true today as it was then, try to describe how you would see your life if you did not have some faith in and/or knowledge about Jesus. Would you be different? How?**
>
> **3) In any group of people there is always the temptation for some people to reject others because of things such as the way these others dress, where they are from, what they look like, their color, religion, or sex. In short, we find ourselves rejecting people because of externals—very often these are people we hardly know. Make a list of people whom you have rejected in some way—mostly because they were different from you. Next to the name, write down what it was or is that causes you problems about the person. Clearly, we cannot be "best friends" with everyone, but are your reasons valid for rejecting these people? Then, make up a prayer for those whom you have rejected.**

Other Questions and Activities for Discussion

1) To reinforce the comprehension of the problems involved in Gentiles' following Jewish laws, have the students read through Leviticus and find other regulations that would be very difficult for people today to follow. Considering the passages found by the students and the passages cited in the student text, discuss these questions:
- How would your day-to-day life be different if you had to follow these laws? [Then cite one or two particular laws from Leviticus.]
- Considering the poor sanitation and lack of refrigeration in the years before, during, and immediately after the life of Jesus, would any of these regulations promote better health?

4

- While some of the laws may make a good deal of sense on the basis of health, could a Gentile see any religious significance to these laws?
- Would there be many Christians if all of these laws had to be followed?

2) To appreciate the need for some source of unity in the community of Christians, ask your students to consider these queries:
- What problems can arise in a family when a family member marries into a different social class, a different religion, a different ethnic group, or a different culture? Think of some particular examples of difficulties that can occur when this happens.
- What actions and attitudes can preserve unity in the family in these situations?
- What could some of the effects be if unity is not preserved?
- Is it fair to reject those who do marry out of the ordinary circle of family life?

3) Set up a panel of four or five students. Each student is to formulate his or her criteria for deciding what characterizes someone who is a Christian. The students must include in their formulation comments on these two questions:
- Is it enough to merely say, even if sincerely, that one is a Christian?
- How can one verify one's claim of being a Christian; are rituals or good works required?

The panelists should explain their responses to the class.

Chances are that the panelists will come up with different descriptions and, of course, some common elements. However, this exercise will illustrate that it is hard to have unity on such a complex question. Thus, when the Jewish Christians wanted Gentiles to follow their laws, they did so to promote some sort of common practice that would show one's Christianity. After all, devout Jews believed that if one followed the Law, one was a good Jew. Jesus' teachings did not have such precise laws, and so, it took considerable adjustment for Jewish Christians to accept the latitude of actions allowed under the two great commandments to love.

4) To further analyze the different outlooks on law versus the spirit of the law, the following case might help students experience the complexities of decision-making:

Mrs. Schneider faces a tough decision. Sitting across her desk is Teri Hilger. Teri has been regularly sent to the office for various problems that she has caused her teachers. Recently she had been caught cheating on a business math test, and when the teacher confronted her about it after class, Teri acted nastily toward the teacher. Today, Mrs. Schneider is faced with Teri's most serious offense: At lunch hour Teri had been caught drinking beer in her car in the school parking lot, and besides being slightly drunk, she was abusive to the dean of students.

The school's student handbook is very clear; students caught drinking on school property could and should be expelled from school. In fact, one month before, a friend of Teri's had been kicked out for drinking. However, Mrs. Schneider has just had a call from the pastor of Teri's parish. He told her that Teri's parents are in the midst of a very bitter divorce proceeding. At issue is the custody of Teri. At present the father is jobless and would have a hard time supporting her; but the mother, although a middle-level manager in a small business, is a heavy drinker, if not an alcoholic. The mother is mean when drunk, and frequently Teri has to spend the night at a friend's house when her mother gets drunk.

- If you were Mrs. Schneider, what would you do? Make sure you list all the issues involved.
- What should be considered more important here, law (designed to protect society) or mercy?

After all the students have made individual decisions and written down their reasons, take a vote on courses of action. Then divide the class into groups according to the courses of action taken; for example, those who would expel Teri would be one group, those who would suspend her another group, and so on. Each group should establish a rationale for its course of action. Then direct each group to appoint a representative to debate the issue.

5) Here is another case that shows how changing membership rules changes a group, and yet, justice may demand the altering of traditions:

Bob Smith belongs to a prestigious civic service organization with branches all over the country. Since its founding eighty years before, the group has, according to its constitution, been composed of all men, usually selected from well-known firms or academic institutions. An invitation for an executive to join this group has always been considered a real honor and a sign that this man was on the way up the corporate ladder.

Two months ago something shocking happened—a woman applied for membership. She is vice-president of a medium-size bank and has a law degree from a prominent university. In her application she cites her desire to serve and the many talents that she can offer the organization. If she were a man, there would be no question as to her acceptance. Even though the constitution clearly excludes women from membership, the rules require that the membership committee consider all applications. Bob is on the membership committee. The woman's application is before him. She is qualified and could clearly make a contribution.
- If you were Bob, what would you do?
- What changes would take place in the organization if women were admitted?
- What ethical considerations are there in the case?
- Is it right to exclude women? (It might be important to consider that membership in the organization helps the careers of members.)

The main point here is that, to some extent, the case parallels the situation of the early Christian community. In practice the community had been composed of Jews. Adding Gentiles would alter the composition of the Christian community, but was it right to exclude anyone from the People of God just because of their previous religious practice? Although the change to more open admission was the correct course to take, it was a difficult transition.

6) Read the story of Jesus and the Samaritan woman from John 4:1–42. Then discuss with the students the following questions:
- Considering this passage, what seems to be Jesus' attitude toward non-Jews?
- Would Jesus require Gentiles to follow Judaic Law?

7) To point out that the tendency for church groups to become closed communities still continues today, discuss with your students these queries:
- What are some examples of how the Church or a parish can sometimes seem closed to others who share in the Word of God (just as the Jewish Christians were closed to the Gentile Christians)?
- What are some ways in which the Church can and does extend itself to all people?

8) Have the students write an imaginary dialogue between a Jewish Christian and a Gentile Christian from Antioch who are discussing the issue of following the Law of Moses. You might wish to review the laws of Leviticus again. The Gentile Christian might need to refer to the Christian Scriptures for support for his or her position. Students could then role-play their dialogues, and other class members could critique the accuracy of the discussion.

4

9) Give your students the following assignment about church councils:

List as many effects of the Second Vatican Council as you can. If you need some information or reactions, ask your parents or relatives about their opinions as to the effects. Were the effects they described similar to the effects of the Jerusalem Council?

Once the students have completed the assignment, discuss their findings in class.

Activities for Concept D

4

During Paul's second journey, he spread the Good News in Europe: Philippi, Thessalonika, Athens, and Corinth. Despite more hardships, vibrant Christian communities were founded. (Pages 61–63 of the student text.)

Review Questions and Exercises from the Student Text

Question 9: What significant events happened to Paul in Philippi? Why did he have to leave the city? What pattern does this seem to establish for Paul and his companions?

Answer: Paul did not have to work to support himself in Philippi; this was a break from the usual pattern. Most importantly, we see Paul doing good—expelling the evil spirit in the slave girl. But in doing good works, he disturbed people and thus got himself into trouble. As often happened, Paul was beaten and thrown into prison. Fortunately, he escaped, but even in doing so, he made a convert of the jailer. Paul preached fearlessly to everyone.

Question 10: What charges were brought against Paul in Thessalonika?

Answer: Paul was charged with treason for denying the worship of the Roman emperor. [*Teacher's note:* Later, Christians were charged with treason because they refused to make sacrifices to the Roman gods. For this, they were martyred.]

Question 11: What made Athens such an important city? Why did the Christian message fail to stir most of the Athenians?

Answer: Athens was the center of Greek philosophy and culture, as well as a center of business. The Athenians loved to debate just about any issue. However, when Paul talked about the Resurrection, the Athenians thought he was crazy. Aristotle taught, and most Athenians believed, that all knowledge came through the senses. If something could not be proven through sensate knowledge, it was suspect. Few of the Athenians could believe in the Resurrection because they could not imagine experiencing such a phenomenon.

Question 12: In the events of this chapter, how did you see the Church as Herald? Servant? Institution? Sacrament? Mystical Body?

Answer: The work of Paul, Barnabas, and the other missionaries illustrates the Church as Herald. The decision to admit Gentiles freely into the Church shows the Church acting to be Sacrament. With the collection from Antioch being delivered to the Christians in Jerusalem, we have an example of the Mystical Body, or People of God, acting as Servant. Finally, Peter's summary of the decision of the Council of Jerusalem institutes the practice of councils as meetings to decide important issues; the Church as Institution has maintained this method of conflict resolution up until the present.

Other Questions and Activities for Discussion

1) Assign each student to research one of the various Greek and Roman gods and goddesses, for example, Diana, Zeus, Apollo, Athena, Neptune, Aphrodite, Bacchus. When the students have given brief reports about these ancient deities, discuss ways in which the gods and goddesses of the Greeks and Romans were radically different from the Judeo-Christian notion of God.

Then pose this problem for discussion with your class:

- Considering what you found out about the many gods and goddesses of the Greeks and Romans, why do you think the Gentiles of those times found Paul's message so appealing? What would attract them about the life and message of Jesus?

2) Christianity became a "movement"—a group that formed around belief in a new way, a new lifestyle. To further understand how movements get started, examine with your class the causes of some contemporary movements, for instance, religious cults, a new fashion in hair or clothes, new styles in music. Movements usually form because of some perceived need in people. What needs were answered by Christianity?

Summary Activities for the Chapter

1) Have the students reflect on and write in their journals about ways in which they have been Herald, Servant, and Sacrament during the past week.

2) If you have not already used the questions for daily quizzes, distribute to the class Student Handout 4–A, "Quiz on Chapter 4" (found at the end of this chapter). The answers for the quiz are as follows:

1) b	5) c	9) b	13) b
2) a	6) a	10) a	14) a
3) c	7) d	11) c	15) a
4) d	8) b	12) d	

3) You may wish to end this unit with the prayer service on Student Handout 4–B, "Prayer Service: A Prayer of Unity from Saint Paul" (found at the end of this chapter).

4

Quiz on Chapter 4

_____ 1) Paul escaped arrest in Damascus **(a)** by knocking out a guard **(b)** by being lowered over the walls in a basket **(c)** by tunneling under a gate **(d)** through an angel leading him past the guards.

_____ 2) Barnabas asked Paul to help him in Antioch because **(a)** there were too many converts for him to minister to **(b)** Barnabas was falling sick **(c)** Barnabas was in prison for treason **(d)** Paul could speak Greek.

_____ 3) Paul and Barnabas brought money to the Jerusalem community because **(a)** they had to pay a tax to the central Christian community **(b)** they had to ransom some Christians in jail **(c)** the Christian community in Jerusalem was suffering through a famine **(d)** the Jerusalem community had to pay a special tax to the Romans.

_____ 4) Before Paul and Barnabas traveled to Asia Minor, they were in **(a)** Crete **(b)** Sicily **(c)** Egypt **(d)** Cyprus.

_____ 5) Paul made a practice of preaching to the Jews first because **(a)** they understood Aramaic **(b)** they kept the Judaic laws **(c)** they understood the prophecies about the Messiah **(d)** he did not have money to stay in inns.

_____ 6) The Christian community in Antioch was upset about **(a)** the demand of some Jewish Christians that Gentiles follow Judaic Law **(b)** the mismanagement of the money sent to the Jerusalem community **(c)** the refusal of the Apostle Matthew to preach to them **(d)** new taxes from Rome.

_____ 7) The problems of the Christian community in Antioch were solved through **(a)** a decree of Herod **(b)** Paul's decision to leave the city **(c)** Peter coming there and silencing the critics **(d)** the council of Christians in Jerusalem discussing the problem and coming to a solution.

_____ 8) To be considered Christians, Gentiles had to **(a)** be circumcised **(b)** refrain from food sacrificed to idols **(c)** visit the Temple in Jerusalem once **(d)** eat no pork.

_____ 9) Who of these was _not_ a companion of Paul on his second missionary journey? **(a)** Silas **(b)** Bartholemew **(c)** Timothy **(d)** Luke

_____ 10) Paul departed from his usual custom in Philippi by **(a)** not working as a tentmaker **(b)** preaching to the Gentiles first **(c)** using Latin **(d)** discussing Christianity with the local Roman governor.

_____ 11) In Philippi, Paul got into trouble because he **(a)** preached in a Greek temple **(b)** told the Jewish community they should not pay Roman taxes **(c)** expelled an evil spirit from a slave girl **(d)** cured a woman of epilepsy.

_____ 12) The officials in Philippi freed Paul because **(a)** no one would testify against him **(b)** as a Roman citizen they could not arrest him legally **(c)** his accuser was killed by lightning **(d)** an earthquake opened up the prison and everyone was afraid of him.

_____ 13) Most Athenians rejected Paul's preaching because of **(a)** the idea of virgin birth **(b)** the Resurrection **(c)** Jesus' dying like a common criminal **(d)** fear of Roman gods.

_____ 14) Corinth was **(a)** filled with prostitution and gambling **(b)** a quiet farming town **(c)** composed mostly of immigrant Jews **(d)** situated near a volcano.

_____ 15) Paul left Corinth with **(a)** Aquila and Priscilla **(b)** Thomas and Helen **(c)** Mark and Agrippina **(d)** Thor and Dido.

Prayer Service:
A Prayer of Unity from Saint Paul

Reading Adapted from Galatians 3:26–29

All: In you, O Christ, we are all children of God through faith. All of us who have been baptized into Christ have clothed ourselves with you. . . . We are all one in you, Lord. And if we belong to Christ, we are the descendants of Abraham, which means we inherit all that was promised.

Leader: In silence, let us pray for those whom we have rejected. [Pause.] Now let's pray for those who support us when we share what we have with others. [Pause for silent prayers of thanksgiving.]

Prayer Adapted from Colossians 3:11–15

Left: Here there cannot be distinctions between Greek and Jew, circumcised and uncircumcised, barbarian, Scythian, slave, and free. For you are all and you are in all.

Right: We are God's chosen ones, holy and beloved. God, help us be compassionate, kind, calm, and patient.

Left: Show us how to forgive; as you, Lord, have forgiven us, so may we also forgive one another.

Right: And above all these may we put on love, which binds everything together in perfect harmony.

All: And may your peace rule in our hearts. May we be thankful. Amen.

CHAPTER 5

The Lasting Legacy of the Apostles

Major Concepts

A. To keep in contact with the Christian communities that he founded, Paul began writing them letters filled with advice, correction, and loving concern. Because these letters had such a powerful effect on the communities, they were preserved, copied, and studied. Paul's Epistles are the earliest written parts of the Christian Scriptures.

B. While continuing to write his letters, Paul embarked on his third missionary journey. During this time, Paul became involved in the issue of whether or not Jewish Christians needed to obey Judaic Law.

C. Paul returned to Jerusalem, and there he was arrested. Claiming Roman citizenship, Paul was sent to Rome for trial. After a long wait he was freed, but he and Peter were later martyred during Nero's persecution of the Christians.

D. The Gospels form a lasting legacy for Christians. They were based on stories of eyewitnesses to the life of Jesus and were written because the early Christians did not want the truth about Jesus' life to be forgotten.

E. With the destruction of Jerusalem in A.D. 70 by the Romans, Jews were dispersed. Fearing that their identity would be lost if they allowed diversity in belief and practice, Jews no longer tolerated the presence of Christians in their communities. This caused a bitter split between Christians and Jews that has yet to be fully healed.

Activities for Concept A

To keep in contact with the Christian communities that he founded, Paul began writing them letters filled with advice, correction, and loving concern. Because these letters had such a powerful effect on the communities, they were preserved, copied, and studied. Paul's Epistles are the earliest written parts of the Christian Scriptures. (Page 70 of the student text.)

Review Questions and Exercises from the Student Text

Question 1: Why did Paul write his two letters to the Christians in Thessalonika?

Answer: Many of the people in Thessalonika imagined that Jesus was coming again soon. Consequently, they stopped work and dropped out of the world around them. Paul wanted them to go about their business.

Question 2: Why did the communities of Christians who received letters from Paul—as well as Peter, James, John, and Jude—cherish them, copy them, and exchange them with others?

Answer: Receiving any sort of letter was unusual. Few people could read and write. Thus, any letter was a rare treat, but one from the Apostles of Jesus was very special. Paul and the other missionaries were important to the life of the Christian communities, and their words were taken seriously.

Question 3: Describe the ways in which Paul wrote his letters.

Answer: Some letters Paul dictated word by word. Others were paraphrased by scribes. A few of the letters might be attributable to his closest associates and were probably written after his death, but they accurately represent his thought.

Personal Reflection Exercises

1) Paul wrote letters to his friends in Corinth, Galatia, and the other places where Christian communities depended on him for encouragement. Write a letter to someone you know who could use some encouragement or just a greeting from you. Try to let them know how important they are to you and how much you care about them. Mail this letter.

2) Reread the letter to Diognetus (see p. 71). If you were writing to a friend of yours and you wanted to describe contemporary Christians, what would you say? Try to view today's Christians as if you were an outsider. Use the topics mentioned in the letter to Diognetus as suggestions of points to consider. Then, write your reflections down as the outline of a letter.

Other Questions and Activities for Discussion

1) It is easy to forget that Paul's Epistles are really letters written to people he cared for a great deal. To illustrate the affection he had for his correspondents, ask your students to read the greetings at the beginnings of the Epistles and to read the closing lines. Paul was a friend, leader, prophet, and healer to the early communities; these relationships are apparent in his letters. You might wish to begin with 1 Thess. 1:1–3 and 5:23–28. Students could be assigned to read out loud the other greetings and farewell passages. Finally, here are some discussion starters:

- In most of the greetings, what facts about his role does Paul make very clear?
- What feelings does Paul have toward the people to whom he is writing? Give some examples of his feelings as expressed in the letters.
- To the early Christians, receiving a letter from Paul was special. What persons today would give you the same feeling if you were to receive a letter from them?
- Today we have instant communication with television, computers, the telephone, and the radio. With all of these methods available to him, do you think Paul would write a letter to the Thessalonians? Why is a printed letter still a useful way of communicating important matters?

What is so obvious in Paul's greetings and farewells is his tremendous commitment to and care for the early communities. Apparent too is his stature in the early Church; he clearly sees himself being a messenger of Jesus Christ. Today receiving a letter from the pope might be somewhat like getting a letter from Paul. The advantages of a printed letter are that it can be read by many people over and over; it is portable and can be easily copied for wide distribution; and there is something permanent about a letter.

2) Bring a letter of several paragraphs to class; it may be a business letter or a sales letter, or you may want to select a long passage from one of Paul's Epistles. Divide the class into four groups. While three of the groups are doing some other assignment in class, take the fourth group out of earshot and read them the letter; they may not take any notes, and they should try to remember the whole letter; then tell the group to discuss the meaning of the letter among themselves. After a few minutes of discussion, the group should select one member to pass on the message of the letter to group 2. The first group then returns to the classroom.

Group 2 now assembles out of earshot of the classroom, and the messenger from group 1 tells them the message. Group 2 then follows the same process as did group 1, which is subsequently repeated by group 3.

When group 4 assembles, tell them that a messenger from group 3 will deliver a message to them; they are to listen carefully. When messenger 3 finishes, the members of group 4 are to compose a written transcript of what he or she said. Their transcript should be copied on the chalkboard. Then read the original letter to the whole class.

To process this exercise, ask the following questions:
- What happened to the original message?
- Were there any important omissions? additions? distortions?
- What would have happened to the message if there had been longer time gaps in between deliveries by the messengers?
- How does this help us understand why Paul wrote his Epistles and his followers copied them?

Conclude with these comments:

If a shorter message gets so changed in such a brief amount of time, imagine what would have happened to the message of Paul (or Jesus) over the centuries. The Epistles and Gospels are indispensable in understanding Jesus. This experience should also point to another consideration: while it is helpful to listen to others talk about God and Jesus, a close reading of the Scriptures is essential in forming one's own faith.

3) Have your students write a letter to the universal Church. In the letter they should express their ideas and feelings on what is good, bad, and in need of change in the Church. Some of the letters could be read in class.

4) The letters of many famous people are preserved. They are kept because of the insights they contain about the persons, about their lives, and about life in general. Assign your students a short research project to find and read a few letters of a famous person such as Theodore Roosevelt, Cardinal John Newman, Teresa of Ávila, Walt Whitman, Henry David Thoreau, Franklin Delano Roosevelt, or Dag Hammarskjöld. Then inquire as to how the letters affected the students' images of the writers.

Activities for Concept B

While continuing to write his letters, Paul embarked on his third missionary journey. During this time, Paul became involved in the issue of whether or not Jewish Christians needed to obey Judaic Law. (Pages 70, 72–73 of the student text.)

Review Questions and Exercises from the Student Text

Question 4: On Paul's third journey, he spent a good deal of time in Ephesus. Why?

Answer: Ephesus was a trading center and a crossroads for eastern and western travelers. The Christian message was spread from Ephesus all over the region by those who heard Paul's preaching, believed, and wanted to tell others.

Question 5: The silversmiths in Ephesus almost killed Paul. Why? Does their reaction seem typical of people's reactions to new religions or to ideas that challenge old beliefs? Can you think of some examples to support your position?

Answer: The silversmiths made statues of the goddess Diana. As Ephesians abandoned Diana for the new Christian religion, the silversmiths lost business. Their anger was directed at Paul. Examples of people's reacting negatively to new ideas or religions might include the hostility of some people toward permanent deacons and people's refusal to enact pollution legislation just because it has never been done in the past or because businesses would have to invest in new procedures and equipment.

5

Question 6: What unresolved problem still caused some division in the Church? Why was this problem more complicated than just another religious dispute?

Answer: While Gentiles were freed from observing the Judaic Law, a faction among the Jewish Christians still demanded that converted Jews should follow the Law. This was more than just a religious issue; setting aside the Mosaic Law was seen as being disloyal to Israel, as becoming romanized.

Other Questions and Activities for Discussion

1) Divide the students into three groups. On a large map of the Middle East, have group 1 trace Paul's third missionary journey. Different colored pins may be placed on the key cities at which Paul stopped. Using the scale of miles, the students should estimate the distances between cities along his route. Group 2 can research each of the main cities where Paul preached: Ephesus, Corinth, and Troas. Finally, passages from the Acts of the Apostles describing Paul's work in each town might be summarized by group 3.

2) Assign parts to several readers, and have them perform Acts 19:23–41, the riot of the silversmiths in Ephesus. The class can act as the mob. Relate this incident to people's reaction to anyone who challenges the status quo; here are some questions to start your discussion:

- Can you name some groups who, through demonstrations or public protests of other kinds, cause people to get angry because their protests challenge the normal ways of thinking?
- What sort of economic motives exist that make people want to protect the status quo?
- Do you think Paul would let economic concerns stand in his way if he were preaching the Good News here?

Activities for Concept C

Paul returned to Jerusalem, and there he was arrested. Claiming Roman citizenship, Paul was sent to Rome for trial. After a long wait he was freed, but he and Peter were later martyred during Nero's persecution of the Christians. (Pages 73–78 of the student text.)

Review Questions and Exercises from the Student Text

Question 7: What attitude did Paul have about returning to Jerusalem? What external motivations existed that caused him to go there?

Answer: Paul seemed to have a premonition that prison and persecution awaited him. Nevertheless, he wanted to go to fulfill his mission. He was again bringing money to help the Christians in Jerusalem, and he wanted to talk with the Apostles about the problem of the Jewish Christians observing the Judaic Law.

Question 8: Why was Paul protected by the Romans? Why were the Jews so determined to kill him?

Answer: The job of the Roman troops was to maintain law and order. They protected Paul because he was nearly killed by the mob, and they arrested Paul because he seemed to be the cause of the riot. When the soldiers found out that he was a Roman citizen, they gave Paul all the privileges due him, one of which was trial in Roman courts.

The Jews wanted to kill Paul because he threatened the unity of Israel by preaching that Gentiles should be allowed membership in the Christian community. Also he said that Jewish Christians need not obey the Law of Moses. These positions seemed treasonous to Jews who thought that keeping the Law was a sign of unity against their Roman rulers.

Question 9: Why did Nero persecute the Christians? If you are not familiar with the word *scapegoat*, look it up in a dictionary. Have any groups of people recently been put into the position in which Nero put the Christians? If so, were any of the reasons for making them scapegoats similar to Nero's reasons for persecuting the Christians?

Answer: Nero blamed the Christians for the fire that raged through Rome. He wanted to take the suspicion away from himself. Thus, the Christians became scapegoats. The most applicable definitions of a "scapegoat" are (1) one who bears the blame for others and (2) one who is the object of irrational hostility. (This question is a good lead-in to discussing the holocaust, the mass murder of Jews by the Nazis.) The Nazis blamed the Jews for all of the economic and social problems of Germany. By using the Jews as scapegoats, Hitler was able to unify Germany.

Question 10: What really made the Christians different from their neighbors? Explain.

Answer: The Christians lived as others did, but they shared with others and loved everyone. They were seen as good people, but they were persecuted. In short, they confused others by their goodness in the midst of much corruption and persecution.

Question 11: According to Luke's account in the Acts of the Apostles, Paul gave at least thirteen years of his life to difficult and dangerous travel in order to tell people the Good News, the Gospel of Jesus the Christ. As a good storyteller, Luke gives some very interesting details about Paul's experiences. To appreciate this, read the following passages in Acts and then write a newspaper headline summarizing each episode:

   a) *The first journey:* Acts 14:1–7; Acts 14:8–20
   b) *The second journey:* Acts 16:16–40
   c) *The third journey:* Acts 19:23–41; Acts 20:7–12

Answer: After the students have written their headlines they can read them to the class. Perhaps have the students select the best headlines, the ones that most clearly summarize the events.

Personal Reflection Exercises

> 3) Choose one of the narratives given in question 11 above and, putting yourself in Paul's place, write briefly how you feel about what happened.
>
> 4) Write an imaginary dialogue with a first-century martyr. What sort of questions would you ask, and how do you think he or she would respond?

Other Questions and Activities for Discussion

1) To gain insight into the riot over Paul's speech to the Jews at the Temple, some students may prepare readings of the incident (Acts 21:27—22:29).

2) Discuss with your students what it must have been like for Paul to have been under house arrest for two years.
   • How would your life be different if you were under house arrest?
   • Considering Paul's great zeal for preaching the Word of God, what do you think it was like for him to be under house arrest?

The Romans were in a very ticklish position with Paul. He was a Roman citizen who had all the rights of Roman law. On the other hand, in seeming to protect him,

5

the Romans caused more anger on the part of the Jewish people. Why was house arrest a clever decision on the part of the Roman authorities?

3) The intermixing of religion and government will be a frequent theme in the rest of the student text. Sometimes there is a tendency to confuse patriotism and religion. In other words, not belonging to a specific religion is considered somehow unpatriotic. Certainly the Christians were considered traitors to Rome because they refused to worship Roman gods. Pose these questions to your class:
- Are there times when religion is used to rally groups around what is basically a government issue?
- Is religion used by politicians to persuade the voters that they are the best candidates?
- Have you ever heard of politicians giving basically religious reasons for the way they vote for issues?
- The United States claims that there is separation of church and state, and yet, in the Pledge of Allegiance the phrase "one nation under God" is included. Why do people accept this phrase as part of the pledge?
- Are there any religious groups that are considered unpatriotic? Consider the Muslims or followers of various Indian gurus; do you ever hear comments that they are dangerous to the nation?

4) Tradition tells us that Saint Peter is buried beneath Saint Peter's Basilica. Have the students do some research into why this belief grew into a tradition. Encourage them to bring in pictures of different artists' versions of the martyrdom of Peter. In addition they might be instructed to explain why Peter was believed to have been crucified upside down. Pictures of Paul's martyrdom abound too; ask the students to describe how he is represented in works of art.

5) Assign your students to write an epitaph for Paul's tomb. It can only be ten words or less, and must summarize the main focus of his life. The class can then discuss each epitaph to select the best one.

6) Here is a writing activity that can also be used to help the students summarize their impressions and knowledge about Peter and Paul. Explain as follows:

Imagine that you have been asked to write a eulogy of Saint Paul (or Saint Peter). You are to deliver the eulogy at a memorial service at his tomb. Write and prepare to deliver a five-minute eulogy. It should highlight his accomplishments and include your personal feelings about him.

Activities for Concept D
The Gospels form a lasting legacy for Christians. They were based on stories of eyewitnesses to the life of Jesus and were written because the early Christians did not want the truth about Jesus' life to be forgotten. (Pages 78–81 of the student text.)

Review Questions and Exercises from the Student Text

Question 12: Why were the Gospels composed? How were they used by the early Church?

Answer: The Gospels were composed because only a few people who knew Jesus firsthand were still alive; if their impressions were to survive, they had to be written down. In addition, written documents could be copied and sent to all communities for their edification. The stories were read to congregations, and since almost all information came in oral form, the listeners remembered the stories and passed them on to their friends. In these ways the life and wondrous works of Jesus were kept alive in the Church.

Question 13: How did the communities in which the authors lived influence the writing of the Gospels? Why is the Gospel of John so different from the other three? To get a sense of the difference, read the introduction to John's Gospel and the introduction to Matthew's. How are they different in tone and content?

Answer: Like any good writers, the Evangelists kept their audiences in mind. Mark lived with Gentiles and wrote the Good News for them. Matthew directed his message to both Jews and Gentiles, and Luke was primarily concerned with Gentiles. Since they wrote separately, although depending on earlier versions of the stories, each Gospel offers slightly different perspectives on Jesus. John's Gospel is quite different in tone and focus. The language is more metaphysical because he wanted to show that Jesus was God made flesh. The introduction to John's Gospel talks about Jesus as the Word. Matthew, on the other hand, concentrates more on showing that Jesus was a descendent of David's line and that his birth was a fulfillment of the prophecies.

Question 14: What is similar and what seems different about the liturgy of A.D. 100 and the liturgy you attend at your parish? What do you think accounts for the differences?

Answer: The order of events in the early celebration matches the modern liturgy very closely. What is different is the seeming informality of the early liturgy. The communities of Christians were much smaller; this contributed to the sense of fellowship that existed. Also, since they had to be careful not to be caught by Roman officials, the celebrations had to be held in homes.

Other Questions and Activities for Discussion

1) This exercise is intended to help students understand that our audience makes a difference in how we write an account of an event and that each writer has a somewhat different perspective on the same event.

   a) Select a story from one of the Gospels that is filled with drama, for example, the cure of the paralytic (Luke 5:17–26), the woman who was a sinner (Luke 7:36–50), the prodigal son (Luke 15:11–32), the cure of the epileptic demoniac (Mark 9:14–29).

   b) Ask for volunteers from your students; they will act out the incident described in the Gospel story selected; one of them will be Jesus who does the narration. Give them some time to practice the scene.

   c) When the scene is ready, assign the student audience the role of reporters. They are to witness the scene and write reports on what they saw. Add one other element; assign some of the reporters to write a report for their peers, others for their parents, others for a younger child, others for the police, others for the bishop.

   d) Have the actors perform the scene(s), and give the reporters time to write up their accounts.

   e) Ask the students to read their reports (at least two reports per audience), and then discuss how different reporters emphasized different aspects of the same event according to their audiences and interpretations.

As a variation of and addition to this activity, have another scene acted out in class. Instead of having the students write down their reports immediately, wait for one week and then have them write their accounts. Discuss how time affected their reports.

Clearly in an age when printing was unheard of, people had to develop their memories much more then we are accustomed to. Nevertheless, stories do reflect the audience to whom they are told and the biases of the storyteller. The Gospels, though inspired by the Holy Spirit, were written to particular audiences by unique and different people.

2) Ask each student to write a biography of a person who is special to him or her. The biography should focus on one key event to which the student was an eyewitness. After the biographies are written, have each student read the story to one or two other people. Each listener should try to formulate an impression of the person written about and should give feedback to the writer about ways in which the writer biased the account through word choice or the selection of the events narrated.

Then discuss with the class the fact that most of the time, stories about people we admire are going to be slanted. This is not bad but just shows that it is important when reading the Gospels to remember the audiences to whom each one was written and the biases of each Evangelist. In total, the Gospels give us a wonderful understanding of Jesus, an understanding indispensable to Christian life.

Activities for Concept E

With the destruction of Jerusalem in A.D. 70 by the Romans, Jews were dispersed. Fearing that their identity would be lost if they allowed diversity in belief and practice, Jews no longer tolerated the presence of Christians in their communities. This caused a bitter split between Christians and Jews that has yet to be fully healed. (Pages 82–85 of the student text.)

Review Questions and Exercises from the Student Text

Question 15: Why is it important for Christians to remember that Jesus was a Jew?

Answer: To have an accurate understanding of Jesus we must remember that he was a devout Jew; Jesus came to the Chosen People first. His intention was not to destroy Judaism, but to offer Jews salvation. To hate Jews is to hate Christ.

Question 16: What were the causes of both the split and the later mutual distrust between Christians and Jews?

Answer: Jews blamed Christians for splitting up Israel, and a united Israel was needed to fight the Romans. On religious grounds, Jews did not believe that Jesus was the Messiah. After the destruction of Jerusalem and the dispersion of Jews from their homeland, Jews wanted to maintain their religion by unity of practice of the Torah and by eliminating any factions. When the Christians were excluded from the synagogues, they resented this; some became bitter.

Question 17: How did the events of the first century of Christianity prepare the communities for the second century?

Answer: The Epistles and the Gospels were written down and became well-remembered sources of inspiration for the fledgling Church. There was a structure in each community that provided stability; bishops and deacons were appointed for each congregation. Mutual service within and between congregations was common practice too. In short, they had the strength to maintain themselves in the coming persecutions because they were supported by the Word of God and by the Church in its aspects as Institution, Sacrament, and Body of Christ.

> 5) What sort of stereotypes exist today about Jews? Try to list and describe as many of these as you can. What stereotypes do non-Catholics have about Catholics? List and describe these. How do you feel about these stereotypes? Do they apply to all Catholics? Do they apply to you? Do the stereotypes listed about Jews apply to all Jews? How do you feel about stereotyping? Is stereotyping a helpful process in arriving at a just view of the world?

Other Questions and Activities for Discussion

1) Invite a Jewish rabbi or the diocesan ecumenical officer to speak to your class about present Jewish-Catholic relations. Ask him or her to focus on sources of tension, sources of understanding, and ways to improve relations with Jews.

2) Discuss causes and effects of divisions within groups; perhaps use these questions:
   • Can you identify times when there have been divisions within the class? within the school? within the community?
   • What were the causes of the splits?
   • How do differences and splits on issues often become personal and result in anger and bitterness?

3) As a research project, students could try to find out where the Jews went after the fall of Jerusalem. For instance, why did so many Jews move to Poland, Spain, and Germany? What has been the history of Jewish migration?

Summary Activities for the Chapter

1) Give the students some time to write in their journals about how they were Heralds, the Body of Christ, Sacraments, and Servants during the past week.

2) If you have not already used the questions for daily quizzes, distribute to the class Student Handout 5–A, "Quiz on Chapter 5" (found at the end of this chapter). The answers for the quiz are as follows:

1) b	8) b	15) d	22) b
2) d	9) b	16) d	23) a
3) a	10) d	17) b	24) c
4) d	11) b	18) d	25) d
5) d	12) d	19) d	
6) c	13) b	20) b	
7) d	14) a	21) b	

3) Student Handout 5–B, "Prayer Service: The Children of God" (found at the end of this chapter), may be used to conclude this chapter. For a closing hymn, consider using "Father, We Thank You"; the words were written in the first century and were used as part of the liturgy.

Quiz on Chapter 5

5

_____ 1) Paul's first letter, or epistle, was written to **(a)** Corinth **(b)** Thessalonika **(c)** Athens **(d)** Jerusalem.

_____ 2) None of Paul's letters were written down by **(a)** scribes **(b)** Paul himself **(c)** his followers **(d)** Tacitus.

_____ 3) Ephesus was the center of worship of **(a)** Diana **(b)** Zeus **(c)** Athena **(d)** Neptune.

_____ 4) Which of these groups threw Paul out of Ephesus? **(a)** the magicians **(b)** the Jews **(c)** the priests **(d)** the silversmiths

_____ 5) At Troas a young man fell out of a window because **(a)** he was drunk **(b)** someone nudged him **(c)** the place for liturgy was too crowded **(d)** he fell asleep during one of Paul's sermons.

_____ 6) One reason Paul went to Jerusalem was **(a)** to see Peter who was ill **(b)** to make his biannual visit to the Temple **(c)** to discuss whether or not Jewish Christians had to follow the Judaic Law **(d)** to rest from his travels.

_____ 7) Paul knew he would run into trouble in Jerusalem because **(a)** Roman officials had warned him **(b)** Luke wrote him a warning letter **(c)** Peter sent him a message **(d)** the Holy Spirit made it clear to him.

_____ 8) Paul went to the Temple in Jerusalem because **(a)** it was the Sabbath **(b)** he wanted to show that he respected the Law **(c)** he was meeting some old friends there **(d)** he wanted to preach about the Resurrection.

_____ 9) The mob that attacked Paul became especially angry when he said that **(a)** Jewish laws were insane **(b)** he was sent to preach to the Gentiles **(c)** the Romans were good rulers **(d)** Judaism was a dying religion.

_____ 10) Paul was escorted to Caesarea by two hundred soldiers because **(a)** he was known to have escaped from prison before **(b)** the Romans considered him a dangerous criminal **(c)** this was a common practice **(d)** forty Jewish men had sworn to kill him.

_____ 11) Paul wanted to be tried in Rome because **(a)** he wanted a free trip there **(b)** he could not get a fair trial in Jerusalem **(c)** he had a divine revelation that he should go there **(d)** he had agreed to meet Peter there.

_____ 12) Paul was shipwrecked on **(a)** Crete **(b)** Cyprus **(c)** Sicily **(d)** Malta.

_____ 13) Paul was a prisoner in Rome for **(a)** one year **(b)** two years **(c)** three years **(d)** four years.

_____ 14) Nero blamed the Christians for the fire that devastated Rome because **(a)** he needed a scapegoat **(b)** a Christian named Aquila started the fire **(c)** his wife wanted all the Christians dead **(d)** the Christian areas of the city were spared.

_____ 15) Peter, according to legend, was (a) beheaded (b) drowned (c) thrown to the lions (d) crucified.

_____ 16) In Greek, the word *church* means (a) a place of worship (b) sacrifice (c) ritual (d) assembly.

_____ 17) The word *gospels* means (a) letters (b) good news (c) thoughts (d) holy words.

_____ 18) The Gospels were complete around the year A.D. (a) 64 (b) 75 (c) 90 (d) 100.

_____ 19) Which of these people did not write one of the Gospels? (a) Matthew (b) Luke (c) John (d) Peter

_____ 20) Mark wrote his Gospel primarily for (a) Jews (b) Gentiles (c) women (d) men.

_____ 21) James was killed when (a) famine hit Jerusalem (b) he was thrown from the roof of the Temple and stoned (c) an earthquake hit Jerusalem (d) Nero persecuted the Christians.

_____ 22) The Temple was destroyed by the Romans in A.D. (a) 66 (b) 70 (c) 74 (d) 76.

_____ 23) The Jews increasingly demanded conformity in belief and practice of Judaism and rejected Jewish Christians because (a) they needed to unify Judaism to survive as a religion (b) they feared Roman infiltrators (c) Jewish Christians decided to eat pork (d) Jewish Christians were growing into a majority group.

_____ 24) Jews were persecuted for centuries in part because Christians (a) thought them sources of disease (b) did not want to follow Judaic Law (c) blamed them for Jesus' death (d) were told to do so by various popes.

_____ 25) The early church liturgy was different than today's in that (a) deacons performed the consecration (b) none of the congregation could receive communion (c) singing was not allowed (d) it was generally more informal.

Prayer Service: The Children of God

Leader: Recorded in the Gospels was the prayer Jesus taught his disciples when they asked him how to pray. Let's pray together the Our Father.

Reading of 1 Timothy 4:12–16

Leader: In a moment of silence, let's think about the many gifts of personality or character that we have and of how we can help others with these gifts. [Pause.]

Prayer Adapted from 1 John 3:1–24

Leader: Think of the love that the Father has lavished on us by letting us be called God's children; and that is what we are.

All: In this way we distinguish the children of God from the children of the devil: anyone not living a holy life and not loving one's brother and sister is no child of God's.

Leader: If a man who was rich enough in this world's goods saw that one of his brothers or sisters was in need, but closed his heart to him or her,

All: how could the love of God be living in him?

Leader: Our love is not to be just words or mere talk,

All: but something real and active.

Leader: Let us love one another

All: since love comes from God. Amen. Alleluia.

Closing Hymn

CHAPTER 6
Gold Tested in Fire

Major Concepts

A. Small Christian communities sprang up all over the Roman Empire; they were united by a strong common faith, by mutual charity, and by evolving structures such as the roles of the bishops and deacons. While life was fairly peaceful for most Romans, many Christians were martyred for their faith.

B. Apologists—"defenders of the faith"—wrote, preached, and taught about Jesus; they tried to state clearly the truths of Christianity.

C. As the year 200 approached, the Roman Empire was disintegrating. Decius, Diocletian, and other emperors used the Christians as scapegoats on whom to put blame for the decline of Rome. More persecutions tested the faith of Christians.

D. In A.D. 312, the Church entered a new era when Constantine granted it freedom of worship and gave it lands and buildings. Persecution ended; Christianity began to be the religion of the empire.

E. Arianism divided the Church, but the creed formulated at the Nicene Council clarified central truths about Jesus, even if it did not bring unity.

6

Activities for Concept A
Small Christian communities sprang up all over the Roman Empire; they were united by a strong common faith, by mutual charity, and by evolving structures such as the roles of the bishops and deacons. While life was fairly peaceful for most Romans, many Christians were martyred for their faith. (Pages 90–93 of the student text.)

Review Questions and Exercises from the Student Text

Question 1: Describe the three groups with whom the Christian community had to contend.
Answer: The Christians had to deal with the Romans, who were suspicious of them and later persecuted them; the Jews, who rejected them; and the barbarians, who raided Roman territories.

Question 2: What helped hold the Christian communities together during the years A.D. 100–312?
Answer: The early Christians celebrated the breaking of the bread, listened to the Word of God, and built relationships in community. In addition, each community was led by a carefully selected bishop, or supervisor, and served by deacons.

Question 3: Why were the Christians persecuted? Try to put yourself in the shoes of the Roman emperors. Why did the Christians stand out?
Answer: The Christians preached publicly. They refused to worship the Roman gods and thus were considered disloyal to Rome. Also, they lived differently, and like people who do not conform today, they were subject to suspicion. If a Roman emperor needed to turn people's attention away from problems in the empire, he could blame

the Christians. After all, if they were loyal subjects they would pray to the Roman gods for blessings on the empire.

Personal Reflection Exercise

> 1) Try to think of some examples from everyday life of what your life would be like today if you could be sent to prison for being a Christian. How would this threat influence your emotions and your actions?

Other Questions and Activities for Discussion

1) Here are some research projects that will fill out your students' information about this period. Instruct the students to complete some of the following:
   a) Bring in pictures of barbarians as they have been represented in books and magazines.
   b) Find out about the population of the ancient city of Rome—size, ethnic makeup, percentage of slaves, and so on.
   c) Prepare a report about how Christians were martyred.
   d) Build a model of the Roman Colosseum.
   e) Build a model of a typical Roman house in ancient times.
   f) Report on what sort of sacrifices were made to the Roman gods.
   g) Report on the life of Ignatius or Polycarp.

2) To help the students understand why deacons were so important in the early Church, point out to them that there were no social service agencies or welfare programs run by the governments of the times. People had to depend on their families. If something happened to their families, they had to rely on friends, and since almost everyone lived from hand to mouth, few people had much to share. Women were kept pregnant much of the time because people needed children to ensure their maintenance when they reached old age. Since the infant mortality rate was very high, people had to have many children to guarantee the survival of a few offspring. The life expectancy for men was less than for women because men were often called upon to fight in armies or to fight just to protect themselves. The Roman army offered citizens some protection, but not much. Consequently, the Christian community would, of necessity given the times, have to help many widows and orphans. Deacons became a very important element in the communities. They also helped the sick because there were no hospitals as we know them and certainly no insurance. If persons could not work because of illness, they had to rely on their families or, in the case of Christians, the community acting through the deacons.

3) Some students could be appointed to act out the trial and execution of Polycarp.

4) There are several points about Polycarp's trial (see p. 92 of the student text) that you may wish to pursue further:
   • Why does the proconsul tell Polycarp to say "away with the godless," and why does Polycarp say it?
   • Why does the proconsul say that Polycarp was taking him lightly when Polycarp said, "But it is a splendid thing to change from cruelty to justice"?
   • Which punishment does the proconsul think worse: beasts or fire? Which do you think is worse?
   • Through studying Polycarp's final prayer, what conclusions can you draw about the early Christian ideas about martyrdom?

In this scene of Polycarp's trial, several points are well summarized. First, Christians were considered godless because they did not believe in the Roman gods. Second,

Polycarp could say "away with the godless" because he meant it, but his perspective was different from the proconsul's. Third, Polycarp's little joke seems especially ironic given his situation but a brave joke nonetheless. Next, clearly the proconsul thought that fire was worse than beasts. If the students get into a discussion of which punishment is worse, have some students research what it is like to die by fire and then present their findings. Finally, Christians believed that martyrdom was a direct way to heaven; this remains part of our tradition.

5) These next questions may be used for discussion or for a written journal reflection:
- Have you ever been in a situation where you felt the need to hide from someone or, in a sense, to go underground?
- Why did you feel this way? What caused your need to hide?
- Did you seek support from anyone?
- What feelings dominated you during this time?
- How did you resolve the situation?

Here are some additional discussion or reflection queries:
- Have you ever put your neck on the block for something? Have you ever stood up for an unpopular cause or person?
- What happened to you because of your stand?
- Did taking this stand make you a different person? If so, how?
- Is it important to stand up for what one believes?

Activities for Concept B
Apologists—"defenders of the faith"—wrote, preached, and taught about Jesus; they tried to state clearly the truths of Christianity. (Pages 93–94 of the student text.)

Review Questions and Exercises from the Student Text

Question 4: Who were the apologists? What service did they perform for the Church?
Answer: The apologists taught and wrote commentaries about the Christian faith. They were "defenders of the faith." Often, they were well educated in Greek and Roman literature and philosophy. People like Justin and Irenaeus fought intellectual battles with Romans and with heretics like the Gnostics. In effect, they began an intellectual element in the Church that fleshed out many areas of thought about Christianity.

Question 5: Explain the problems encountered with the Gnostics.
Answer: Gnostics believed that all things material were bad. And they thought that they were special because they had a secret knowledge of the divine spark that would be released from their bodies upon death. For the Gnostics, salvation was not a gift from Jesus but a special privilege for a select few. Clearly these beliefs were contrary to the revelation of Jesus.

Other Questions and Activities for Discussion

1) Have your students look up the words *apologist, apologize, apology, apologetic.* It is important that they realize the positive implications of these words. Apology and apologize frequently are understood only for their pejorative meanings.

2) In our growing up we sometimes get into arguments with other people about our religion versus theirs. Maybe these types of arguments are less common today, but in many places fundamentalists, charismatics, and members of cults engage Catholics in arguments about religion. Some of your students may have had to be

6

"apologists." In order to understand the work of these early defenders of the faith, have your class examine this case:

Joan and Margie live in a small town. They are stars on their high school softball team and want to play in the local summer softball league. Both women are Catholics. They have been invited to play for the Bellvue Baptist Church team, a team that has won the regional championships for three years in a row and that promises to be tops again this year. They are very honored to be invited, and they decide to join the team. Practices go very well, and Joan and Margie seem to be getting along well with the other players. The only irritant is that they are asked to pray with the other women before and after games and have been invited to attend services on Sunday. Joan and Margie tell the other team members that they are Catholic and go to Mass. This fact is received well by all the team members except for one woman who begins challenging Joan and Margie about different matters of faith, especially about the infallibility of the pope. She says that this doctrine cannot be found anywhere in the Bible and must be false. Pretty soon other team members begin asking questions too; some of the questions express a sincere interest in the differences between Catholic and Baptist beliefs, but others are really challenges to Joan and Margie.

- If you were Joan or Margie, how would you deal with your teammates?
- Where would you go for help in answering questions?
- How would these questions make you feel?
- Should you quit the team?
- How could these challenges actually help your religious commitment?

3) Now reverse the case presented in activity 2 above. Pose the case as if two Baptist girls had joined a Catholic church team and some of their teammates had begun arguing with them about the fact that the Bible cannot be taken literally. Ask your students these questions:

- Should Catholics challenge the faith of other people?
- How would these challenges make the Baptist women feel?
- Would you blame these women if they quit the team?

Finally, end the discussion of activities 1, 2, and 3 with a summary statement like this one:

A person's faith is a private matter between him or her and God. In charity and in respect for other persons' rights, we should not go out of our way to challenge their religious beliefs. On the other hand, sometimes when our beliefs are challenged, we need to be educated enough about our faith to represent the Church and ourselves well, to be apologists. God's ways are not the ways of humans; sometimes having to explain our own faith to others who have different views can actually strengthen our own convictions. The apologists in the early Church were talking to people whose religion was vastly different from Christianity—far more dissimilar than Baptist faith and Catholic faith are. Also, Christianity was a new religion; many of its concepts were just being formed. In many ways, challenges to Christian faith helped crystallize the thought of the apologists and consequently were very helpful in the growth of Christian belief.

4) The Gnostics' abhorrence of the material world might be the subject of reflection; here are some discussion starters:

- What would life be like if we really believed that the material world was bad? Try to think of some practical examples of how we might live our lives differently.
- Can you think of some arguments that would show that the material world in itself is not evil?
- What are some passages from both the Christian and the Hebrew Scriptures that show the goodness of the material world?

6

Activities for Concept C

As the year 200 approached, the Roman Empire was disintegrating. Decius, Diocletian, and other emperors used the Christians as scapegoats on whom to put blame for the decline of Rome. More persecutions tested the faith of Christians. (Pages 94–97 of the student text.)

Review Questions and Exercises from the Student Text

Question 6: After A.D. 200, what was beginning to happen to the Roman Empire?

Answer: The Roman Empire was disintegrating. The army deposed and appointed emperors in rapid succession. Taxes burdened the people. Corruption flourished. The economy was a mess. Diocletian temporarily stopped the decline, but upon his resignation, the chaos increased throughout the empire.

Question 7: Who were the apostates, and what dilemma did they pose for the early Church? Who was important in settling this issue?

Answer: Apostates were people who had renounced their Christian faith in order to save their lives during the periods of persecution. Some Christians did not want to accept them back into the Church, even if they repented. Stephen, the bishop of Rome, was important in the final decision to readmit them. The role of the bishop of Rome was becoming more prominent.

Other Questions and Activities for Discussion

1) Two very important cities in the Roman Empire were Alexandria and Carthage. Assign students to prepare reports on these two cities as they were during the first and second centuries A.D.

2) Scapegoats have been discussed before, but to reinforce the understanding of them, here are some inquiries to make of your students:
- Have you ever been held responsible for something bad happening that you did not do or could not prevent?
- How did you react to being held responsible?
- Were you tempted to blame the incident on someone else?
- What happened to you as a result of the incident?

Then, have groups of four or five students write skits depicting one of the incidents that happened to a group member. Have the groups act out the incidents before the class. Then discuss the effects on the scapegoats.

3) Ask the students to write an interior monologue on the following scenario:

The Colosseum in Rome was the site of the death of many Christian martyrs. Imagine that you are scheduled to die in the Colosseum in one hour—martyred for your faith. What would you be thinking about; what concerns would you have; what would be your hopes? Think about these questions for a few moments and then write down your reflections; include a prayer in your monologue.

4) Set up a debate in class that would outline the pros and cons of readmitting apostates into the Church. Designate two people in support of readmission and two against. Here is the case:

Lucius is the father of four children. His wife died several years ago from a mysterious fever. He is very devoted to raising his children as Christians. The small Christian community to which he belongs was exposed to the Roman authorities by a spy who wormed his way into the group. At the trial before the proconsul and after some coercion, Lucius decides in great mental anguish to offer sacrifice to the Roman gods. Almost all the other members of his community

are burned at the stake, dying as Christians. Two years have passed, and now Lucius wants to rejoin the Christian community.
- The issue before the class, who are to act as a council to the presiding bishop, is whether Lucius should be readmitted. If he is, should he do penance, and if so, what penance should he do?

If those who are arguing for his readmission forget, after the debate has ended, examine Jesus' forgiveness of Peter, the woman caught in adultery, the woman at the well, and so on. On the other side, remind the class that the Romans did plant spies in communities, spies who could cause even more Christians' deaths. The early communities had to be very careful in readmitting Lucius and others who had renounced the faith.

5) Here is another problem that can be discussed in groups, after which the entire class can come to a consensus solution:

Diocletian's persecution is raging throughout your local area. Christians are hiding out, and those not known to be Christians are very afraid of exposure. You are the president of the local Christian community. Helena has come to you with a serious dilemma. Her husband, Cassius, a newly converted Christian, has fallen madly in love with Agrippina, a pagan and the wife of a Roman military commander. Helena has tried to confront Cassius about the matter, but each time, he has gotten extremely angry with her. In his anger, Cassius has said that before they became Christians, he could have easily divorced her according to Roman law. He says he believes in Jesus but still wants to have this relationship with Agrippina. Helena does not want to drive him to break with her or with the Church, but she does not know what to do. She has come to you for advice, and hopes that you will intervene and bring Cassius to his senses before he does something rash.
- What will you do?

There are lots of problems in this situation. If Cassius leaves the Church because he is angry at their interference, he might denounce the community to the Roman authorities who would surely persecute the group. If the Church does not act, Helena will be hurt and disillusioned; after all she should be able to turn to the community for help. Also, the Church is concerned about the soul of Cassius; renouncing his faith is a serious matter, and then, there is the prospect of divorce.

6) Priscilla describes her reactions to the early Christian rite of initiation (see pp. 96–97 of the student text). You might wish to read the contemporary Rite of Christian Initiation of Adults and then compare it to Priscilla's experience. Discuss differences and similarities with your students. One difference is the baptistry construction; we no longer use a pool. You might ask your students about this:
- Do you feel that actually walking down into the water would be a more effective experience of Baptism than sprinkling water on the head like we do now?
- Why was the rite such a secret in early Christian times?

Activities for Concept D
In A.D. 312, the Church entered a new era when Constantine granted it freedom of worship and gave it lands and buildings. Persecution ended; Christianity began to be the religion of the empire. (Pages 98–99 of the student text.)

Review Questions and Exercises from the Student Text

Question 8: Describe how Constantine's conversion altered the future of Christianity. What positive changes followed his conversion? What negative results occurred?

Answer: Constantine issued the Edict of Milan in A.D. 313, which granted freedom of worship for all Christians in the Roman Empire. Eventually, Christian clergy were exempted from taxes. Constantine built churches and gave lands to the Church. The negative effects centered around the tendency of Constantine to interfere in matters of the Church. [*Teacher's note:* While the Council of Nicaea was helpful, Constantine's calling of it signaled a change in church-state relations that would color the history of the Church until the nineteenth century when the Vatican lost all church lands and again became a spiritual authority, not a secular one.]

Other Questions and Activities for Discussion

1) Constantine's putting off Baptism until near the end of his life seems odd to us today. Certainly, the concept of Baptism as a purification of sin from our souls is integral to the sacrament, but the idea that one can only be forgiven once and only through Baptism must have caused great anxiety among those who held this view. Gradually, the Sacrament of Reconciliation developed and provided a means to signify forgiveness and reconversion. To illustrate this point, discuss with your students these queries:
- Imagine what it must have been like to think that only at Baptism could sins be forgiven. What do you think you would feel like?
- Would people behave better if they held this view?
- Is this concept of onetime forgiveness consistent with what we know of Jesus' forgiveness?
- Why would someone like Constantine want to put off his Baptism? What does it seem to say about him that he delayed?

2) Point out Istanbul, Turkey, on a map, and remind your students that it was called Constantinople and before that Byzantium. Some students might do a report about modern Istanbul and about the fate of Constantinople after Constantine founded it. This city plays a part in the history of the Church for many centuries.

3) The effects of Constantine's legalizing Christianity and of its eventually becoming the religion of the empire cannot be overestimated. After three centuries of persecution, Christians suddenly found themselves to be in power, to have status. Try to help your students appreciate this enormous change; here are some examples you might use:

Put yourself in this situation: You have just come into high school. Your first week is a bit lonely because you do not know any of your classmates. Some people talk with you, but you would still like to make some friends, especially with one group that seems like your sort of people. The members of this group are quite popular, better than average students, and just generally the sort of people you like.
- What would you gain by being accepted as a group member?
- Would you have to give up anything (other nonmember acquaintances, ideas, habits, likes and dislikes, etc.)?

Now, ask the students to think of examples in which a group who has been picked on, powerless, and looked down upon has gained power and/or prestige. (You might have them scour the newspapers and news magazines for examples: poor people who won the lottery, countries like Iran and the OPEC nations who had the West over a barrel, etc.)
- How did these people act after they gained power? Did it make them different? Were they better off?
- How did they treat their old friends? How were they treated?
- Is there a tendency for the newly rich or powerful to flaunt or misuse their wealth or power?

6

In summary, after Constantine legalized Christianity, the Church was relieved of the terrible persecutions. The Good News could be preached more widely; all could hear the Word of God. Places of worship could be fixed for regular use. There must have been tremendous joy in the hearts of Christians in A.D. 313. However, power tends to corrupt, and clearly, as we see in history, the Church was subject to the corruptions of power too. It is essential that students understand that the Church, while guided by the Holy Spirit, sometimes does not listen too well; it is, after all, composed of human beings like us.

4) Some of your literary students might be encouraged to write a skit depicting Constantine and the bishop of Rome negotiating and bargaining over the conditions for allowing Christians to publicly practice their religion or for making Christianity the official state religion. We do not know what was said, but Constantine (being the clever politician that he was) must have wanted some influence in church affairs. The skit would give students a chance to examine what they would want if they were Constantine and what they would want to protect if they were the bishop of Rome.

5) Religion and politics still influence each other. Have your students make a list of the political decisions that must have affected the Church at the time of Constantine and how religion probably influenced politics at the time. Then, in a second list, have students draw parallels to the present political-religious scene.

6) In the United States, there used to be a lot of suspicion about Roman Catholics who held public offices because a common belief was that the pope could control Catholic politicians. Alfred E. Smith lost his candidacy for president in large part because he was a Catholic. The election of John F. Kennedy changed the situation considerably. To understand what it must have been like for Catholics to be denied political power because of their religion and to understand religious prejudice, students can be instructed to interview parents, grandparents, or others who remember the days before Kennedy's presidency.

Activities for Concept E
Arianism divided the Church, but the creed formulated at the Nicene Council clarified central truths about Jesus, even if it did not bring unity. (Pages 99–103 of the student text.)

Review Questions and Exercises from the Student Text

Question 9: Arianism represented the most serious threat to the Church in its history to that point. Why? How was Arianism dealt with?
Answer: Arianism denied the divinity of Jesus. Certainly Christ's divinity is an essential belief. Arians could not believe that a human being could also be "one in Being with the Father," both God and human. In the fashion begun at the Council of Jerusalem, a council was called to deal with the problem. After stormy debate, Arianism was condemned.

Question 10: What is heresy? What are its positive and negative results?
Answer: Heresy is a belief held clearly in opposition to the official teachings of the Church. Most often a heresy begins with someone teaching a partial truth or emphasizing one element of faith to the detriment of the whole faith. The positive results of heresies are the reclarifications and recommitments to the faith that occur. The negative results are divisions among Christians, sometimes hate developing, and denial of the fullness of the Good News.

Question 11: How does Athanasius represent the positive and negative effects of religion's becoming institutionalized in a country?

Answer: Emperors were so involved in the problem of Arianism that they used force to suppress it or to promote it. Athanasius was forced into exile by some emperors and placed back at the helm of his diocese by other emperors. It is good that government protects religion from persecution, but it is wrong to force people to believe a certain way.

Personal Reflection Exercises

2) Reflect on what was said about women's place in the Church as seen in the history of the Church. Read Ephesians 5:21–33. Would Jesus agree with the way in which women have been treated in the Church? What changes might take place in the status of women in the Church during your lifetime? How do you think women should best participate in the Church?

3) There is a sort of daily martyrdom that takes place in many of our lives. Think about the events in your life during this last week. Have your beliefs in Christianity caused you to suffer in any way? Did the suffering enrich your life in any way?

6

Other Questions and Activities for Discussion

1) Have a student look up the meaning and etymology of *heresy*. Examine with your students what would happen if people could believe anything they wanted and still call themselves Catholic.

2) The Nicene Council wrote a creed that is still used by Catholics. Have your students write a creed.
   a) Divide the class into several groups. Each group should write a summary of what they believe about Jesus. These statements should be written out neatly and then read to the class.
   b) Have one representative from each group sit in an inner circle to decide on a correct (orthodox) statement for everyone to accept. The final statement should represent the ideas of all the groups.
   c) Have the rest of the class sit in an outer circle, listening to the inner circle's discussion. There should be one empty chair in the inner circle so that class members from the outer circle may enter into the discussion if they think that their representatives are missing some key points.
   d) When no new elements are emerging in the discussion, instruct the group in the inner circle to decide on a final statement.
   e) The final "creed" should be read as part of a class prayer service.
   f) Compare the class creed to the Nicene Creed. What was overlooked? What was added? Are any parts at odds?

3) After the students have read "Women in the Early Church" (pp. 102–103 of the student text), invite a woman who is engaged in church ministry to talk to your class about the roles of women in the Church today.

Summary Activities for the Chapter

1) Ask the students to write in their journals about ways in which they have heralded the Word, served others, and contributed to the building of the Body of Christ during the past week.

2) If you have not already used the questions for daily quizzes, distribute to the class Student Handout 6–A, "Quiz on Chapter 6" (found at the end of this chapter). The answers for the quiz are as follows:

1) d	6) c	11) d	16) c
2) a	7) a	12) d	17) b
3) b	8) a	13) c	18) a
4) c	9) c	14) c	19) a
5) b	10) c	15) d	20) a

3) A prayer service with which to end this chapter is contained in Student Handout 6–B, "Prayer Service: Prayers from the Martyrs" (found at the end of this chapter). For the closing prayer, you may wish to use the class creed; either someone can read it prayerfully or the whole class could pray it together.

6

Quiz on Chapter 6

_____ 1) Which of these groups did *not* present problems to the Christians? **(a)** the Romans **(b)** the barbarians **(c)** the Jews **(d)** the Assyrians

_____ 2) "Barbarian" comes from a word meaning **(a)** hairy ones **(b)** monsters **(c)** savages **(d)** people from Barbary.

_____ 3) "Bishop" comes from the word that means **(a)** holy person **(b)** supervisor **(c)** merchant **(d)** high priest.

_____ 4) In the early centuries these people were the only other official church personnel besides the bishops: **(a)** priests **(b)** nuns **(c)** deacons **(d)** brothers.

_____ 5) After the fall of Jerusalem, the bishop of this city was considered most important of all the bishops: **(a)** Carthage **(b)** Rome **(c)** Alexandria **(d)** Antioch.

_____ 6) The Roman Empire was threatened by **(a)** famine **(b)** the Egyptians **(c)** frontier nomadic tribes **(d)** drought.

_____ 7) Because they would not sacrifice to the Roman gods, Christians were considered **(a)** atheists **(b)** barbarians **(c)** foreigners **(d)** ignorant.

_____ 8) Apologists were **(a)** defenders of the faith **(b)** Greek philosophers who fought Christianity **(c)** a group who denied there was a god **(d)** Roman priests who worshiped Apollo.

_____ 9) A group who taught that all things material are bad and that only a few people who have a secret knowledge can be saved were **(a)** Anabaptists **(b)** Dionysians **(c)** Gnostics **(d)** Agnostics.

_____ 10) A statement that summarizes what people believe is called a **(a)** synod **(b)** treaty **(c)** creed **(d)** diatribe.

_____ 11) This emperor required that all citizens carry a certificate showing that he or she had sacrificed to the Roman gods: **(a)** Nero **(b)** Severus **(c)** Marcus Aurelius **(d)** Decius.

_____ 12) People who renounced their faith to save their lives during the persecutions were called **(a)** antediluvians **(b)** apodictics **(c)** amoralists **(d)** apostates.

_____ 13) For better management Diocletian split the empire into groups of provinces called **(a)** territorialities **(b)** states **(c)** dioceses **(d)** proconsulates.

_____ 14) Diocletian persecuted the Christians because **(a)** he thought they were cannibals **(b)** they burned down Rome **(c)** he wanted to unify the country using religion **(d)** he considered them weak.

_____ 15) Priscilla was baptized on **(a)** Christmas **(b)** Advent **(c)** Pentecost **(d)** Easter.

_____ 16) Constantine had these Greek letters painted on his soldiers' banners and shields: **(a)** *AO* **(b)** *INRI* **(c)** *XP* **(d)** *PAX.*

_____ 17) Freedom of religion was granted to Christians in the Edict of **(a)** Rome **(b)** Milan **(c)** Pisa **(d)** Illyria.

_____ 18) At the Council of Nicaea this heresy was condemned: **(a)** Arianism **(b)** Gnosticism **(c)** Pelagianism **(d)** Modernism.

_____ 19) The heresy condemned at Nicaea said that **(a)** Jesus was not divine **(b)** Mary was not the mother of Jesus **(c)** the Holy Spirit did not exist **(d)** the Resurrection was not true.

_____ 20) The many exiles of Athanasius are good examples of **(a)** the interference of the state in church affairs **(b)** his heretical teachings **(c)** the power of deacons **(d)** his unpopularity with the bishop of Rome.

Prayer Service: Prayers from the Martyrs

A Prayer for Apostates by Cyprian of Carthage (who died in A.D. 258, during the persecutions of Decius)

All: Let us pray for those who have fallen away,
    that they may recover their footing.

Left: Let us pray for those standing firm,
    that they may not be tempted to their downfall.

Right: Let us pray for those of whose fall we have been told,
    that they may admit the gravity of their sin
    and realize that the remedy it calls for is anything but superficial.

Left: Let us pray that when they have received full forgiveness,
    they may do penance,
and remembering their guilt,
    may decide to be patient for a time.

Right: The Church is still unsteady. May they not upset it altogether, its own members turning to persecution within it and crowning their many sins with the sin of trouble-making.

A Prayer Written by Afra of Augsburg (who was martyred during the reign of Diocletian). She had lived a sad and disoriented life before her conversion.

Reader: Lord God almighty, Jesus Christ, you did not come to call the just; you came to call sinners to repentance.

Your promise is clear; it admits of no doubt. You were so good as to say that as soon as a sinner turned away from his evil deeds, you would say no more about his sins. Accept, then, as a sign of my repentance, the sufferings I am now undergoing, and by this fire that is waiting to burn my body for a time, deliver me from the eternal fire that burns body and soul alike. . . .

Thanks be to you, Lord Jesus Christ: in your mercy you have chosen me to be a victim for the glory of your name—you who offered yourself on the cross as a victim for the salvation of the whole world, you the innocent for us the guilty, you the good for us the wicked, you the blessed for us the cursed, you the sinless for all us sinners.

To you I offer my sacrifice, to you who are one God with the Father and the Holy Spirit, with whom you live and reign, as you always will, age after age. Amen.

Leader: Let us reflect on the ways in which we are called to be martyrs in our small daily sufferings. [Pause.]

Closing Prayer: The Class Creed

CHAPTER 7

Building the City of God

Major Concepts

A. As the age of martyrdom gave way to an age of power for the Church, some men and women desired to draw apart from the world to live solely in silent communion with God. In the fourth century, monasticism began taking on a distinct character and became an integral part of church life.

B. Even though the Roman Empire was on the verge of destruction in the West, Ambrose of Milan was writing works of theology and Jerome was translating the Hebrew and Christian Scriptures into Latin. Their works formed a key part of the foundation of Christian thought.

C. After a dissolute youth, Augustine converted to Christianity and turned his vast talents to the service of God. He formulated a monastic rule that is still followed by religious orders today, was pastor to a diocese, and wrote theological works like *The City of God* that are still avidly studied.

D. Saint Patrick established a novel method for his missionary work. He built monasteries throughout Ireland from which monks and nuns could spread the Word of God. This method not only converted Ireland but also was used by later missionaries on the continent of Europe.

E. Pope Leo the Great established the primacy of the bishop of Rome. He assumed the title "Pontifex Maximus," a title used by the Roman emperors to signify that they were chief among all priests. At the Council of Chalcedon, Leo and his supporters rejected the heresy declaring that Jesus was not human. And Leo saved Rome from destruction by the Huns when he faced down Attila.

Activities for Concept A

As the age of martyrdom gave way to an age of power for the Church, some men and women desired to draw apart from the world to live solely in silent communion with God. In the fourth century, monasticism began taking on a distinct character and became an integral part of church life. (Page 108 of the student text.)

Review Questions and Exercises from the Student Text

Question 1: What motivated people to become monks or cloistered nuns? What developments in the Roman Empire contributed to the growth of monastic life?

Answer: In the fourth century, as now, women and men entered monastic life to find God in silence, solitude, and simplicity. Since the Church was legalized and, indeed, was gaining power and prestige, some thought that a new "martyrdom" was called for, a life in which a person gave up everything for God.

Question 2: How have monasteries been part of the Church as Servant?

Answer: The wisdom of monks and nuns was a source of consolation and advice for simple people and emperors. Monasteries were oases for the poor and sick too, although this was not their main function.

Other Questions and Activities for Discussion

1) Sometimes people have the mistaken idea that monastic life is escapist or that people enter monasteries because they are running away from the world. Ironically, monastic life—especially the life of a hermit—is a harsh confrontation with oneself and with God. To aid your students in understanding monastic life, here is an exercise that may prove helpful.

If possible, take your students to the chapel or outside if the weather is suitable. Have them spread out so that each one has plenty of room. They may bring nothing with them (except maybe a copy of the Christian Scriptures). Tell them that they will have one-half hour to meditate alone; they should talk to no other person.

When the half hour is up, ask them to write in their journals on the following topics:

- List the topics that came into your mind during your meditation and then try to describe in detail what you were thinking about each topic.
- Put an *X* next to topics about which you wanted to think or about which you frequently daydream.
- Put a check mark next to topics about which you did not want to think or about which you infrequently think.
- Did you come to a point in the meditation at which you wished, for example, that you could turn on the radio or during which you began to hum a song? If so, about what topic were you thinking when this desire hit you? Why would you wish to change "the subject" of your thoughts?
- Did you learn anything new about who you are or about how you think? If so, what did you learn?
- What topics did you refer to God? How did God enter into your meditations?
- Would you like to have a period of quiet like this every day? If so, why? If not, why not?
- From this experience, what do you think it would be like to live a whole life of silent meditation? Do you think it would be easy or hard? Do you think that someone who wanted to escape the real world could be a monk or nun?

After your students have finished their journal reflections, discuss with them the last two questions of the reflection exercise and any other relevant questions that are brought up because of their experiences. A lot of us fear silence; there is an urge to escape the quiet listening to ourselves and to God. Students need to understand that monks are not escapists and, in fact, have to face the toughest persons to face—themselves!

2) In the last twenty years, we have seen the rise of interest in various Eastern gurus and even in homegrown messiahs who have founded cults that seem to promise complete happiness. Some of your students have probably had dealings with cultists of one sort or another. Analyze with your students the difference between reasons for joining a cult and the fundamental notions about going into the desert to pray.

Most of the early monks went alone and lived alone. A person like Antony did not rule the lives of the monks and did not try to attract a following. Certainly he lived as simply or even more simply than most of the other monks, unlike the gurus who ride around in Mercedes and demand complete obedience of their followers. The early monks were free to come and go as they pleased; each monk had to follow the promptings of the Holy Spirit as he perceived it. There was little, if any at all, of the "group-think" that so characterizes cults. Instead of finding the type of neurotic comfort in constant group stroking—all designed to brainwash a person into passivity—the monks freely decided to come to grips with themselves and God in silent prayer and meditation.

Eventually, as is explained in this chapter, monks did form groups with rules and with a superior. However, the rules were rather general and were derived from the experiences of the monks themselves for the most part. And the superior was elected by the monks who freely submitted to his guidance in living out the rule. The abbot

7

was not a guru whose words in and of themselves were of value; he was empowered to ensure that the monks prayed to God and kept the rules, and he was to set an example for all.

3) To examine why monks wanted some sort of rules for their lives, begin with these questions:
- If you were to form a community of people, why would a rule of life be so important?
- What would have to be some of the rules that you would need to ensure an atmosphere of charity, prayer, and reconciliation in a monastery? in any group of Christians?

At this point, divide the class into small groups. Each group is responsible for writing rules or general guidelines that would be necessary to ensure a charitable, prayerful, healthy life in the monastery. Give each group a different area of life for which to write rules: prayer schedule and type of prayer, work around the monastery, meals, communication with the outside world and between each other, clothing and other personal needs, study and spiritual reading, methods by which decisions are to be made in the monastery, and ways in which superiors are to be elected. After the groups are done, have the students report on their "rule." You might even make copies of the rule so as to compare it later to the rules of Augustine, Benedict, and Francis. Then conclude this topic by discussing these questions:
- Why would the monks give up ownership of personal property? What would be gained by doing this? Is it necessary for monastic life? What problems does ownership of personal property cause you? For example, what are some of the negative effects of owning your own car?
- Why would monks find it necessary to freely vow to stay single? What would be gained by being celibate as a monk? Is it necessary for monastic life?
- Why would monks put themselves under the authority of superiors? What would be gained by doing this? What problems would arise in a monastery if they did not have a superior?

4) Students may be assigned to bring in pictures of monasteries and to report on what sort of buildings composed the monastery.

5) Student Handout 7-A, "Quotations from Basil, Ambrose, and Jerome" (found at the end of this chapter), has four short quotations from Saint Basil's writings. You might wish to discuss these passages with your students; they are good illustrations that "there is nothing new under the sun." They also show that abortion is a very old issue in the Church.

Activities for Concept B
Even though the Roman Empire was on the verge of destruction in the West, Ambrose of Milan was writing works of theology and Jerome was translating the Hebrew and Christian Scriptures into Latin. Their works formed a key part of the foundation of Christian thought. (Pages 109–111 of the student text.)

Review Questions and Exercises from the Student Text

Question 3: How were bishops selected during the fourth and fifth centuries? What is your reaction to the way in which Ambrose was made bishop of Milan? Could good bishops be selected this way now?

Answer: Bishops were frequently elected by popular acclamation. This seems very odd to us because the process of selecting bishops is now much more secretive. Today bishops are nominated by other bishops, and advice is given by selected people in the local church where a prospective bishop resides. Names of capable priests are sent to the papal nuncio and then forwarded to Rome with his recommendation. From there on the decision is made in the Vatican. Dioceses frequently have bishops who were previously unknown to them.

Question 4: Using Ambrose's life as a bishop as a guideline, write a job description of a bishop. Then, list as many characteristics as you can for a good bishop.

Answer: Ambrose had to be a theologian, preacher, pastor, financial manager, social welfare director, sacramental administrator, and mediator.

Question 5: What kind of relationship between church and state do you see developing in this chapter? Give examples that describe this relationship.

Answer: The emperors tried more and more to impose their decisions on church authorities. If the emperor was an Arian, the Church suffered. In a confrontation with the Arian ruler, Ambrose had to rely on his people's faithfulness and support in order to maintain his role as the head of the diocese.

Question 6: Why is Jerome's work as a religious scholar so important even to our time? Why are religious scholars important people in the life of the Church?

Answer: The Vulgate Bible, which is Jerome's Latin translation, has been used for centuries as a guide to understanding and translating the Hebrew and Christian Scriptures. Accurate translations are indispensable aids in learning the Word of God, the wellspring of Christian life. As scholars help us better comprehend our faith, we can become better informed messengers of the Word.

Question 7: Why was Alaric's sacking of Rome such a shocking event?

Answer: For centuries Rome had ruled supreme in the Western world. Rome had finally fallen to the barbarians; its era of power was finished. The empire would now have to find new order.

Other Questions and Activities for Discussion

1) Have some students find Milan, Italy, on a map and do a report about the city.

2) Clearly, bishops play an important part in the life of our local church. The selection of a bishop like Ambrose was rather informal in the 300s because he led a much smaller group of people in a smaller area than a modern bishop would. Lest your students idealize the method of selecting bishops by acclamation of the people, discuss these two questions:

- Would the election of a bishop by acclamation be practical today?
- Why was acclamation by the people the only realistic way of selecting bishops in the 300s?

Today, with dioceses so spread out and with many priests functioning in each diocese, people would find it difficult to know each priest sufficiently in order to make a good decision through an acclamation. In the 300s, communication was very poor and each diocese was much more autonomous; in addition, the bishop of Rome just did not have complete information on who would be the best candidates. The process used today to select bishops would take months, if not years, to complete given the state of communication in the fourth century.

7

3) Ambrose's congregation staged a sit-down strike to protect their bishop and their right to remain faithful to the official teaching of the Church. Have your students find examples of church persons using nonviolent resistance to protest injustice and/or to protect the rights of people. Assign students to look for articles in the diocesan, local, and national newspapers. Discuss the use of nonviolence to confront injustice; it is certainly well within the Church's tradition.

4) Discuss public penance. Remind the students that the early communities required reconciliation only after very serious, and usually public, sins. Most sins were more or less public because towns were small and Christian communities would know about any serious moral failing. Besides, the early Christians had a keen sense of sin's being a socially significant act as well as an act against God. Every serious sin negatively affected the whole community. Therefore, reconciliation with the whole community was called for. Ambrose showed tremendous courage when he refused the sacraments to the emperor, but the emperor's crime was terrible. After any other explanation that you see fitting, ask your students:

- Should public penances be reinstated for public sins?
- Would people submit to public penances today? If so, why? If not, why not?
- Are public acts of repentance and reconciliation better for Christian communities? for the penitent person?
- How do you respond to being corrected publicly at school? Should schools enforce public penances?

To bring the situation closer to home, describe the following case to the students:

Let's say that a student is caught spray painting profanities on the side of the school building. The paint must be sandblasted off, at considerable expense to the school. In effect, this student's act has cost you—as a tuition payer—a portion of your fees to the school.

- Should this student have to do some sort of public penance?
- What penance would serve to show his or her repentance and yet allow for his or her reconciliation with the school community?
- What would happen if there were no sort of public repentance? Would the whole school suffer?

5) At this point, refer the students to the short passage from Ambrose's writings that states clearly his views about church-state relations (see Student Handout 7–A, found at the end of this chapter).

6) Jerome was the spiritual director for a monastery and several convents, as well as a full-time scholar. He undoubtedly had a severe personality and did not mince words when he thought someone needed a good scolding. On Student Handout 7–A (found at the end of this chapter), Jerome's letter to Sabinian demonstrates his toughness of character. The letter also exemplifies Jerome's concern for the soul of even this most lecherous priest, and it shows that, once again, nothing is new. If people think that we have declined morally as a people, let them read the words of Jerome.

7) Also on Student Handout 7–A, three passages from Jerome's letters to his friends illustrate dramatically the effects on people of the fall of Rome to Alaric. These letters also give us a sense of what the fall of Rome was like. Ask your students to read these passages; then discuss them.

- Based on Jerome's letters, what were some of the effects of the fall of Rome?
- Why would Jerome be so distraught because of its fall?
- Are there any modern parallels to illustrate the fate of refugees after the fall of a country?

Activities for Concept C

After a dissolute youth, Augustine converted to Christianity and turned his vast talents to the service of God. He formulated a monastic rule that is still followed by religious orders today, was pastor to a diocese, and wrote theological works like *The City of God* that are still avidly studied. (Pages 112–117 of the student text.)

Review Questions and Exercises from the Student Text

Question 8: In your own words, describe the conversion of Augustine. What was it about his personality that made him first a great sinner and then a great saint?

Answer: Augustine was brilliant and passionate. After his conversion, all the energy he had spent on "lust," the study of philosophers, and non-Christian amusements was turned to Christian purposes. His brilliant mind had been looking for satisfying answers to the meaning of life; once he found such answers in the Christian Scriptures, he became single-minded and poured his whole being into living as a Christian.

Question 9: You have read some passages from Saint Augustine's *The Confessions* and Thomas Merton's *The Seven Storey Mountain*. Why would these two very great Christians write about their reckless young adulthoods and their mysterious conversions? What elements are similar in their processes of conversion?

Answer: Both Augustine and Merton wrote about their conversions in order to show the wonder of God's ways. If God could call them to new life, then God could call anyone. They also wanted to show the goodness of the new life to which they were called, to show how much better it was than the old lives they had led. Both Augustine and Merton were brilliant students who led reckless lives in their youth. Both were clearly looking for something that would satisfy them intellectually, emotionally, and spiritually. Eventually, both men found Christian writers who inspired them, and both found the Christian Scriptures. An "inner voice" spoke to both men.

Question 10: What were Augustine's homilies like? Why is there such little interaction between the priest and the congregation during homilies today?

Answer: Augustine's homilies were rather informal. People shouted questions and comments, and he would often share asides. Augustine also spoke for long periods of time. There is little interaction in homilies today for many reasons. Our congregations are much larger, making informal interchange less practical. Homilies tend to be short, certainly much shorter than Augustine's. They are short because the presumption is that Catholics have had some religious instruction in school or in parish programs; therefore, parishioners do not need formal instruction through homilies. Finally, during Augustine's time, most of his audiences would be adults; thus, he could talk at greater length and about more complicated issues.

Question 11: Describe the three groups that Augustine opposed. What beliefs did they hold that were contrary to Augustine's belief?

Answer: The Manichaeans believed in a good god, who created good, and a bad god, who created evil. Humans were caught in the middle between these gods and therefore could not be held responsible for their acts. Augustine became convinced that there was a single, spiritual God and that humans shared part of that spiritual nature.

The Donatists refused to readmit into the Church those who had denied their faith during the Roman persecutions. Especially in North Africa, Donatist churches had survived for nearly a hundred years since the last persecution. Augustine clearly agreed with the decision to readmit people who denied their faith and, therefore, opposed the Donatists. Donatists also taught that sacraments administered by sinful persons were invalid. Augustine knew that all people are, in varying degrees, sinful; but God's love transcends our weaknesses.

7

Finally, Pelagians believed that they could get to heaven using their own free will and human powers; grace was not required. Augustine knew that God's love was the source of our salvation.

Question 12: Why did Augustine write *The City of God?*

Answer: Augustine wanted to remind people that evil will always exist in the "City of Man" where greed, hatred, lust, and selfishness abound. Through God's grace, Christians can build the "City of God," but it will only come to completion in the next life. His book was an argument against those who blamed Christianity for the fall of the Roman Empire.

Personal Reflection Exercise

> **Both Saint Augustine and Thomas Merton describe times when they felt helpless to change their lives—times when they felt sinful, alone, directionless—times of searching. Think back in your own life to a time when you were feeling helpless. Describe where you were, who was with you, what you were doing, and what had most recently happened to you. What helped you come out of this feeling? What place did God have in your experience?**

Other Questions and Activities for Discussion

7

1) The area of Africa stretching along the Mediterranean Sea was part of the Roman Empire; the people living there in Augustine's time were more Roman than African. Ask some students to report on the situation of North Africa now.
   - What North African countries border the Mediterranean?
   - What religions are practiced there?
   - What sort of governments do they have?

2) Augustine founded a type of communal monastic life and wrote some general instructions for the monks and nuns who lived in the monasteries and convents he founded. Some of these guidelines are quoted on Student Handout 7–B, "Saint Augustine's Thoughts on Religious Life" (found at the end of this chapter). Ask your students to compare these guidelines with the "rule" they wrote earlier in this chapter for concept A, activity 3.

3) In his *Confessions,* Augustine admits that he was going to marry, in large measure, to regulate his "lust." He needed to settle down, and a wife was considered necessary. Of course, the marriage never occurred, but the incident demonstrates a mentality of the times about the functions of a wife and of marriage itself. Ask your students the following questions:
   - How would you evaluate Augustine's motivations for marriage?
   - What stereotypes about women does this attitude demonstrate?
   - Do some men today still have the same mentality about marriage, that is, "If I get married, my wife can straighten me out"?

4) Augustine's early life might be more appealing to some students than his life as a celibate bishop, monk, preacher, and scholar. Explore with your students how media in modern life try to seduce us into thinking that a life like Augustine's young adulthood is the road to true happiness. Students might bring in advertisements for alcoholic beverages, clothing, colognes, vacations, music, bars, nightclubs, and so on, that demonstrate the allure of the "macho" life. The students could create a collage on the bulletin board called "Augustine's Flaming Youth." Then discuss how all this—the "macho" life—can be a dead end, as was the case for both Augustine and Merton.

5) Pelagianism is worth considering in more depth. There is an element of Pelagianism in the work ethic, and/or, maybe the work ethic carries over into our notions about salvation. The tendency to think that we have to work our way to heaven is common. The practice of buying indulgences to pay one's way to heaven demonstrates a Pelagian attitude too. Here are some questions to raise with your students:
- Why would people be tempted to be Pelagians?
- If we have been saved by Jesus and if faith in Jesus' saving power is what is required for salvation, why would people not depend on God's grace?
- What are some examples of people who seem to be trying to work their ways into heaven?

Activities for Concept D

Saint Patrick established a novel method for his missionary work. He built monasteries throughout Ireland from which monks and nuns could spread the Word of God. This method not only converted Ireland but also was used by later missionaries on the continent of Europe. (Pages 117–118 of the student text.)

Review Questions and Exercises from the Student Text

Question 13: Who were the Celts? How were they different from people living in the Roman world?

Answer: The Celts were a people who had been pushed from northern Europe into England and Ireland by Germanic tribes. They resisted the Romans, but eventually the only independent Celts were those living in Scotland and Ireland. They maintained their own customs and religion, which were different from the Romans'.

Question 14: What approach did Patrick take to missionary work among the Irish?

Answer: Patrick brought monks with him to Ireland. From the monasteries, the monks taught the people to read and write Latin and Celtic, and eventually they taught the Irish about the Christian religion. The monasteries provided a secure base for these missionary monks.

Question 15: Many legends abound about Patrick. Why do people create fables about saints or heroes? What positive values do legends have—even if they are not literally true?

Answer: Legends about saints and heroes are made to glorify and honor the saint or hero. The value for people is that these saints then become models of behavior.

Other Questions and Activities for Discussion

1) Have some students research the Druids and early Irish religious practices. A panel of the researchers could present reports on what Patrick had to face in Ireland. Other students could find out about legends told of Saint Patrick. Then they could narrate the legends to the class like storytellers acting out the drama.

2) Bring to class some pictures of illuminated manuscripts to show your students the painstaking work that monks and nuns did so many centuries before the printing presses.

3) The feast of Saint Patrick is celebrated with great enthusiasm just about everywhere. People of all nationalities become Irish for one day each year. What accounts for Saint Patrick's popularity? Students could interview grandparents, aunts, uncles, and parents asking these queries:

7

- Why is Saint Patrick's Day so popular?
- What stories have you been told about the life of Saint Patrick?
- What has he meant to Irish people over the centuries?

Then the students could report their findings to the class.

4) Patrick used monasteries to spread the Word of God. Ask your students these questions:
- What would a contemporary "Patrick" find himself doing in the Church today?
- Where would "Patrick" be found today?
- How would a contemporary "Patrick" spread the Word of God today?

5) Every Mormon young man must do two years of missionary work somewhere away from his home. Most of us have seen pairs of clean-cut, neatly dressed young adult men walking through neighborhoods visiting with people and spreading the Mormon message. Ask these questions of your students:
- If the Mormons can do this, why don't Catholics require two years of missionary service of all young adults?
- Should people be required to be missionaries?
- The Mormons have grown in numbers over recent years. How do you think people feel about the dedication of these young men who spread the Mormon message?
- Are there equivalent ways in which Catholic young adults can serve the Church and the People of God?

Have some information available about lay Catholic volunteer programs and religious orders; Catholics do have ways of spreading the Word too.

If your class could profit from it, invite two Mormon missionaries to talk to the class about the experience of being a missionary; your classes could learn some valuable lessons about dedication. And, if you know of some young people who are Catholic lay volunteers, invite them to discuss being missionaries in the modern world.

Activities for Concept E

Pope Leo the Great established the primacy of the bishop of Rome. He assumed the title "Pontifex Maximus," a title used by the Roman emperors to signify that they were chief among all priests. At the Council of Chalcedon, Leo and his supporters rejected the heresy declaring that Jesus was not human. And Leo saved Rome from destruction by the Huns when he faced down Attila. (Pages 119–122 of the student text.)

Review Questions and Exercises from the Student Text

Question 16: How did Leo I influence the role of the bishop of Rome? What do the titles "pope" and "Pontifex Maximus" mean? How did the changes in the pope's position come about? What were the forces that altered his role?

Answer: Leo gave the position of pope much more prominence. The word *pope* comes from *papas,* meaning dad or papa. When Leo took the title "Pontifex Maximus," a title previously used by Roman emperors, he wanted to indicate that the bishop of Rome was the high priest for all Christians. With the fall of the Roman Empire, more and more leadership was assumed by the pope because he was the only one who could influence all the tribes that were ebbing and flowing across the continent, yet even his influence was limited.

Question 17: What issues did Eutyches's teachings raise? How were these problems settled?

Answer: Eutyches taught that Jesus was not really a human being; the divine somehow had absorbed the human part of Jesus. In settling the matter, the nature of the authority of the bishop of Rome, the role of the emperor in theological disputes, the growing split between the Eastern and the Western schools of thought, and the ranking of the Christian bishops were all raised as problems facing the Church. The Council of Chalcedon met to settle the theological disputes, but it did not really solve all these problems.

Question 18: Based on the decisions of the Council of Chalcedon, describe the authority of the pope at this time.

Answer: The bishop of Rome was given a preeminence in the Church, but his input into the council was only one opinion among many expressed. Leo was influential but could not order the council around. When the council declared the patriarch of Constantinople second in eminence to the bishop of Rome, Leo did not like it but had to accept the decision.

Question 19: Why were Leo's confrontations with Attila and then the Vandals so important?

Answer: Leo saved thousands of lives through his actions, and he minimized the destruction of Rome. He was the only defense strong enough to protect the Western empire.

Question 20: Why did priests become more numerous in the fourth and fifth centuries?

Answer: The Church was growing rapidly, and thus more ministers of the sacraments were needed, especially in small towns and villages. Bishops lived mostly in large cities.

7

Other Questions and Activities for Discussion

1) Discuss which view of the pope dominates today—papa or supreme high priest? Students might profit from interviewing some older people about how they remember the pope. Ask the students to describe where their own images of the pope come from.

2) The Coptic Church lives on in Ethiopia. Students might do research about Coptic rites, membership figures, special feasts, distinctive garb, and so on. If they can bring in some pictures of things Coptic, it would be helpful.

3) Concerning the heresy preached by Eutyches, ask your students these questions:
- Would it make a tremendous difference in your belief if Jesus had, indeed, been only divine and not human?
- What if Jesus had simply been human and not divine? How would our religion be different then?
- Are there people today who, through the ways they treat Jesus, seem to believe that Jesus was not human?

4) Stage a debate in which one side represents the majority of bishops at Chalcedon, who teach that Jesus was human and divine in one person, and in which the other side speaks for Eutyches, who denies Jesus' humanness. Both sides would have to do some research beforehand. Clearly, you would need rather bright students to do this activity.

5) On a large wall map of Europe, have some students trace the different battle routes of Attila and the Huns. Other students can be charged to find some pictures of how the Huns must have looked.

6) Ask the students to write a dialogue of Leo I trying to talk Attila out of sacking Rome. What would Leo have said? Then, the dialogues can be read or acted out in class.

Summary Activities for the Chapter

1) In their journals, students should record their reflections about how they have been Servant, Herald, Body of Christ, and Sacrament.

2) If you have not already used these questions for daily quizzes, distribute to the class Student Handout 7–C, "Quiz on Chapter 7" (found at the end of this chapter). The answers for the quiz are as follows:

1) c	8) b	15) b	22) d
2) d	9) c	16) b	23) b
3) b	10) c	17) d	24) a
4) a	11) d	18) b	25) b
5) d	12) a	19) c	
6) b	13) d	20) d	
7) d	14) a	21) a	

3) A prayer service for closing this chapter is contained on Student Handout 7–D, "Prayer Service: Our Dependence on God" (found at the end of this chapter). A song that would go well with this service is "City of God" by Dan Schutte in *Glory and Praise,* vol. 3 (Phoenix: North American Liturgy Resources, 1982).

7

Quotations from Basil, Ambrose, and Jerome

Statements from Saint Basil's Letter to the Bishop of Iconium (A.D. 374)

- A woman who has deliberately destroyed a fetus must pay the penalty for murder.

- A man who, in a fit of temper, used an axe on his wife is a murderer.

- Those also who give drugs causing abortions are murderers themselves, as well as those who receive the poison which kills the fetus.

- Our Fathers did not reckon killings in war as murders, but granted pardon, as it seems to me, to those who were fighting in defense of virtue and piety. Perhaps, however, they should be advised that, since their hands are not clean, they should abstain from Communion for a period of three years.

Saint Ambrose Preaches About Church-State Relations (A.D. 386)

The tribute that belongs to Caesar is not to be denied. The Church, however, is God's, and it must not be pledged to Caesar; for God's temple cannot be a right of Caesar. That this is said with sentiments of respect for the emperor no man can deny. And what is there more full of respect than that the emperor be styled a son of the Church? . . . For the emperor is in the Church, not over the Church; and far from refusing the Church's help, a good emperor seeks it.

Saint Jerome Scolds the Priest Sabinian

Sabinian, that belly of yours is your god, not Christ. Lust's slave are you. All your glory rests in your shame; and, like a victim for sacrifice, you continue to fatten yourself for the slaughter, imitating the behavior of those ignorant of their approaching torment. Do you not realize that the goodness of God calls you to repentance? . . .

. . . Certainly you are vigorous, healthy; and when you are discovered for what you are in one city, like a new apostle of the Antichrist, on to the next you move. Money you do not need; no crushing blow strikes you: you do not deserve the afflictions other men bear who are not, like you, an irrational beast. Pride elevates you, lust covers you like some fine vestment. Out of your bloated, flabby carcass wheeze words of death. You never consider that one day you must die, nor do you ever feel the slightest twinge of remorse after you have satisfied your lust. Truly, you have more than the heart you desire!

And so that you may not feel lonely in your evil ways, you invent scandals about people who are God's servants. In so doing, you fail to realize that you are blabbering iniquity against the Most High, setting your mouth against heaven. . . .

Saint Jerome Writes About the Fall of Rome

A letter to the nun Principia (A.D. 412)

. . . a terrifying rumor reached us from the West. Rome had been besieged. Citizens were ransoming their lives, we were told, and after being stripped of their wealth, they were once again attacked: first material possessions, then their very lives were lost in the sack of the city. My voice sticks in my throat, words fail as I dictate this.

The city which had captured the whole world is captured herself. Indeed, Rome perished from hunger before being put to the sword. Only a handful were found living to be taken captive. Hunger's frenzy, erupting, sent men to feed on strange, hideous food: they tore and gnawed at each other's limbs. . . .

. . . Meanwhile, amid all the confusion, a group of blood-smeared barbarians forced their way into Marcella's house. . . . Marcella met them with an unperturbed countenance. When they demanded gold and hidden valuables, she merely pointed to her shabby dress. Refusing to believe such voluntary poverty, they beat her with clubs and riding-whips. . . .

A letter to Gaudentius, father of Pactula (A.D. 413)

Shame on us Christians! The whole world crashes down in ruins, and still we remain firm in our sins. Head of the great Empire, the glorious city blazes in one tremendous conflagration. No part of the earth lacks exiles from Rome. Churches once held sacred collapse, broken down into cinders and smoldering ashes. Yet our minds are buzzing with schemes to accumulate money! Live for today, tomorrow you may die—this is our attitude. But we continue to build homes as if we were going to reside in this world forever. . . . Yet huddled among the famished, naked, destitute people at our doors, Christ Himself lies dying. . . .

Such are the times, then, into which your Pactula has been born. Slaughter and death are the toys of her childhood. She will know tears before laughter, sorrow before joy. Scarcely arrived on the stage of this world, soon she must exit. That the world was always like this—what else can she believe? Of the past she knows nothing; from the present she flies; she longs only for the future.

Refugees arrive at Bethlehem (A.D. 410–414)

. . . the sight of the refugees was extremely painful, and I simply could not continue my commentary and usual study. I was longing to transform the words of the Scripture into action. . . . Such a mighty political power, once careless of its wealth, reduced to such extremities. . . . Yet there are some here so vicious and hard-hearted that they break open the refugees' bundles and shabby luggage, hoping to find gold among the pitiful belongings of mere captives.

Saint Augustine's Thoughts on Religious Life

Excerpts from a Letter of Augustine to a Group of Religious Women (about A.D. 423)

These are the rules which we prescribe for the observance of those of you who have been admitted to the monastery. In the first place, as you are gathered into one community, see that you dwell together in unity in the house and that you have "one heart and one soul" toward God; that you do not call anything your own, but that you have all things in common. Let your Superior distribute food and clothing to each one of you, not equally to all, because you are not all of the same bodily strength, but to each one according to her need. . . .

Be instant in prayer at the hours and times appointed. Let no one do anything in the oratory but that for which it was made and from which it takes its name, so that if some of the Sisters have time and wish to pray even outside the appointed hours, those who wish to do something else there may not be a hindrance to them. . . .

Subdue your flesh by fasting and abstinence from food and drink as far as your health allows. . . . From the time when you come to the table until you rise from it, listen without noise or argument to what is read according to custom; let it not be only your mouth that takes food, but let your ears also drink in the word of God.

Let your garb be inconspicuous; do not aim at winning favor by your garments, but by your conduct. . . .

. . . no one will work at anything for her own use, . . . but let all your work be done for the common good, with greater zeal and more constant eagerness than if you were making things for your own use. . . . And so, the more care you take to promote the general good rather than your own, the more progress in perfection you will know that you have made. . . .

. . . The washing of the body, also, and the use of baths is not to be too frequent, but may be allowed at the usual interval of time, that is, once a month. . . .

. . . Refrain, therefore, from harsh words; if any slip from your mouth, do not be ashamed to utter healing words from the same mouth that caused the wounds. . . .

Quiz on Chapter 7

_____ 1) Saint Antony became a monk in the desert of **(a)** Syria **(b)** Palestine **(c)** Egypt **(d)** Turkey.

_____ 2) People who became monks wanted **(a)** to escape the real world **(b)** to hide from responsibilities **(c)** to be alone **(d)** to live in silent meditation and study to draw closer to God.

_____ 3) The first person to formulate some rules for monks was **(a)** Athanasius **(b)** Basil **(c)** Augustine **(d)** Mark.

_____ 4) Saint Ambrose became bishop of Milan when **(a)** the people acclaimed him bishop **(b)** the pope appointed him **(c)** the emperor chose him **(d)** he was elected by the local bishops.

_____ 5) Even under orders from the emperor's mother, Ambrose still refused to turn a church in Milan over to the **(a)** Donatists **(b)** Pelagians **(c)** Monophysites **(d)** Arians.

_____ 6) Ambrose made Theodosius do penance for **(a)** divorcing his wife **(b)** ordering the killing of several thousand Thessalonikans **(c)** attacking people hiding in a church **(d)** public profanity.

_____ 7) Jerome's translation of the Bible is called the **(a)** Standard Version **(b)** Jerusalem Bible **(c)** Rheims-Douay **(d)** Vulgate.

_____ 8) This person led the Goths in the sack of Rome: **(a)** Ali Baba **(b)** Alaric **(c)** Aloysius **(d)** Alphonsus.

_____ 9) Augustine was born in **(a)** Rome **(b)** Antioch **(c)** North Africa **(d)** Palestine.

_____ 10) Those who believe in a good god and an evil god are called **(a)** Monophysites **(b)** Aesthetes **(c)** Manichaeans **(d)** Ascetics.

_____ 11) Monica brought Augustine under the influence of **(a)** Antony **(b)** Leo **(c)** Athanasius **(d)** Ambrose.

_____ 12) In order to get his life organized, Augustine decided to **(a)** take a wife **(b)** study Plato **(c)** have a child by his mistress **(d)** read _The One-Minute Manager._

_____ 13) At the moment of his conversion Augustine was **(a)** almost drowning in the Tiber **(b)** listening to a famous preacher **(c)** arguing with his mistress **(d)** listening to children chanting a little song.

_____ 14) This heresy taught that apostates could not be readmitted into the Church: **(a)** Donatists **(b)** Pelagians **(c)** Manichaeans **(d)** Monophysites.

_____ 15) This heresy taught that people did not need grace to get to heaven, but could be saved through their own works: **(a)** Donatists **(b)** Pelagians **(d)** Manichaeans **(d)** Monophysites.

_____ 16) In this book Augustine makes clear that evil will always exist as long as people are selfish and hateful; on this earth we can only build for the next life: **(a)** _The Confessions_ **(b)** _The City of God_ **(c)** _Apologia pro Vita Sua_ **(d)** _The Perfect Life._

_____ 17) Patrick was born in (a) Ireland (b) Gaul (c) Holland (d) Britain.

_____ 18) These people were pagan priests, judges, and advisers to tribal Irish kings: (a) Droogans (b) Druids (c) Trolls (d) Wizards.

_____ 19) To help with his missionary work, Patrick brought (a) a carriage (b) a band of soldiers (c) monks and nuns (d) a letter from the pope.

_____ 20) When Leo I became bishop of Rome, he assumed this title that was not used by his predecessors: (a) pope (b) patriarch (c) holiness (d) Pontifex Maximus.

_____ 21) The heretical group led by Eutyches believed that (a) Jesus was not human (b) Jesus was not divine (c) Jesus was only a prophet (d) Jesus was born in Jerusalem.

_____ 22) The Council of Chalcedon decided that the patriarch of this city was second in eminence to the bishop of Rome: (a) Alexandria (b) Antioch (c) Jerusalem (d) Constantinople.

_____ 23) The Huns originated in (a) North Africa (b) North China (c) Turkey (d) Siberia.

_____ 24) Leo struck a bargain with the Vandals; they could steal, burn, and take slaves, but they could not (a) kill people unless attacked (b) loot the pope's house (c) pollute the Tiber (d) desecrate churches.

_____ 25) The word *catholic* means (a) holy (b) universal (c) religious (d) true.

Prayer Service: Our Dependence on God

Opening Prayer by Saint Ambrose

All: O God, who cannot change nor fail,
        Guiding the hours as they roll by;
    Brightening with beams the morning pale,
        And burning in the midday sky.

    Quench Thou the fires of hate and strife,
        The wasting fever of the heart;
    From perils guard our feeble life,
        And to our souls Thy peace impart.

Reading from Saint Augustine's New Year's Day Sermon

Reader: And so, many will struggle to-day in their hearts with the words they have heard. For we said, "Do not give New Year's presents; give to the poor." It is not enough that you give only so much; give even more. You do not want to give more? Well, give at least that much.

But you say to me, "When I give New Year's presents, I receive them in return." What? When you give to a poor person, do you receive nothing in return? . . .

Now, there certainly are among you those who liked to hear His words, standing with others who did not like to hear them. I am now speaking to true Christians: if your faith is different from that of others, if your hope is different, if your love is different, then lead different lives and show by your different conduct that your faith, hope, and charity are really different. . . .

Leader: Let us pause for a few moments of reflection on ways in which we might believe, hope, and love better.

Closing Prayer by Saint Patrick

All: I arise today:

in the Might of God	for my piloting;
in the Power of God	for my upholding;
in the Wisdom of God	for my guidance;
in the Eye of God	for my foresight;
in the Ear of God	for my hearing;
in the Word of God	for my utterance;
in the Hand of God	for my guardianship;
in the Path of God	for my precedence;
in the Shield of God	for my protection;
in the Host of God	for my salvation.

CHAPTER 8

Church Growth in a Crumbling Empire: 400–700

Major Concepts

A. While the Eastern empire remained stable, the Western empire dissolved into two major kingdoms—the Goths under Theodoric and the Franks under Clovis—and many minor tribal groups. Despite the dissolution of the Western empire, Christianity flourished.

B. Saint Benedict founded the abbey of Monte Cassino and gave his monks a rule that would be the cornerstone of Western monasticism.

C. The Emperor Justinian ruled the Eastern empire vigorously, giving it the magnificent Hagia Sophia and the Justinian Code. However, after his rule, the Eastern empire began a slow decline.

D. Pope Gregory the Great strengthened the Church by his preaching and example, his emphasis on education for the clergy, his diplomatic missions, his missionary zeal, and his reforms of the liturgy. During this period, the everyday lives of average Christians were very difficult. They relied heavily on the strength and comfort provided by the Church.

E. Islam was spread throughout the Middle East, North Africa, and Spain. By the time Charles Martel stopped Islamic advances at the Battle of Tours, most of the Eastern empire and some of the West had been converted to the new religion.

8

Activities for Concept A
While the Eastern empire remained stable, the Western empire dissolved into two major kingdoms—the Goths under Theodoric and the Franks under Clovis—and many minor tribal groups. Despite the dissolution of the Western empire, Christianity flourished. (Pages 126–128 of the student text.)

Review Questions and Exercises from the Student Text

Question 1: What were the main differences between conditions in the Western and Eastern empires? How did these differences influence the roles that the Church played during this period?
Answer: The Eastern empire was much more stable than that of the West. The West was plagued with invasions, pirates, terrible shortages of goods and services; and it was being carved up into tribal kingdoms. In the West, the Church, through the offices of several strong popes, gave leadership to the people and served as a stabilizing influence—functions associated with governments. In the East, the emperors tended to oversee the Church, sometimes heavy-handedly.

Question 2: What services did the Church in the West provide in the West? Why was the Church's position so central to life during this period?
Answer: The Church provided a common set of moral principles to guide the lives

of the people, no matter from which tribe they came. This common code of values and a sense of membership in the one Church gave different groups common ground; thus, the Church could be a mediating influence.

Question 3: How was the conversion of Clovis an important event in the spread of the faith? What custom and what larger process were set into motion when Clovis converted?

Answer: Since his kingdom was very large, many people were influenced by Clovis. When Clovis converted, many of his subjects followed suit. After all, what was good enough for the king was very good indeed for his subjects. Naturally, Clovis also used a common religion as a means of unifying his kingdom, and so Catholic Christianity replaced Arianism in those tribes that were influenced by him. [*Teacher's note:* But problems were also caused by the conversion of the Franks. First, there were too few trained clerics to deal with the masses of converts. Second, many of the converts were ignorant about the faith, and their motivation for converting was politically influenced.]

Question 4: What creations of Denis the Short are still important to us today? Why would a pope command Denis to work on these projects?

Answer: Denis created a new calendar beginning with the date of Christ's birth. This new calendar signified a shift of emphasis away from the importance of the Roman Empire and toward the centrality of Christianity in the lives of all people in that area of the world. Denis also collected the teachings of the various councils and synods, which were the beginning of canon law. Surely the pope saw this project as providing a common source to which to refer in decision-making and a tool for unifying the people.

Other Questions and Activities for Discussion

1) All too often we think of the present as a dangerous time, far more treacherous than "the good old days." Despite the many threats that do exist today, life is peaceful, relative to the fifth and sixth centuries for example. To give your students a further sense of what it was like in the days of Theodoric and Clovis, have them read the incidents on Student Handout 8-A, "Sygismund and the Conversion of Clovis" (found at the end of this chapter). These incidents were recorded by Gregory, bishop of Tours, France (a.d. 538–594), in his *History of the Franks.* Point out to your students that Gregory was seeing events as a person living then would; that is, he accepted violence perhaps more readily than we would, and he praised kings more uncritically than we would. Nevertheless, the stories give us an idea of the mentality of the times.

After the students have read the incidents, here are some questions you might raise to spur discussion:
- We do not know if Clovis's conversion happened exactly like this, but why would people at that time accept this sort of account?
- What other famous person was converted because Jesus helped him achieve victory?
- Why would Gregory want to connect Clovis so clearly to the conversion of Constantine?
- Why would people of that time follow their king to Baptism?
- What effect would this sort of mass Baptism have on the quality of religious practices of the time?
- What sort of picture of the political situation and morality of the day does the story of Sygismund's killing his son give us? For instance, why would it be important to mention that Sygismund had been married to the daughter of Theodoric, king of Italy?
- Would a king get away with killing his own son today? Why was it so different back then?

Gregory tells the story of Clovis's conversion so that Clovis comes off like a new Constantine; in fact, a bit later Gregory says about the Baptism of Clovis, "another Constantine advanced to the baptismal font. . . ." Gregory was definitely stretching the story just to make the grandeur of Clovis's conversion even greater. The troops converted because if Jesus was good enough for the king, he was good enough for them. Most people believed that a king ruled by divine right—certainly Gregory thought that was the case with Clovis.

Sygismund's murdering his son would not have shocked too many people in those times; sons plotted against fathers; brothers killed one another with frightening regularity; poison was a favorite tool of power-hungry queens. Kings were absolute authorities in their kingdoms—as long as they were tough enough to hold on. Sygismund's marriage to Theodoric's daughter was certainly politically inspired, and sons were insurance that the throne would stay in the family. Chances are that Sygismund had little to do with the son he killed. These were hard, brutal days. A sign that the Church was making some inroads into the consciences of people was that, at least, Sygismund did penance and admitted wrongdoing. Before Christianity he would have hardly considered the matter from any moral position. Progress in changing people's customs takes centuries.

2) Student Handout 8–B, "Two Accounts of the Treatment of the Jews" (found at the end of this chapter), is also from Gregory's *History of the Franks.* These readings are instructive as to the persecution and even forced conversion of Jews during this period. After the students have read the passages, these questions could be used for discussion:
  - Would Jesus have approved of the forced conversions?
  - In a sense, how could Priscus be considered the best person of all in the first story?
  - In the second story, we see a Jewish moneylender being killed, and his Christian murderer being treated leniently. Why were the Jews involved in moneylending as a business? Why would they be so unpopular for doing a job that was obviously much in demand by Christians? How could the murderer get away with such a deed?
  - How do these stories match many of the stereotypes people have about Jews even today?

The Frankish king forced conversions so that everyone would conform to his religion. Of course Jesus would not approve of forced conversions, but then, during these times most people would have accepted the use of force; they lived lives dominated by royalty. Priscus held firm to his Jewish faith; this took courage and faith. Jews ended up being moneylenders because Christians needed loans but were forbidden to loan and charge interest. Since there was no profit in loaning money at no interest, Christians were not in the moneylending business, and they despised the Jews who took on this service. Jews were excluded from many jobs by prejudicial laws throughout most of Europe; in many countries, they could not own land. Thus, to live, they had to enter into mercantile business.

3) Students could do some additional research into the following topics: Clovis, Theodoric, the small kingdoms that came to be France, what people wore at this time, the armaments of a king of the period, church constructions during this time.

4) Denis the Short put together the decisions of councils. These were the start of canon law. Canon law is the set of rules or legal system with which the Catholic Church guides its members. The word *canon* comes from the Greek *kanon* meaning "norm" or "rule." Canon law became more and more necessary as the Church grew larger. Without a common practice and understanding the identity of the Church would likely suffer. In addition, norms were needed, especially since, for many centuries, the training of clergy was very unregulated and often quite short.

8

Student Handout 8-C, "The New Code of Canon Law: Selected Canons" (found at the end of this chapter), lists some passages from the new code. After the students have read the handout, discuss the positive nature of these norms. They certainly are supportive of persons' rights to religious education. Also, the canon about Sunday Mass can be seen as a positive support. On the other hand, a multiplicity of laws has, as British historian Arnold Toynbee pointed out, accompanied the decline of civilizations or groups. Ask your students the following:

- What does it indicate when a group makes many rules?
- As more laws are made within a society or group, what is lost?

Activities for Concept B

Saint Benedict founded the abbey of Monte Cassino and gave his monks a rule that would be the cornerstone of Western monasticism. (Pages 128–131 of the student text.)

Review Questions and Exercises from the Student Text

Question 5: Why was Benedict's Rule so essential to monastic life?

Answer: The monks who came to Benedict wanted some guidance about how to grow in holiness. If any group is to live together peacefully and constructively, it must have some sort of rule of life. Drawing on the wisdom of Antony and Basil, Benedict's Rule is a marvel of common sense and spiritual wisdom.

Personal Reflection Exercise

> There has been much discussion in this chapter about the role of monks in the Church. Monks and nuns who lead a contemplative life spend most of their lives silently praying and meditating on God's presence. This very focused type of existence may, at first or even second glance, seem terribly boring or maybe even meaningless. Nevertheless many women and men today are entering monasteries all over the world.
>
> Reflect on your own life during the last couple of weeks. Try to list some times when you just wanted time to think—time to be silent with yourself. Did you find the silence you wanted? Were you tempted to turn on the radio, TV, or stereo to drive away the silence? If so, why did you want to distract yourself? What did you think you would find in the stillness? Would you and/or people around you be better off if they had some time or took some time to meditate, pray silently, or think quietly?

Other Questions and Activities for Discussion

1) Invite a member of a Benedictine congregation into your class to speak about the Benedictines today.

2) Divide the class into groups of five or six members. Here is a case that your students should analyze and then to which they can write solutions:

Imagine that you and your group are Benedict and a handpicked group of monks who are going to advise him about a rule for a new band of monks who have asked to join him. Some of the men can read but many cannot. The men range in age from fifteen to thirty-nine. Monte Cassino is getting crowded by newcomers. Rations are short because little work is done with any consistency. There is a housing shortage too; the caves are filled, and there is not much timber around for huts. In short, there is much sincerity but no order. Benedict has called you together to (*a*) write a statement of purpose for all these would-be monks and (*b*) write a list of guidelines for the monks' prayer, work, study, and daily needs.

For help in creating their rules, remind your students that they can look at the rules they composed during chapter 7 (see concept A, activity 3 in this manual) and the selected rules included in the student text.

When the students' rules are completed, each group should first read its mission statement to the class. Discuss similarities and differences in the mission statements and arrive at a consensus statement. Then, examine each group's rule; point out similarities and differences, and finally compose one list of guidelines.

If you wish to explore the rule of Benedict further, you might assign some class members to compare the "class rule" to that of Benedict and then to report back to the class on their findings.

3) One aspect of Benedictine life that was certainly integrated well was *ora et labora,* or "prayer and work." Benedict saw no contradiction between the two: work, if done with dignity in the presence of God, was a kind of prayer. Unfortunately, work is too often seen as an interference with prayer. These queries could help your students examine their attitudes toward work:

- Does the word *work* have more positive or negative overtones when people use it?
- What could be the cause of a negative attitude about work as such?
- In what ways could work be a prayer?
- What are you doing, in the long term, when you work?

Close with a comment like the following:

When we build the earth, provide service for others, our work can be a kind of prayer if we recognize that the talents we use are from God and if our intent is to serve God's people. Our work can also be enriched if we remind ourselves of God's presence no matter where we are.

4) The abbey of Monte Cassino was almost completely destroyed during World War II. Ask some students to report on why the Allies bombed the monastery and on what the reactions of people were.

Activities for Concept C
The Emperor Justinian ruled the Eastern empire vigorously, giving it the magnificent Hagia Sophia and the Justinian Code. However, after his rule, the Eastern empire began a slow decline. (Pages 132–134 of the student text.)

Review Questions and Exercises from the Student Text

Question 6: The Justinian Code illustrates another way in which the Church influenced the lives of people in this period. Explain.

Answer: Reflecting Christian principles, the Justinian Code protected women and children from the complete tyranny of husbands and fathers. Marriage was protected from easy divorce.

Question 7: What other contributions did Justinian make to the Church? In what ways did he cause problems for the Church?

Answer: Justinian built many churches, most notably the Hagia Sophia. He made laws to improve public morality and for the protection of orphans. However, he frequently interfered with church matters, once even keeping the pope under arrest. And he persecuted Jews and other non-Christians.

Other Questions and Activities for Discussion

1) Justinian; his wife, Theodora; and his famous general, Belisarius, are all interesting characters. Students could do additional research about them and then give reports in class.

2) If possible, gather together pictures of Jesus, Mary, and the saints that were created during the years 400–700. Some of the best examples are mosaics done in churches built during this time. Then discuss the ways in which Jesus, Mary, and the saints are portrayed. Are they friendly, warm, or what?

3) The penalties listed in the Justinian Code and mentioned in the student text seem brutal to us today. Or, do they? This may be a good time to discuss capital punishment and other punishments for crimes. Here is a case that students should first respond to individually. When everyone has finished his or her individual response, groups can be formed. Give each group one of the penalties to defend—even if members disagree with the penalty they are to defend. The exercise should be looked upon as role-playing. Each group is to formulate a rationale for its position. After the rationales are completed, students should debate the proper penalty. (Note: There are historical precedents for each of the penalties listed.)

> Bob is sixteen. His parents are middle-class folks who get by (but they don't vacation in the Rockies each summer). Bob has been caught committing petty theft before but was released by the store owners. Now he has been arrested for shoplifting at a large department store. Bob managed to grab an expensive watch out of a display case while the clerk was busy with another customer. However, a store detective caught Bob. He is standing before the judge who must sentence him. Which of the following penalties should the judge give?
> a) amputation of one of his hands
> b) a term of one year in the juvenile correction center
> c) life imprisonment
> d) two to five years in an adult prison
> e) probation for two years

After the debate and discussion, reflect with your students on which penalty, if any, is most Christian. This case certainly raises the question about the relationship between a society's need for laws and punishment and a Christian community's expression of love and forgiveness.

4) Justinian's prohibition of selling one's children into slavery was certainly a step forward for children's rights. And permitting women and children to hold property in their own names must have seemed daring in those days. Some of your students might do a short research project on the status of women's rights in your state. For example, are women protected by law from acts of discrimination if they want to buy a house or rent an apartment, take out a loan or open a business?

Activities for Concept D

Pope Gregory the Great strengthened the Church by his preaching and example, his emphasis on education for the clergy, his diplomatic missions, his missionary zeal, and his reforms of the liturgy. During this period, the everyday lives of average Christians were very difficult. They relied heavily on the strength and comfort provided by the Church. (Pages 134–139 of the student text.)

Review Questions and Exercises from the Student Text

Question 8: How did Gregory demonstrate the changes that had taken place in the roles that a pope was supposed to fill?

Answer: Gregory was a diplomat, pastor, spiritual leader, businessman, landowner, and government official who acted with enormous influence throughout the western part of Europe and with considerable power even in the East. Gone were the days when the bishop of Rome was a local pastor of souls. [*Teacher's note:* Now the pope was Pontifex Maximus indeed.]

Question 9: What was life like for the average Christian during these centuries from 400 to 700? How did the Church help make life meaningful?

Answer: Christians went to Mass, prayed for good health and abundant harvests, and celebrated the sacraments much like we do today. However, their lives were hard. Life expectancy was short; diseases could wipe out entire towns because of unsanitary conditions. Thus, people of these times relied on God with a kind of directness and lack of embarrassment. They knew that God—not humans—controlled all things. The Church provided comfort, protection, and guidance, and kept before them the promise of heavenly blessings.

Question 10: Describe some of the difficulties in the selection and training of priests.

Answer: Education of the clergy was very hit-and-miss. Priests were still chosen by local congregations, by a local bishop, or often by a local lord. The criteria for the selection of priests therefore varied tremendously. Communications were slow; as a result, each priest was often left to his own devices without the support of the larger Church. [*Teacher's note:* With so many people converting to Christianity, priests were in short supply. There was no system of seminaries or colleges. All this, along with the above-mentioned factors, contributed to the general low quality of diocesan clergy.]

Other Questions and Activities for Discussion

1) Gregory was a great diplomat. Recent popes have acted in diplomatic capacities too. Have the students find examples of some actions of recent popes that were attempts at peacemaking or bringing about justice.

2) Find a recording of the Benedictine monks of Solesmes singing Gregorian chant. Students might enjoy hearing some of the chant. Then discuss what mood it suggests to them.

3) Invite the diocesan vocation director to discuss with your students the present program for training diocesan clergy. Ask him to describe changes that have taken place in the training of priests. In addition, have him include in his speech a list of the qualifications a person should have who is seeking admission into the seminary. In Gregory's time women were excluded from the priesthood; your guest speaker might want to address this topic too.

8

4) The veneration of saints became more and more common in the religious life of people in the Church. There was no complicated process for the selection of saints. Most of the time saints were selected by popular acclamation and traditions grew up about the saints. Sainthood honors women and men who have led exemplary Christian lives. People did not and do not worship saints. From the fifth century to the beginning of the twentieth century, people frequently prayed to the saints to intercede with God for them. The average person probably felt that saints were more accessible to humble people than God was. Similarly, poor people could seldom address their lords directly, but usually had to use intermediaries. Thus, this same attitude about talking to God through the saints prevailed.

To pursue this issue of veneration of saints further, ask your students to do some of the following:

a) Write short reports describing the saints whose names they were given at Confirmation and/or whose names they were given for their first names. Some students might do research about the saints whose names were given to their parishes. And other students could find out whose relics are used in their parishes' altar stones and why relics were placed there in the first place.

b) Interview parents, grandparents, or other older adults to find out what stories they were told about saints when they were kids, who were the most popular saints, why saints are less often referred to now, and so on.

c) Make a matching test or survey to give to other students to find out about their knowledge of saints. For example, the students could use the research on their names to form items like these:

_____ 1. Saint Joseph

    a. founded an order of brothers who run schools, colleges, and other educational projects

_____ 2. Saint John Baptist de La Salle

    b. the husband of Mary

When the results of the matching survey have been compiled, your class should have a sense of whether or not their peers know much about saints. The class could then compile brief biographies for posting in the school halls or library so that other students, if interested, could find out about the saints after whom they are named.

Activities for Concept E

Islam was spread throughout the Middle East, North Africa, and Spain. By the time Charles Martel stopped Islamic advances at the Battle of Tours, most of the Eastern empire and some of the West had been converted to the new religion. (Pages 139–142 of the student text.)

Review Questions and Exercises from the Student Text

Question 11: How did the Muslims change the course of church history? How did Muslim control of the Mediterranean Sea exaggerate the differences between the Western Church and the Eastern Church?

Answer: Most of North Africa, the Middle East, Spain, and other parts of Europe submitted to Islam. The Church found itself on the defensive from this aggressive religion. With Muslim control of the Mediterranean, the churches in the East and West found it much harder to communicate with each other.

Question 12: Why was it so easy for the Muslims to conquer so much territory? Why was Spain particularly vulnerable?

Answer: The Muslims were united in one faith and one vision, and their leadership was united too. On the other hand, the Middle East, Europe, and especially Spain were divided into small kingdoms often warring with each other. In fact, a faction of Spanish Goths had sought the help of the Muslims, enabling the Muslims to gain control of a part of Spain; from this foothold, Islam conquered all of Spain.

Question 13: Describe the system of land ownership later called feudalism. What were the advantages and disadvantages of this system?

Answer: The system of land ownership later called feudalism was based on lords and vassals. A poor man would go to one of the rich landowning lords and ask to become his vassal. If accepted, the vassal would work the lord's land and, when necessary, fight in the lord's small army. In this system, everyone had his or her place. The peasant had some land to work and was protected by the local lord. The lord provided the vassal and his family with food, clothing, and a small house. Since most kingdoms were small, Europe was hard put to fight a unified group like the Muslims.

Question 14: How did the Church model itself as Servant? Sacrament? Herald? Institution? People of God? Which model of the Church seemed to suffer most because of the enormous growth of the Church?

Answer: As Servant, the Church educated people in monasteries and church schools and helped poor people. As Sacrament, the Church mediated between God and the individual. Yet as People of God, the sense of community, the Body of Christ, which was so strong in the early Church, now became less obvious as the Church grew larger and as Christian lords proceeded to fight each other for land and power. Also, the difference between the Western Church and the Eastern Church seemed to be growing as communications became more difficult. As Herald, the Church worked through monks like Augustine and his followers. Huge groups converted in the West when their leaders decided to become Christian. The role of the Church as Institution expanded: the Church mediated between the warring factions of Europe; the pope's roles increased, as did the Church's land and property. The model of Church as People of God seems to have suffered the most because of the enormous growth of the Church in this period.

8

Other Questions and Activities for Discussion

1) *Islam* (National Film Board of Canada, 19 min., black and white), while somewhat dated, is a very useful film with which to introduce students to Islam—who Muhammad was, what the main beliefs of Muslims are, where the holy places of Islam are, what motivates fervent Islamic belief. This presentation of the history and belief of Islam is very clear and balanced. Even though the film is in black and white, the photography is so well done that students should find it appealing. *Islam* is available through ROA Films.

2) On a large wall map, have the students identify the countries of the world that are now Islamic, and have them locate Tours, France, the site of Charles Martel's victory over the Muslims.

3) Distribute to your class Student Handout 8-D, "Passages from the Koran" (found at the end of this chapter). Have the students read these passages; then discuss them.
- Which of the passages sound very Christian?
- What attitude does Muhammad have toward infidels, nonbelievers?
- In what way does the Koran demonstrate an attitude about violence that is different from the Christian Scriptures' attitude?
- After reading these passages, do you somewhat understand the attitude toward the West held by Iran, Syria, Saudi Arabia, and other Muslim countries?

Summary Activities for the Chapter

1) Have the students spend some time writing in their journals about how they have been Servant, Herald, Sacrament, and People of God this week.

2) If you have not already used these questions for daily quizzes, distribute to the class Student Handout 8–E, "Quiz on Chapter 8" (found at the end of this chapter). The answers to the quiz are as follows:

1) b	8) a	15) c	22) c
2) a	9) a	16) a	23) c
3) d	10) d	17) d	24) c
4) a	11) d	18) b	25) d
5) d	12) b	19) d	
6) d	13) a	20) d	
7) c	14) c	21) b	

3) Student Handout 8–F, "Prayer Service: Psalm 97 in the Tradition of the Monks" (found at the end of this chapter), is offered as a closing activity for this chapter. To accompany the readings, you might want to sing the hymn "Holy God, We Praise Thy Name." The words to this hymn are attributed to Saint Nicetas who lived during the early 400s. "Where Charity and Love Prevail" is a beautiful song that is adapted from a Gregorian chant; it can be found in many hymnals, like *The People's Mass Book*. Another contemporary song that fits nicely with this service is "Turn to Me" by John Foley, in *Glory and Praise,* vol. 1 (Phoenix: North American Liturgy Resources, 1977).

8

Sygismund and the Conversion of Clovis

Passages from *History of the Franks* by Bishop Gregory of Tours

The Conversion of Clovis

The queen did not cease to urge [Clovis] to recognize the true God and cease worshiping idols. But he could not be influenced in any way to this belief, until at last a war arose with the Alamanni, in which he was driven by necessity to confess what before he had of his free will denied. It came about that as the two armies were fighting fiercely, there was much slaughter, and Clovis's army began to be in danger of destruction. He saw it and raised his eyes to heaven, and with remorse in his heart he burst into tears and cried: "Jesus . . . who art said to give aid to those in distress, and to bestow victory on those who hope in thee, I beseech the glory of thy aid, with the vow that if thou wilt grant me victory over these enemies, . . . I will believe in thee and be baptized in thy name. . . ." And when he said this, the Alamanni turned their backs, and began to disperse in flight. And when they saw that their king was killed, they submitted to the dominion of Clovis. . . . And he stopped the fighting, and after encouraging his men, retired in peace and told the queen how he had had merit to win the victory by calling on the name of Christ. . . .

    . . . And the king was the first to ask to be baptized by the bishop. . . . And of his army more than 3000 were baptized.

King Sygismund Kills His Son

Now on Gundobad's death his son Sygismund held his kingdom, and he built with great skill the monastery of St. Maurice. . . . And losing his first wife, the daughter of Theodoric, king of Italy, he married another, and she began to malign his son bitterly and make charges against him as is the custom of stepmothers. From this it came about that on a day of ceremonial when the boy recognized his mother's dress on her, he was filled with anger, and said to her: "You are not worthy to have on your back those garments which are known to have belonged to . . . my mother." And she was set on fire with rage and she stirred her husband up with crafty words, saying: "The wicked boy wishes to possess your kingdom, and he plans when you are killed to extend it as far as Italy, forsooth, that he may possess the kingdom which his grandfather Theodoric held in Italy. For he knows that while you live he cannot accomplish this; and unless you fall he will not rise." Sygismund was aroused by these words, and taking the advice of his wicked wife he became a wicked parricide. For when his son had been made drowsy by wine he bade him sleep in the afternoon; and while he slept a napkin was placed under his neck and tied under his chin, and he was strangled by two servants who drew in opposite directions. When it was done the father repented too late, and falling on the lifeless corpse began to weep most bitterly. . . . Nevertheless he went off to the holy Saint Maurice and spending many days in weeping and fasting he prayed for pardon. After establishing there a perpetual service of song he returned to Lyons, the divine vengeance attending on his footsteps.

Two Accounts of the Treatment of the Jews

Passages from *History of the Franks* by Bishop Gregory of Tours

Priscus and Phatir: Converted Jews

King Chilperic ordered many Jews to be baptized that year and received a number of them from the sacred font. Some of them however were purified in body only, not in heart, and lying to God they returned to their former perfidy so that they could be seen to observe the Sabbath as well as honor the Lord's day. But Priscus could not be influenced in any way to recognize the truth. The king was angry at him and ordered him to be put into prison, in the idea that if [Priscus] did not wish to believe of his own accord [the King] would force him to hear and believe. But Priscus offered gifts and asked for time until his son should marry a Hebrew girl at Marseilles; he promised deceitfully that he would then do what the king required. Meantime a quarrel arose between him and Phatir, one of the Jewish converts who was now a godson to the king. And when on the Sabbath Priscus . . . was retiring to a secret place to fulfill the law of Moses, suddenly Phatir came upon him and slew him with the sword together with the companions who accompanied him. When they were slain Phatir fled with his men to the church of St. Julian. . . . While they were there they heard that the king had granted to the master his life but ordered the men to be dragged like malefactors from the church and put to death. Then, their master [Phatir] being already gone, one of them drew his sword and killed his comrades and then left the church armed with his sword, but the people rushed upon him and he was cruelly killed. Phatir obtained permission and returned to Gunthram's kingdom whence he had come. But soon after he was killed by Priscus's kinsmen.

Armentarius: A Jewish Moneylender

. . . Armentarius, a Jew, with one attendant of his own sect and two Christians, came to Tours to demand payment of the bonds which Injuriosus, ex-vicar, and Eunomius, ex-count, had given him. . . . And calling on the men, he received a promise to pay the sum with interest, and they said to him besides: "If you will come to our house we will pay what we owe and honor you with presents also, as is right." . . . when the feast was over and night come, . . . the Jews and the two Christians also were killed by Injuriosus's men, and thrown into a well which was near his house. Their kinsmen heard what had been done and came to Tours and information was given by certain men and they found the well and took the bodies out, while Injuriosus vigorously denied that he had been involved. . . . After this it came to trial, but as [Injuriosus] denied it with vigor . . . and they had no means of proving him guilty, it was decided that he should take oath that he was innocent. . . . [And Injuriosus] returned home.

The New Code of Canon Law: Selected Canons

Canon 97—(1) A person who has completed the eighteenth year of age is an adult, below this age, a person is a minor.

Canon 98—(1) An adult person enjoys the full use of his or her rights.

(2) A minor person remains subject to the authority of parents or guardians in the exercise of his or her rights, with the exception of those areas in which minors by divine law or canon law are exempt from their power. . . .

Canon 225—(2) Each lay person in accord with his or her condition is bound by a special duty to imbue and perfect the order of temporal affairs with the spirit of the gospel; they thus give witness to Christ in a special way in carrying out those affairs and in exercising secular duties.

Canon 795—Since a true education must strive for the integral formation of the human person, a formation which looks toward the person's final end and at the same time toward the common good of societies, children and young people are to be so reared that they can develop harmoniously their physical, moral and intellectual talents, that they acquire a more perfect sense of responsibility and a correct use of freedom, and that they be educated for active participation in social life.

Canon 798—Parents are to entrust their children to those schools in which Catholic education is provided; but if they are unable to do this, they are bound to provide for their suitable Catholic education outside the schools.

Canon 800—(2) The Christian faithful are to foster Catholic schools by supporting their establishment and their maintenance in proportion to their resources.

Canon 1247—On Sundays and other holy days of obligation the faithful are bound to participate in the Mass; they are also to abstain from those labors and business concerns which impede the worship to be rendered to God, the joy which is proper to the Lord's Day, or the proper relaxation of mind and body.

Passages from the Koran

- Set not up another god with God, lest thou sit thee down disgraced, helpless.

- Thy Lord hath ordained that ye worship none but him; and, kindness to your parents, whether one or both of them attain to old age with thee: and say not to them, "Fie!" neither reproach them; but speak to them both with respectful speech. . . .

- And to him who is of kin render his due, and also to the poor and to the wayfarer; yet waste not wastefully,

    For the wasteful are brethren of the Satans, and Satan was ungrateful to his Lord. . . .

- Kill not your children for fear of want: for them and for you will we provide. Verily, the killing them is a great wickedness.

- Have nought to do with adultery; for it is a foul thing and an evil way:

- Neither slay any one whom God hath forbidden you to slay, unless for a just cause: and whosoever shall be slain wrongfully, to his heir have we given powers; but let him not outstep bounds in putting the manslayer to death, for he too, in his turn, will be assisted *and avenged.*

- And give full measure when you measure, and weigh with just balance.

- Verily those who believe not, and who pervert others from the way of God, and then die in unbelief, God will not forgive.

    Be not fainthearted then; and invite not the *infidels* to peace when ye have the upper hand: for God is with you, and will not defraud you *of the recompense* of your works.

- And when ye go forth to war in the land, it shall be no crime in you to cut short your prayers, if ye fear lest the infidels come upon you; Verily, the infidels are your undoubted enemies!

- God doth not forbid you to deal with kindness and fairness toward those who have not made war upon you on account of your religion, or driven you forth from your homes: for God loveth those who act with fairness.

    Only doth God forbid you to make friends of those who, on account of your religion, have warred against you, and have driven you forth from your homes, and have aided those who drove you forth: and whoever maketh friends of them are wrongdoers.

Quiz on Chapter 8

_____ 1) The last Western Roman emperor was deposed by **(a)** Justin **(b)** Odovacar **(c)** Theodora **(d)** Aloysius.

_____ 2) Most of the Goths under Theodoric were **(a)** Arians **(b)** Monophysites **(c)** Manichaeans **(d)** Modernists.

_____ 3) Clovis was king of the **(a)** Visigoths **(b)** Goths **(c)** Lombards **(d)** Franks.

_____ 4) Christianity spread quickly when **(a)** Clovis converted **(b)** Theodoric converted **(c)** Albanus converted **(d)** Gregorius converted.

_____ 5) Denis the Short was responsible for formulating **(a)** the Justinian Code **(b)** a new Mass formula **(c)** the chant **(d)** canon law.

_____ 6) Benedict's first monastery was built at **(a)** Monte Carlo **(b)** Monte Falco **(c)** Monte Athos **(d)** Monte Cassino.

_____ 7) _Ora et labora_ means **(a)** bread and labor **(b)** song and work **(c)** prayer and work **(d)** sweat and toil.

_____ 8) Benedict allowed the monks to drink some wine with meals because **(a)** the monks could not be persuaded otherwise **(b)** wine is good for digestion **(c)** wine would help them sleep **(d)** the water was bad.

_____ 9) The Justinian Code was a great change because **(a)** it had a more Christian orientation **(b)** it allowed for divorce **(c)** it could be taught all over the empire **(d)** it taxed the churches.

_____ 10) The famous church Justinian built was called **(a)** Saint Basil's **(b)** Hagia Maria **(c)** Saint Nicholas's **(d)** Hagia Sophia.

_____ 11) Immediately before becoming pope, Gregory had been a **(a)** governor of a province **(b)** rich merchant **(c)** bishop **(d)** monk.

_____ 12) Gregory was elected pope by **(a)** the cardinals **(b)** the people of Rome **(c)** other Italian bishops **(d)** the emperor.

_____ 13) Gregory's main missionary accomplishment was the mission to **(a)** Britain **(b)** Spain **(c)** Sweden **(d)** Russia.

_____ 14) This form of singing became part of the religious services of the times: **(a)** hymns in harmony **(b)** polyphonic choruses **(c)** Gregorian chant **(d)** Antony's melody.

_____ 15) Gregory reformed **(a)** the circuses **(b)** taxes **(c)** the training of the clergy **(d)** monasteries.

_____ 16) Gregory took this new title for the pope: **(a)** Servant of the Servants of God **(b)** Pontifex Maximus **(c)** Holy Father **(d)** Very Reverend.

_____ 17) Followers of Muhammad are called **(a)** Animists **(b)** Pelagians **(c)** Copts **(d)** Muslims.

_____ 18) The holy book of Islam is the **(a)** Torah **(b)** Koran **(c)** Book of Kells **(d)** Kowloon.

_____ 19) Followers of Islam believe in **(a)** the Trinity **(b)** Jesus as God **(c)** God the Father and the Holy Spirit **(d)** one God.

_____ 20) By A.D. 700, which part of the world was *not* yet conquered by Islam? **(a)** Egypt **(b)** North Africa **(c)** Syria **(d)** Constantinople

_____ 21) Spain was easier to conquer for Islam because **(a)** it was almost uninhabited **(b)** the Goths were fighting among themselves **(c)** a pestilence was raging **(d)** the army was too busy fighting the Franks.

_____ 22) Shipping in the Mediterranean was dominated by **(a)** Romans **(b)** Franks **(c)** Muslims **(d)** Phoenicians.

_____ 23) The Gauls were led into battle against the Muslims by **(a)** Clovis **(b)** Charles I **(c)** Charles Martel **(d)** Clotwaldo.

_____ 24) The advance of Islam into France was halted at **(a)** Lyons **(b)** Lille **(c)** Tours **(d)** Toulouse.

_____ 25) The Church lost some of its sense of being the People of God because of its **(a)** loss of revenue **(b)** losses to Islam **(c)** lack of leadership **(d)** size.

Prayer Service:
Psalm 97 in the Tradition of the Monks

Opening Hymn

Psalm 97

Leader: A blessing Lord, pray bestow on us.
Yahweh reigns.

All: Let the earth rejoice.

Left: Yahweh, you reign; let the earth rejoice; let the many coastlands be glad.

Right: Clouds and thick darkness are round about you, righteousness and justice are the foundation of your throne.

Left: Fire goes before you,

Right: Your lightnings lighten the world; the earth sees and trembles.

Left: The mountains melt like wax before you, before the God of all the earth.

Right: The heavens proclaim your righteousness; and all the peoples behold your glory.

Left: All worshippers of images are put to shame, who make their boast in worthless idols; all gods bow down before you.

Right: Zion hears and is glad, and the daughters of Judah rejoice, because of your judgments, O God.

Left: Because you, Lord, are the most high over all the earth, you are exalted far above all gods.

Right: You, Yahweh, love those who hate evil; preserve the lives of the saints and deliver them from the hand of the wicked.

Left: Light dawns for the righteous, and joy for the upright in heart.

Right: Rejoice in Yahweh, O you righteous and give thanks to God's holy name!

All: Yahweh reigns; let the earth rejoice.

Closing Hymn

CHAPTER 9

New Challenges, New Solutions: 700–1000

Major Concepts

A. While some Irish and English monks like Bede were copying and authoring important books, others like Boniface were spreading the Good News throughout northern Europe. As a result of Boniface's work, Pepin the Short gave the Church a section of Italy that formed the basis of the Papal States.

B. Divisions grew between the Eastern and Western Church over the issue of "images," and when the pope crowned Charlemagne emperor of the Roman Empire, the conflict deepened. Charlemagne united more of Europe, encouraged learning, and protected the Church, but he also interfered with church management.

C. Under Charlemagne's weak successors, the Roman Empire splintered again. Consequently, feudalism became established as the only governmental system that granted some stability and protection.

D. Storming down from the north, the Vikings conquered huge areas of eastern and western Europe. As they settled in the West they accepted the Christianity already entrenched there. In the East, Cyril, Methodius, and their successors spread the Good News to the Slavs, Magyars, and other groups; codified the Slavic language; and helped formalize the unique liturgical rites of the Eastern Church.

E. Civil rulers and church officials in both the East and the West progressively interfered more in each others' affairs. The Cluniac reform reminded the Church of its spiritual mission.

Activities for Concept A

While some Irish and English monks like Bede were copying and authoring important books, others like Boniface were spreading the Good News throughout northern Europe. As a result of Boniface's work, Pepin the Short gave the Church a section of Italy that formed the basis of the Papal States. (Pages 146–149 of the student text.)

Review Questions and Exercises from the Student Text

Question 1: Why was the work of Bede so significant, especially in light of what was happening all over Europe?

Answer: While wars raged all over Europe, the preservation and development of learning went on in monasteries. Without the efforts of the monks and nuns, one can only wonder if the ancient works that we cherish today would have survived at all. Specifically, Bede's works give us a good understanding of his times and of the early history of the Church, people, and culture of England.

Question 2: Veneration of saints is still common today but less so than in this period from 700 to 1000. Why do you think that people today are skeptical about miracles happening?

Answer: People then were more helpless in the face of nature and other people. For example, they understood little about the nature of diseases. While our understanding today is still limited, we can cure many illnesses that killed people in those times. As we have gained more power over nature, our sense of mystery and miracle has changed, weakened, and for some people disappeared altogether. We tend to look for scientific answers first and seldom seek the hand of God working in human affairs.

Question 3: What were the major contributions of Saint Boniface? Try to imagine what it would have been like for him to cross from Amsterdam to Munich in those times. How many miles would he have traveled? Describe what the roads would have been like. Where would he have slept at night? What dangers would he face? If necessary, do some research about this period.

Answer: Saint Boniface converted many Germanic groups, established monasteries and dioceses all over Germany, and organized the Church among the Franks. In a straight line, Amsterdam is 450 miles from Munich. Clearly, travelers could not go in a straight line, so the trip must have been far longer. During Boniface's travels, he would have had to cross mountains, ford rivers, sleep in the open, fend off bandits, walk, and walk some more. Most of the roads would have been little more than rough footpaths.

Question 4: Why was Pepin such an important figure in the church history of this period? of later centuries?

Answer: Pepin protected Rome from the Lombards. Pepin's gift of the land in Italy that became the Papal States made the popes temporal rulers of a country. The Papal States were the cause of strife for the Church over the centuries. [*Teacher's note:* Boniface set a precedent by crowning Pepin as king of the Franks. From now on, would-be rulers would try to gain the approval of the Church and would often seek to be crowned by the pope or a bishop—signifying that God and the Church approved of his kingship. As rulers of a country (i.e., the Papal States), popes began imposing taxes, policing the territories, and raising armies to defend their country. The Papal States were run by the Church until the 1800s when Pope Pius IX was forced by the Italian republicans to give them up.]

9

Personal Reflection Exercise

People in the early Middle Ages had a real sense of their dependence on God. They knew that some Divine Being ruled the universe. God punished but also performed miracles. How would you describe people's reactions to the idea of miracles happening today? How do you react to the idea of miracles? Do you ever pray for something miraculous to happen? What would it say about someone's attitude toward God if he or she did not believe that miracles were possible? Do you think that there are miracles happening now right in front of you that you just are not seeing?

Other Questions and Activities for Discussion

1) Here is a map exercise that should help your students further understand the complexities of running the Church from 700 to 1000. Split your class into seven teams, and name the teams according to the city in which they reside: Paris, Aachen (Germany), Warsaw, Madrid, Istanbul, Prague, and London. Then read the students this case that they are to solve:

Bishop X has to send an urgent message to Pope Y in Rome: "Your Holiness! As we long expected, King Z is insisting that he appoint the other bishops. He also wants to reduce his support of the parish priests because the local lords are tired of supporting them; they claim that the priests should be working in the

fields when not saying Mass. In addition, the king is raising the tithes from the monasteries, and as you know, the monasteries are already paying more than in other domains of Holy Mother Church. What has complicated the problem is that the crops this year have been damaged by some scourge, and a sudden freeze at planting did not help. Of course the king blames the Church because we did not bless the fields properly, so he says. What are we to do?''
- How long would it take Bishop X's messenger to walk to Rome and back? to ride a horse there and back? How many boundaries of national frontiers would he have to cross? List as many obstacles as possible that might hold him up.
- Considering the position of the Church at this time, what do you think the pope would tell this bishop?

When the students have finished their research and discussion, each group should present a written report to you and an oral report to the class.

2) Invite an art teacher or a calligrapher to demonstrate calligraphy to your class. If possible, have the students try writing in calligraphy a very short passage from the Christian Scriptures. Note the approximate time that it takes them to write one line. Then, approximate how long it would take to write one of the Gospels in this manner.

3) Have some students bring in a map of the Papal States and report to the class on the following questions:
- How many square miles did the Papal States cover?
- What state in the United States would be a comparable size?
- Were there many large towns located there?
- What kind of land did this area include?

Activities for Concept B

Divisions grew between the Eastern and Western Church over the issue of "images," and when the pope crowned Charlemagne emperor of the Roman Empire, the conflict deepened. Charlemagne united more of Europe, encouraged learning, and protected the Church, but he also interfered with church management. (Pages 149–151 of the student text.)

Review Questions and Exercises from the Student Text

Question 5: Why did the crowning of Charlemagne as Holy Roman emperor by the pope change the relationship between the Eastern and Western empires and parts of the Church?

Answer: There had not been an emperor in the West in three centuries. During that time, it was accepted that the Eastern ruler was emperor of both the West and the East. Thus, when Charlemagne was crowned by the pope, it signaled a secession from the Eastern empire.

Question 6: What is an iconoclast? How did the dispute over icons illustrate the splits that were growing in the Church?

Answer: An iconoclast is a "breaker of images," that is, a person who opposes the use of representations of religious persons—especially God. Iconoclasm was practiced with the encouragement of the Eastern emperor. Even though iconoclasm was eventually condemned in the East, the Eastern emperor sent a fleet of ships to force the pope in Rome to condemn images. In addition, the rejection by the Council of Frankfort of the decrees by the Council of Nicaea (II), because of the bad translation, showed that West and East were losing the ability to communicate effectively.

Other Questions and Activities for Discussion

1) Student Handout 9–A, "Charlemagne: A Glimpse into His Life" and Student Handout 9–B, "A Plot on Charlemagne's Life Is Uncovered" (found at the end of this chapter), contain passages from two early histories of Charlemagne that give a vital sense of his rule. These can be handled in several ways. You might simply duplicate them, have your students read the passages, and then discuss them. However, I would recommend that you pick some good interpretative readers from your classes. Assign the various parts of these actor-readers. In readers' theater style, the actors can deliver the passages. Students might even bring in props and costumes—perhaps borrowed from a madrigal choir, but these are not necessary.

After the readings are done, here are some questions to raise during discussion:
- Why did Charlemagne have the right to appoint bishops? What does this say about the institutional organization of the Church during this period?
- What does the story about Pepin the Hunchback tell us about the state of the royal court during Charlemagne's time? Does this type of intrigue exist in modern governments?

2) If you have time and a video recorder, rent a videotape of the movie *Pippin*. This play is a fanciful version of Pepin the Hunchback's life, but it does raise interesting questions about how one finds one's identity and meaning in life. Also, it gives a good sense of what court intrigue was all about. Finally, it is a wonderful play full of excellent songs—a nice way to celebrate the middle of a church history course.

3) Instruct your students that when they next go to Sunday Mass in their parish churches, they should bring pad and paper and list every statue or image in the church. They should count the number of stained-glass windows and write down the persons or scenes represented in them. They might also list the saints' statues that are found on the outside of the church.

After the lists are complete, ask the students to interview their parents, brothers, and/or sisters in order to determine what these people think about statues. Particular questions should be formulated in class.

Follow up the interviews with a debate in class about icons, statues, pictures, mosaics, and carvings in church: Do they bring us to God, or do they turn Catholicism into a worship of idols?

4) A visit to an Eastern rite or a Greek Orthodox church might be arranged. In lieu of a visit, slides or pictures of Eastern icons could be shown to your students. Then discuss the similarities and differences between Eastern and Western art—particularly as it represents Jesus, Mary, and the saints. Which do your students prefer? Why?

Activities for Concept C
Under Charlemagne's weak successors, the Roman Empire splintered again. Consequently, feudalism became established as the only governmental system that granted some stability and protection. (Pages 152–156 of the student text.)

Review Questions and Exercises from the Student Text

Question 7: Describe what feudalism was and how it operated. Why did this system of society emerge? What was the role of the Church in feudal society? Are there any societies today that are feudal? For instance, look into countries like El Salvador. How could they be considered feudal?

Answer: Feudalism was a system of local government and defense. The serfs worked the lands of a vassal who had been given the land by a lord who was given

9

his land by the king. The lords raised an army of vassals in time of war. This system emerged because communications were poor, but the Vikings and other marauders were many. Protection had to be local and swift. The Church's bishops and abbots were lords in effect. People were served by priests who were dependent on local lords. In some countries, feudalism still exists today but in a different form. Now it is seen where a small minority of very wealthy families owns a majority of the country's land and controls its economy and government.

Question 8: Why was it so difficult to have common practice of the sacraments during this time span? What developments took place in the celebration of Baptism? Reconciliation? Why did changes take place with these sacraments?

Answer: Poor communications accounted for most of the problems in having a common liturgical practice.

When families would convert, the whole family wanted Baptism. Therefore, it became common for infants to be baptized with their families. Later, infants were baptized without the whole family being involved. Infant mortality was very high, and parents wanted to guarantee salvation for their babies. As the notion of original sin became popular, Baptism was seen as wiping away sin; this was another reason for infant Baptism.

While public penances were still used for the most serious sins, private confessions and penances were common by this time. Private reconciliation allowed priests to give guidance to people on a more regular basis. This practice grew because infant Baptism was common, and so adults needed a means to have their sins forgiven. Penitential books came into use during this time too.

Other Questions and Activities for Discussion

1) Some students might report on different aspects of castles, complete with pictures and drawings. Castles were not the romantic places to live that movies often make them out to be. The reports should include information about floor plans, building materials, kitchens, halls, bedrooms, toilets, chapels, barns, stables, servants' quarters, fortifications, and so on. If the students can find out about heating, furniture, and other amenities, the reports would be enhanced.

2) We might think that feudalism is a long-finished way of life, but today feudalism exists in a different form in some countries, especially in countries where immensely rich families have control of the economies and governments. Students could study the feudal systems of countries like El Salvador and Guatemala.

3) To dramatize the tough life of serfs, this simple exercise might be effective (if not a bit corny). Bring in some field corn (this might be difficult for city dwellers to find) complete with husks and kernels still on the cob—very hard corn is best. Give the students one ear each to husk and shuck (that is, to remove the kernels by twisting the corn in gripped palms). Ask them to imagine themselves shucking a whole field of corn. Actually, in some places, shucking was common even up to this century. Then have the students mill the corn with a wooden instrument (a baseball bat might do, but don't take one of the coach's Louisville sluggers) and a flat stone. Ask the students to imagine doing this every day—otherwise they don't eat. In fact, in many developing countries, corn is still milled by hand like this. Thus, this exercise is a way of talking about feudalism and technology's effects on us.

4) To increase your students' understanding of private confessions and the penitential books, some examples of penalties and commutation are listed below. William Bausch, in *A New Look at the Sacraments* (Notre Dame, IN: Fides/Claretian, 1977), gives the following example about the sin of gluttony from a penitential book: "He

who suffers excessive distention of the stomach and the pain of satiety shall do penance for one day. If he suffers to the point of vomiting, though he is not in a state of infirmity, he shall do penance for seven days" (pp. 173–174).

Later on, penances could be commuted. A rich person could hire someone to take his or her penance—especially if he or she was so sick that it was impossible for the penitent to do the penance. And other penalties were sometimes substituted for the original ones. Soon the practice of commutation had been corrupted, for example:

> One year of fasting can be commuted to 3,000 lashes
> But ten psalms can be recited while inflicting 1,000 lashes
> Therefore 30 psalms can be recited from inflicting 3,000 lashes
> Therefore one year of fasting = 30 psalms
> Therefore five years of fasting = 15,000 lashes = one recitation of the Psalter.
> (Bausch, *Sacraments,* p. 174)

Here is a more exaggerated example of commutation showing how a seven-year penance could be satisfied in three days: "The penitent will pay twelve men to fast three days for him on bread, water, and vegetables. Then he will get 7×120 men to fast three days. The total of $(12 \times 3) + (120 \times 7 \times 3) = 2,556$ days = 7 years" (ibid.).

To discuss penitential acts further, pose some of the following situations to your students. Then, in groups, ask them to decide on a fitting "penance" that would express a person's determination to change, to convert, and that would also be a reconciling act.

a) Theft of someone's wallet out of his locker
b) Writing graffiti in a washroom stall
c) Cheating on a test
d) Coming to school drunk
e) Having premarital sex
f) Starting a fight during which someone was hurt

Activities for Concept D

Storming down from the north, the Vikings conquered huge areas of eastern and western Europe. As they settled in the West they accepted the Christianity already entrenched there. In the East, Cyril, Methodius, and their successors spread the Good News to the Slavs, Magyars, and other groups; codified the Slavic language; and helped formalize the unique liturgical rites of the Eastern Church. (Pages 156–160 of the student text.)

Review Questions and Exercises from the Student Text

Question 9: How did the Vikings aid the spread of Christianity?

Answer: As the Vikings explored, raided, and conquered various Christian regions, they became acquainted with and many accepted Christianity. When they returned home they talked about their new religion. Eventually missionaries journeyed to Scandinavia.

Question 10: Why was it that some central and eastern European countries used Latin, others Slavonic, and others Greek? How did politics, in part, determine the development of the Church in these areas?

Answer: Latin was used in areas converted by missionaries from the Western Church. Slavonic was developed by missionaries who worked among Slavic people. Greek, of course, was the language of the Eastern empire and had an ascendancy over the other two languages because much of the Christian Scriptures were written in Greek. Politics played a part because the country from which the missionaries came often influenced political alignments.

Question 11: What major contribution did Cyril and Methodius make toward the heralding of the Word to the Slavs?

Answer: Cyril and Methodius composed the first Slavic alphabet [*teacher's note:* also known as the Cyrillic alphabet] into which they translated the Christian Scriptures. Instead of forcing people to learn Greek or Latin, they made the Good News accessible in the people's own language.

Other Questions and Activities for Discussion

1) Assign some students to do a little research into the Vikings on such topics as their dress, boats, explorations (including the tales that they even sailed to North America), pre-Christian religion, customs, and the actual territory that they terrorized. After the reports, discuss the similarities and differences between the reality and the stereotypes about Vikings.

2) To understand the Eastern Church better, try to arrange a field trip to an Eastern rite or Greek, Serbian, or Russian Orthodox church. Ask someone from the church to explain the church structure, liturgy, and so on. If you cannot go to a church, invite someone to come to your class to talk about these topics.

3) Show your students the differences between the Cyrillic alphabet and our alphabet. Actually there are many similarities because our alphabet was developed from the Greek. The volume *Byzantium* of the Great Ages of Man series from Time-Life Books (pp. 12–13) has the Cyrillic alphabet.

4) The conversion of the Vikings is another good example of the ways of humans not being the ways of God. Few if any humans would have planned the conversion of these warriors through their gradual assimilation of Christianity. If they had not been such courageous seafarers and warriors, they would not have explored south and then been converted as soon as they were. God's will is done in strange and unexpected ways. You might ask your students to reflect on ways in which they have been moved to do good things that they might not ordinarily have done. They could write on this in their journals.

Activities for Concept E
Civil rulers and church officials in both the East and the West progressively interfered more in each others' affairs. The Cluniac reform reminded the Church of its spiritual mission. (Pages 160–162 of the student text.)

Review Questions and Exercises from the Student Text

Question 12: Why did the Church have to rely so much on various kings and nobles? How did this reliance harm the Church and its ability to be the Sacrament of Christ present in the world?

Answer: All people living in someone's domain were directly under the local ruler. In the feudal system that was so necessary for mutual protection, church officials had to depend on kings and nobles. In turn, nobles wanted to appoint churchmen who would support them. Lands were given by the lord to people; thus monasteries existed due to the benevolence of kings and nobles. This reliance on civil authority often interfered with church activity. For example, when the pope called on German emperor Otto I for help, the pope pledged loyalty to the German emperor, and the Church became more German than universal.

9

Question 13: Why did people welcome the reforms of Cluny?

Answer: Cluny was virtually free from political concerns because it was independent of control by a local lord. The monks and graduates of Cluny were formed to lead holy lives free from the concerns of courts; they had refocused their mission on the welfare of people's souls.

Other Questions and Activities for Discussion

1) Discuss what could happen to the Church if either or both of these two practices occurred: (*a*) offices such as that of bishop or abbot were sold to rich people, or (*b*) parishioners were allowed to elect their own priests and bishops. Simony was condemned, and there were good reasons; what were they?

2) Ask some students to do research on Cluny. Have them bring in pictures of Cluny and tell what has happened to the monastery over the centuries.

3) Monastic reforms like Cluny affected kings and nobles during that period. Religious groups are influencing government now, in very direct ways. Each religious group has a different interpretation of a just, peaceful, and Christian society. So that our students understand that there are religious lobbyists, assign some students to research these groups: NETWORK, Center for Concern, Community for Creative Non-Violence, Moral Majority, and others (new religious lobbyists seem to pop up constantly).

4) Many of our traditional actions such as kneeling, genuflecting—the general pomp and circumstance of the Church—reflect the manners and customs of the medieval royal court. Much of the religious garb worn commonly until Vatican Council II, especially among monastic orders, also originated in this period. Have students research the costume of the period 700–1000, focusing on the origins of episcopal costumes, and bring in pictures with an accompanying oral report. If your school has a madrigal group, they may have actual costumes to display. After the report about garb is done, direct the other class members to interview five people each, asking them these questions:

- Why do you think the Church maintains the custom of priests wearing vestments that originated centuries ago?
- How would you react if priests could wear contemporary clothes for Mass?

Summary Activities for the Chapter

1) In their journals, students should write their reflections about how they were Herald, Sacrament, part of the People of God, and Servant this week. Clearly, you may want to add other items for reflection too.

9

2) If you have not already used the questions for daily quizzes, distribute to the class Student Handout 9-C, "Quiz on Chapter 9" (found at the end of this chapter). The answers to the quiz are as follows:

1) c	8) a	15) d	22) d
2) b	9) b	16) d	23) a
3) b	10) b	17) a	24) a
4) a	11) c	18) a	25) c
5) c	12) a	19) d	26) b
6) d	13) b	20) c	27) d
7) d	14) c	21) c	28) b

3) Student Handout 9-D, "Prayer Service: Life's Daily Miracles" (found at the end of this chapter), contains a service for closing this unit. Two hymns you might wish to use are "O Come, O Come Emmanuel" (plainsong) or "All Glory, Praise, and Honor" (attributed to Saint Theodulph, c. 820), which were written during this time period and are known to students. Since the prayer is about the miracles of everyday life, ask the students to prepare at least two thanksgiving prayers of a sentence or two each. These will be shared during the prayer service. Contemporary hymns you might use are "Glory and Praise to Our God" by Dan Schutte, in *Glory and Praise,* vol. 1 (Phoenix: North American Liturgy Resources, 1977), and "Morning Has Broken" by Cat Stevens.

9

Charlemagne: A Glimpse into His Life

The following tales about Charlemagne are taken from two accounts written near the time of the emperor's life. One account was written by the monk Eginhard, who lived at court. The other story was written by a person who is simply called the Monk of Saint Gall.

Reader 1: [Charlemagne's] body was large and strong; his stature tall but not ungainly, for the measure of his height was seven times the length of his own feet.

Reader 2: The top of his head was round; his eyes were very large and piercing. His nose was rather larger than is usual. . . . Although his neck was rather thick and short and he was somewhat corpulent this was not noticed. . . .

Reader 1: He was temperate in eating and drinking, but especially so in drinking; for he had a fierce hatred of drunkenness in any man, and especially in himself or in his friends. He could not abstain so easily from food, and used often to complain that fasting was injurious to his health. . . .

Reader 3: His daily meal was served in four courses only, exclusive of the roast, which the hunters used to bring in on spits, and which he ate with more pleasure than any other food. During the meal there was either singing or a reader for him to listen to. Histories and the great deeds of men of old were read to him.

Reader 4: He paid the greatest attention to the liberal arts. . . . Charles spent much time and labour in learning rhetoric and dialectic, and especially astronomy, from Alcuin. . . .

Reader 3: He tried also to learn to write, and for this purpose used to carry with him and keep under the pillow of his couch tablets and writing-sheets that he might in his spare moments accustom himself to the formation of letters. But he made little advance in this strange task, which was begun too late in life.

Reader 2: In educating his children he determined to train them, both sons and daughters, in those liberal studies to which he himself paid great attention. Further, he made his sons, as soon as their age permitted it, learn to ride like true Franks, and practise the use of arms and hunting.

Reader 1: He ordered his daughters to learn wool work and devote attention to the spindle and distaff, for the avoidance of idleness and lethargy, and to be trained to the adoption of high principles.

Reader 5: The Romans had grievously outraged Pope Leo, had torn out his eyes and cut off his tongue, and thus forced him to throw himself upon the protection of the King. [Charlemagne], therefore came to Rome to restore the condition of the church, which was terribly disturbed, and spent the whole of the winter there. It was then that he received the title of Emperor and Augustus. . . .

Reader 4: When another prince of the Church died, the emperor appointed a young man in his place. When the bishop designate came out of the palace to take his departure, his servants, with all the decorum that was due to a bishop, brought forward a horse and steps to mount it:

Reader 5: but he took it amiss that they should treat him as though he were decrepit; and leaped from the ground on to the horse's back with such violence that he nearly fell off on the other side.

Reader 2: The king looked on from the steps of the palace and had him summoned and thus addressed him:

Reader 3: "My good sir, you are nimble and quick, agile and headstrong. You know yourself that the calm of our empire is disturbed on all sides by the tempests of many wars. Wherefore I want a priest like you at my court. Remain therefore as an associate in my labours as long as you can mount your horse with such agility."

A Plot on Charlemagne's Life Is Uncovered

Passages Adapted from Two Early Histories of Charlemagne

Characters: Narrator, Charlemagne, Women, Fardulf

Narra: The night of the warning about the plot, Charlemagne was wakeful, listening for the bell that would call him to lauds. In midwinter the darkness lasted until the second hour of the day. His sandglass could not tell him how many hours had passed, when he heard the giggling and bustling of women in the antechamber.

Going to the curtain, he found a bevy of Fastrada's ladies half clad with hair undone, pushing at the outer door.

Charl: (*Demanding*) What are you after?

Narra: They thrust folds of their skirts into their mouths to stifle laughter, crying,

Women: A stripped, scraped, silly, and raving man is trying to push through the door!

Charl: What is he raving?

Women: That he seeks your excellent presence. But he is quaking all over in shirt and hose—

Charl: Let him in and take yourselves out.

Narra: In came a heavy and shorn man, clad as the women said, panting and shivering with cold. He cried, falling to his knees.

Fardu: At each door they tried to keep me from your beneficent presence—first the guards—

Charl: Now that you are here, drink wine, and speak sense.

Narra: His name was Fardulf, a poor deacon of Saint Peter's church in the city.

Fardu: I had merely gone to light the altar candles for the dawn service when in the dark I heard armed men talking low at the very altar, talking of how they would cut down Charlemagne when he came as he did by custom to early prayer. They would make pretense of a drunken brawl, and the blow would appear to be an accident.

Narra: Fardulf heard this because the swordsmen were cautioning each other how to act in the mock brawl.

Fardu: I hid behind the altar; but they discovered me, stripped me of my robe, and made me take an oath that I would lie quiet under the altar. I was shivering and cold and knew that the conspirators would skewer me like a pig the moment your majesty was slain. So I crawled away to warn you.

Charl: Guards, surround the church and man the streets.

Narra: When the conspirators were caught in Ratisbon, the whole of their scheme became known. They planned to slay the boy Louis with the king, while other armed bands attacked his other sons. Then they meant to bring forward Pepin Hunchback, Charlemagne's son of a concubine, as the oldest son and true heir to the throne.

At an assembly of his liege lords in Ratisbon, the conspirators were tried and condemned to death. Charlemagne showed his mercy afterward only to Pepin, his son.

Charl: Pepin, you are to go under guard to the monastery at Prüm for a little while.

Narra: There Pepin spent the rest of his life, alone, laboring in the gardens with his fancies for company.

Some of the accused cleared themselves by the will of God, after undergoing an ordeal. A few Charlemagne spared to go into exile. The rest died by the rope and the sword, or were blinded.

Quiz on Chapter 9

_____ 1) At the Synod of Whitby, the English Church decided on a date for (a) Pentecost (b) the Immaculate Conception's feast (c) Easter (d) Christmas.

_____ 2) The development of the idea of original sin prompted the growth of (a) Confirmation (b) infant Baptism (c) frequent confessions (d) harsh penances.

_____ 3) This English monk wrote valuable histories: (a) Bonaventure (b) Bede (c) Bernadine (d) Bamber.

_____ 4) Like Saint Patrick, Boniface continued the practice of (a) building monasteries from which to evangelize (b) doing miracles (c) driving out snakes (d) arguing with the Druids.

_____ 5) This ruler gave the Church lands that became the Papal States: (a) Pepin the Red (b) Pepin the Bald (c) Pepin the Short (d) Pepin the Fat.

_____ 6) One of Boniface's famous acts was chopping down the tree of (a) Munich (b) Goslar (c) Tübingen (d) Thor.

_____ 7) The king of the Franks saved the pope and Rome from the (a) Saxons (b) Angles (c) Lilliputians (d) Lombards.

_____ 8) Charlemagne means (a) Charles the Great (b) Charles the Tall (c) Charles the Mean (d) Charles the Magician.

_____ 9) When Charlemagne conquered the Saxons, he (a) enslaved all the men (b) forced them to convert to Christianity (c) took their queen for his wife (d) allowed them to live as they wanted.

_____ 10) Iconoclasts were (a) fortune tellers (b) image breakers (c) odd-shaped blood plasma (d) magi.

_____ 11) The Council of Frankfort denied the decisions of the Council of Nicaea (II) in large part because of (a) a group of Spanish cardinals (b) prejudice against Bulgarians in the Eastern church (c) a poor translation (d) heresy in the East.

_____ 12) This act was a sign of the growing split between East and West: (a) Pope Leo's crowning Charlemagne as Roman emperor (b) the Eastern emperor's attack on Rome (c) the stoppage of trade between Alexandria and Rome (d) the use of Greek in the Mass.

_____ 13) The head of Charlemagne's school was (a) Albert (b) Alcuin (c) Adelbert (d) Alvin.

_____ 14) _Vikings_ means (a) marauders (b) land grabbers (c) sea rovers (d) boat makers.

_____ 15) These people paid their rent to the lord in the form of military service: (a) serfs (b) merchants (c) monks (d) vassals.

_____ 16) At the bottom of the feudal class order were the (a) pages (b) counts (c) priests (d) serfs.

_____ 17) Feudalism came into being, in part, because **(a)** kingdoms were not well established **(b)** the Church encouraged it **(c)** certain strong leaders grabbed all the good land **(d)** many feuds lasted for years.

_____ 18) Bishops were often **(a)** rich land owners **(b)** simple men who depended on their congregations **(c)** selected by the pope **(d)** great theologians from seminaries.

_____ 19) These helped priests in the private celebration of the Sacrament of Reconciliation: **(a)** canon laws **(b)** relics **(c)** counseling methods **(d)** penitential books.

_____ 20) The Norsemen almost completely controlled this country: **(a)** Italy **(b)** France **(c)** Ireland **(d)** Austria.

_____ 21) Part of Alfred the Great's treaty with the Vikings demanded that they **(a)** help in an attack on the Franks **(b)** conquer Scotland **(c)** accept Christianity **(d)** share their boat-making techniques.

_____ 22) Croatians, Poles, and Russians are all descendants of the **(a)** Vikings **(b)** Danes **(c)** Magyars **(d)** Slavs.

_____ 23) _Slava_ means **(a)** glory **(b)** victory **(c)** slave **(d)** slayers.

_____ 24) Cyril and Methodius made a major contribution to the people they converted by **(a)** devising a Slavic alphabet **(b)** teaching them Greek **(c)** telling them about new agricultural methods **(d)** making them part of the Western Church.

_____ 25) To keep Poland free of the Germans' rule, King Boleslaw **(a)** allied himself with Russia **(b)** hired Magyars as mercenaries **(c)** became a vassal of the pope **(d)** placed his kingdom under the Eastern emperor.

_____ 26) _Simony_ means **(a)** the sin of being miserly **(b)** selling church offices **(c)** lying to a priest **(d)** refusing to tithe.

_____ 27) Pope John XII asked King Otto I for help against the **(a)** Lombards **(b)** Magyars **(c)** Franks **(d)** Romans.

_____ 28) Cluny was very different from most other monasteries because **(a)** it did not have farmlands **(b)** it was not under the control of a local lord **(c)** it did not answer to the pope **(d)** it was incredibly corrupt.

Prayer Service: Life's Daily Miracles

Opening Hymn

Leader: Let us remember that we are in God's presence. [Pause.]

Reading from Genesis 1:27–31

Reader: God created man in the image of himself, in the image of God he created him, male and female he created them.

God blessed them, saying to them, "Be fruitful, multiply. . . ." And so it was. God saw all he had made, and indeed it was very good. . . .

Reading from Psalm 147:1–12,15–18

All: Praise God, who is good;
    sing praise to our God, who is gracious;
    it is fitting to praise God.

Left: God rebuilds Jerusalem, gathers
    the dispersed of Israel.

Right: God heals the brokenhearted,
    and binds up their wounds.

Left: God tells the number of the stars;
    and calls each by name.

Right: Great is our God and mighty in power;
    to God's Wisdom there is no limit.

Left: Our Creator sustains the lowly and casts
the wicked to the ground.

All: Sing to God with thanksgiving;
sing praise with the harp to our God,

Right: Who covers the heavens with clouds,
who provides rain for the earth;
who makes grass sprout on the mountains
and herbs for the service of the people.

Left: Who gives food to the cattle,
and to the young ravens when they cry.

Right: In the strength of the steed God delights not,
nor is God pleased with the fleetness of humans.

Left: God is pleased with those who reverence,
with those who hope for kindness.

All: Glorify the Creator, O Jerusalem;
praise your God, O Zion.

Right: God sends forth a command to the earth;
swiftly runs the word!
God spreads snow like wool;
and strews frost like ashes.

Left: God scatters hail like crumbs;
before God's cold the waters freeze.
God sends a word and melts them;
God lets the breeze blow and the waters run.

All: Alleluia.

Prayers of Thanksgiving

Leader: Now let each of us share thanksgiving for one of the miracles that we
have experienced.

Closing Hymn

CHAPTER 10

The High Middle Ages: 1000–1300

Major Concepts

A. During the years 1000–1300, Christianity was the unifying religion of Europe. Kingdoms developed and national boundaries became more established. With more peace came an increase in the population, the growth of cities, and the building of the great cathedrals.

B. The Church split between East and West. And even though the Crusades might have unified the Church to fight Islam, the Fourth Crusade particularly made the division seem irrevocable.

C. The first two great orders of mendicant friars—the Dominicans and the Franciscans—were founded, establishing a new model for religious life.

D. The Albigensian heresy and other types of dissent from the Church were suppressed through the institution of the Inquisition.

E. When the great universities were founded, they replaced the monasteries as the centers of scholarship. Thomas Aquinas and other great thinkers found in these universities a fertile setting for sharing their learning.

Activities for Concept A

During the years 1000–1300, Christianity was the unifying religion of Europe. Kingdoms developed and national boundaries became more established. With more peace came an increase in the population, the growth of cities, and the building of the great cathedrals. (Pages 166–172 of the student text.)

Review Questions and Exercises from the Student Text

Question 1: What role did the Church play in the development of towns? Why were towns important in medieval life?

Answer: Towns were often built around monasteries or diocesan seats. The construction of cathedrals demanded many skilled workers. Also, the Church encouraged the formation of the guilds whose members dedicated themselves to certain saints. Towns became mercantile, governmental, and educational centers.

Question 2: How were the cathedrals symbolic of the Church's role in life of the Middle Ages? How is the Romanesque cathedral different from the Gothic cathedral? What purposes did the cathedrals have other than providing a place for worship?

Answer: The cathedrals were the central focus of the towns in which they were built, and the Church was central to the life of Europeans during the Middle Ages. Romanesque cathedrals tended to be more horizontal, heavy, and simple—suggesting peace and solidity. The Gothic cathedrals were taller, lighter, and more decorated—suggesting the mysterious and miraculous nature of God as opposed to the earthbound laboriousness of human life. Cathedrals served as meeting halls, places for pilgrims to rest, classrooms for teaching religion (using the statues and windows), and sources of inspiration.

Question 3: What changes were happening to the governments of Europe after the year 1000? How did these developments influence the Church? Why were the German emperors particularly important to the Church?

Answer: Kingdoms were becoming more centralized and powerful, especially in France and England. Kings could gather larger armies, conquer more territory, and thus gain still more power. Kings wanted more control over the Church and church property. Conflict between the popes and various kings increased as the Church tried to protect itself from civil control. The German emperors considered themselves emperors of the Holy Roman Empire and, therefore, protectors of the popes.

Question 4: What was the role of the papacy during this period?

Answer: The pope was the spiritual leader of the Church, but he was also a civil ruler of the Papal States. He wielded considerable influence with the European rulers.

Other Questions and Activities for Discussion

1) Check at your local library to see if it has a film or slides with a commentary about the building of Gothic cathedrals. The film *Exeter* (National Film Board of Canada, 29 min., color) is about the building of this famous cathedral in England. *Exeter* is available from International Film Bureau Inc., 332 South Michigan Avenue, Chicago, IL 60604; phone 312-427-4545. If your school is located near a college or university, perhaps someone from its art or architecture department would be willing to talk about Gothic cathedrals with your class.

2) Students could prepare reports about other great Gothic cathedrals, such as Cologne, Wells, Rheims, Notre Dame of Paris, Chartres, Salisbury, Winchester, York Minster. The reports should include pictures, the number of years it took to build the cathedral, its dimensions, novel features, famous events that took place there, and so on.

3) To compare medieval cathedrals with our modern churches, discuss these questions with your students:
   - The medieval cathedrals were acts of faith and of inspiration for people of those times and still inspire those who visit them now. Are modern churches in this country built with the same purpose in mind?
   - Has our notion of the purpose of church architecture changed? If so, describe it.

Today our churches tend to be more clearly functional, but many churches are beautiful and reflect the changes in the liturgy. Some churches are multipurpose buildings with movable walls so that the building can be divided up for meetings.

4) As was mentioned in the student text, cathedrals employed sculptures and windows to tell Bible stories; most peasants and even some nobles could not read or write. Another medium of religious education and entertainment was the mystery, or miracle, play. These were originally performed inside the churches, later on the cathedral steps, and finally in courtyards. These medieval plays were precursors to Shakespearean plays and to European drama generally. They were composed for the entertainment and education of the common people; the language and scenes are frequently comic and were familiar to the audiences.

Student Handout 10–A, "Noah's Flood" (found at the end of this chapter), is a cutting from a medieval miracle play. Some of your students might act it out. God has told Noah to build the ark, but poor Noah is having a terrible time convincing his wife to enter the ark because she wants to take her cronies along. The audiences would have appreciated this bit of comedy—biblical education in the medieval mode.

5) One of the most revered medieval saints was Thomas à Becket, the murdered archbishop of Canterbury. Chaucer would later write the *Canterbury Tales,* a book of stories told by pilgrims on their journey to Becket's shrine in the Canterbury cathedral.

10

The case of Becket is very instructive in giving us a sense of the conflicts that existed between Church and kings during this time period. King Henry II, who ruled England from 1154 to 1189, had been a close friend of Thomas à Becket while Henry was still a prince. Becket had been befriended also by the archbishop of Canterbury, who had sent him to study canon law. Becket served as archdeacon of Canterbury from 1154 to 1162. These two friendships would later split Becket's loyalties.

When Henry became king, he tried to tax the Church, to try priests in civil courts, and to appoint priests. Hoping to find an ally in Becket, Henry appointed him chancellor of England, in which post Becket served from 1155 to 1162. Becket was faithful to Henry; he even organized and fought in the war with Toulouse (1159). However, he was also faithful to the Church. Henry grew more and more frustrated with the archbishop of Canterbury, who staunchly refused the taxes Henry wanted to impose and who rejected Henry's right to jurisdiction over clergy who had committed crimes, maintaining that they could only be tried by church courts.

When the archbishop died, Henry manipulated the bishops of England to elect Becket, in the hopes that Becket would be more loyal to him than to the Church. He was totally mistaken. Becket firmly opposed all taxes on the Church and any encroachment by Henry in church prerogatives. Having been such intimate friends, the pain and anger of the conflict was that much greater. Henry, in a drunken rage, cried out, "Will no one rid me of him? A priest! A priest who jeers at me and does me injury. Are there none but cowards like myself around me? Are there no men left in England? Oh, my heart!" Four of his barons took him at his word and killed Becket as he was going to his devotions in Canterbury cathedral. Henry mourned the loss of his friend, did penance at Becket's tomb, and henceforth tried to end his feud with the Church. In 1173, only three years after his death, Becket was canonized.

Student Handout 10–B, "Becket; or, The Honour of God" (found at the end of this chapter), is a cutting from Jean Anouilh's play of the same title. Again, I suggest that you have students act out the scene or do it in readers' theater fashion. The play is a good discussion starter on issues like these:
- Should the Church be tax-free?
- What is the proper relationship between church and state?
- Was Becket's resistance saintly? Is resistance to wrongful actions by a government the work of true saintliness?

A movie version of the play about Becket is quite well done and should be available from video rental stores.

Activities for Concept B
The Church split between East and West. And even though the Crusades might have unified the Church to fight Islam, the Fourth Crusade particularly made the division seem irrevocable. (Pages 172–177 of the student text.)

Review Questions and Exercises from the Student Text

Question 5: In 1054, the Church was split in two. What were some of the causes for this division, and what event brought the final split?

Answer: The Eastern patriarchs believed that the popes had taken authority that was not really warranted by their position. Many other matters—language, customs, liturgical practices—added to the differences. The two parts of the Church rejoined some years later, but when the Crusaders sacked Constantinople in what was supposed to be the Fourth Crusade, the break between East and West was complete.

10

Question 6: Why were the Crusades initiated? How would you evaluate the effectiveness of the Crusades, in terms of their original purpose? What positive effects were there from the Crusades that were not part of the original intent?

Answer: The original intent of the Crusades was to free the Holy Land from the Muslims; in this the Crusaders ultimately failed. The Crusaders learned much from the Muslims, opened trade to India and China, and in short, saw that the world was large.

Question 7: Would present-day Christians rally around the pope and fight a Crusade today? Why or why not?

Answer: Today the Church does not have sufficient persuasive power to rally people to a Crusade, and besides, there are Christians in almost all countries of the world. The popes just do not have the power now that they had during those earlier centuries.

Question 8: What attitudes about war made the Crusades acceptable to people in the Middle Ages?

Answer: [*Teacher's note:* War was a way of life for most people of the Middle Ages. To be strong in battle was a matter of great personal pride. From time immemorial people had taken what they wanted through force of arms; Christian values like love and peace were still new to most people. Besides, fighting infidels was considered a good thing for God, country, and one's family.]

Question 9: In the Middle Ages, was the Christian attitude toward war really all that different from the Muslim attitude? What similarities and differences do you see between their attitudes toward war and our present-day attitudes?

Answer: [*Teacher's note:* Muslims converted by force and so did Christians. Both thought they were doing God's will. Today wars are more motivated by political, nationalistic, and economic matters than by religion, although religion is still a large factor in conflicts, especially with Islam.]

Personal Reflection Exercise

> How did you react to Bertran de Born's declaration about war? If you said something similar in a conversation with friends, and you meant it, how would they react? Then, think about all the comments, scenes within movies and television, words to songs, and so on that encourage or at least approve of violence, especially as a means of solving a problem or winning an argument. Try to list as many of these as you can from the last week or two. Take out a newspaper; look at the first section's stories. How many of these are about war or in defense of military spending? Finally, do you think modern people have a substantially different mentality about war than Bertran de Born? Describe any similarities and/or differences. What would you like your stand to be about war or the uses of violence?

Other Questions and Activities for Discussion

1) To discuss the tragedy of the divisions between the Western and Eastern Church, you could use these questions:
- One of the key issues over which the split occurred was the role of the patriarchs in comparison to the bishop of Rome. If Jesus had been there to mediate the discussion between Patriarch Michael and Cardinal Humbert, what do you think he would have said to both sides? Would he have thought this an issue that should cause such a major split in the Church?

- We have been talking about the Church as the People of God, the Body of Christ. What do disputes within the Church do to the Church? On a very practical level, what are some concrete effects of division among people who call themselves Christian?
- Vatican Council II declared that healing divisions in the Christian community was a top priority. Why?
- Have you seen any signs that tolerance of other people's religions is greater now than in the past?

Students might be grouped together to write imaginary dialogues between Jesus, Michael, and Humbert. Some of the dialogues could be read to the class and then discussed as to which most accurately represents the Christlike way of dealing with the differences of opinion.

Students could be assigned to search the newspapers to find any evidence of cooperation between Christian religions.

2) The word *crusade* has as its root the Latin word for cross—*crux. Crusade* is a derivative of the French word *croisade* or the Spanish word *cruzada.* The Crusaders wore on their tunics and armor a cross and, thus, were "crusaders."

As the cross on their armor signified, the Crusaders were engaged in what they perceived to be a holy war. To examine contemporary feeling about holy wars, pose these queries for dialogue:

- The word *crusade* originally applied only to the Crusades to restore the Holy Land to Christian rule. In what contexts do people use the word *crusade* today?
- Does the word *crusade* still imply holy war? Or, does it imply an effort to win someone to a way of thinking?
- One group that works on college campuses today is called the Campus Crusade for Christ. What is implied by the use of the word *crusade* in this group's name?
- Christians join the Army, Air Force, Navy, and Marines in order to defend the nation. They consider it their duty to fight for their country. Would these same people fight for the Church like the Crusaders did? Why or why not?
- Do you think that Saint Peter or Saint Paul would have joined a Crusade? Would Jesus have approved of a holy war to recapture Jerusalem?

Some students might interview members of the Campus Crusade for Christ to find out why they are named as they are. What does *crusade* imply to them and for their methods of working with students?

3) Have students bring in pictures or descriptions of the armor, weaponry, and battlefield tactics used by the Crusaders and by the Muslims. How were wounds treated? How were armies fed?

4) One of the Crusades' contributions to culture was that they opened up trade with the Far East. Most famous perhaps of the medieval explorers was Marco Polo. He wrote a description of his travels, and others have written novels and biographies and made movies about him. To give the students a sense of the gigantic task he undertook in traveling to China, have some students illustrate on a map of Europe and Asia the route of his journey to and from China. They should estimate the distances. Other students can find a copy of his book or books about him and report on how long his journey took.

Recently a television version of Marco Polo's story appeared. If it is available in video rental stores, you may wish to show the segment during which Marco arrives in the Holy Land, meets the papal legate who is later elected pope, and then journeys to the Holy Sepulcher. This film will give students the flavor of the period—especially of the Crusades.

10

Activities for Concept C
The first two great orders of mendicant friars—the Dominicans and the Franciscans—were founded, establishing a new model for religious life. (Pages 177–179 of the student text.)

Review Questions and Exercises from the Student Text

Question 10: How were the mendicant friars different from earlier religious orders? Why would the mendicant sort of life be attractive at this time in history?

Answer: Earlier religious orders were monastic, that is, their members lived in monasteries. [*Teacher's note:* Their orientation was to the silent life of work and prayer.] The mendicants preached and taught actively among people in towns and in the countryside and depended on the generosity of people for their support, relying on Providence in a radical way. [*Teacher's note:* This sort of life appealed to people because frequently monasteries had become complacent, if not rich.] Also, the friars needed to move about in order to preach and combat heresy.

Question 11: What was the situation of women religious up to this time period? In what ways was Clare quite influential?

Answer: Until the time of Saint Clare, women religious lived in seclusion in convents. [*Teacher's note:* Some of these convents had become rich and powerful too.] Clare's convent maintained the life of silent prayer, but like the "begging" friars, her sisters relied completely on gifts for their sustenance. Clare was a spiritual guide to many influential people—including the pope.

Other Questions and Activities for Discussion

1) Invite a Dominican and/or Franciscan brother, sister, or priest into your class to speak with the students about Dominic or Francis or Clare, and about contemporary Dominican or Franciscan life.

2) *Brother Sun, Sister Moon* is a wonderfully romantic, irrepressibly appealing, beautifully made movie about the lives of Francis and Clare. It illustrates the great gap between rich and poor of their time, the militarism of the Italian city-states, and the connection between respect for creation and love of life. Show the movie if at all possible. It should be available in videocassette. Franco Zefferelli, who made *Romeo and Juliet*, directed the movie.

3) The letters *OFM* behind the name of Franciscans mean Order of Friars (brothers) Minor (little). Francis was never a priest. In fact, Francis was very concerned about those who joined him who wanted to be priests. He was afraid that if his brothers became priests, they would lose the simplicity of lifestyle that he wanted to maintain. Eventually, his concerns seemed prophetic. The Franciscans did become powerful and certainly were not poor beggars like their founder. There were several reform movements within the Franciscans, which called them back to the simple life. Here are some related questions:
- Why would Francis want the brothers to be beggars and to refrain from priesthood?
- Would contemporary Franciscans be more effective preachers and ministers of God's Word if they begged for a living and were not priests?
- Is it necessary for someone to be a priest before he or she can be an effective preacher of God's Word?
- Francis and Clare are still greatly admired saints. Why do people today find them so appealing?

10

- In what ways does the rule of Saint Francis closely resemble many of Jesus' statements in the Christian Scriptures?

Activities for Concept D
The Albigensian heresy and other types of dissent from the Church were suppressed through the institution of the Inquisition. (Pages 179–181 of the student text.)

Review Questions and Exercises from the Student Text

Question 12: Why did civil authorities want to suppress heresy? What was the procedure used to find, try, and prosecute people considered heretics? Why were the Cathars, or Albigensians, heretics? Why were they seen as such a threat? From the medieval point of view, why was the Inquisition acceptable as a sort of necessary evil?

Answer: Religion stabilized kingdoms. Christianity was the official religion of Europe. Heresy disrupted the harmony of a kingdom and was therefore treasonous. People suspected of heresy were usually accused by others. Witnesses gave testimony without the accused's knowing who his or her accusers were. The judges would try to extract a confession from the accused. If a confession was given, the penalty was a fine, a prison sentence, or sometimes even death. If someone was found guilty but did not confess and beg pardon, he or she was often executed by civil authorities.

Heresy was a threat to the salvation of all and to the unity of a kingdom. Medieval people accepted torture and executions at the stake. The Inquisition seemed fair because at least a person was tried before a jury and two witnesses had to make a charge against him or her. In civil cases a noble or king could order an execution at will.

Other Questions and Activities for Discussion

1) Here are some queries to check your students' understanding about the Albigensians:
- Who were the Albigensians, and what did they believe?
- Why were they heretics?
- What methods did the Church use to bring them back to orthodox practice before it used the Inquisition?
- How would the Cathari teachings destroy basic beliefs of Christianity?

2) Bernard Gui was one of the most famous inquisitors. He was born in France in 1261 and became inquisitor at Toulouse in 1306. He died about 1331. Friar Bernard, a Dominican, wrote a treatise about how to conduct an interrogation of suspected heretics. Student Handout 10–C, "An Inquisition by Bernard Gui" (found at the end of this chapter), is an adaptation of a model interrogation that Gui used to instruct future inquisitors. You may wish to have three students act out the scene.

After the scene is completed, discuss the interrogation.
- Gui pictures the heretic as trying to squirm out of admitting his true beliefs. What techniques does the suspected heretic use to avoid answering the inquisitor?
- How do you feel about the inquisitor? Do you think that he is treating the accused fairly?

3) Edgar Allan Poe's story "The Pit and the Pendulum" pictures the terror of a supposed inquisitorial dungeon. Your students might read this story and react to it. Poe, of course, adds his own touches of the macabre, but the story does a good job

10

at projecting the fear that must have passed through the minds of accused heretics. There is also a movie version of this story starring Vincent Price that is quite good.

4) The following questions might be raised with your students regarding the Inquisition:
- Do you think that the Inquisition was effective in getting at the truth?
- If someone retracted his or her unorthodox belief under torture, do you think that he or she could be really sincere?
- Is torture justifiable under any circumstances?
- What do you think Jesus would say about torture?

Activities for Concept E

When the great universities were founded, they replaced the monasteries as the centers of scholarship. Thomas Aquinas and other great thinkers found in these universities a fertile setting for sharing their learning. (Pages 182–186 of the student text.)

Review Questions and Exercises from the Student Text

Question 13: Describe the development of the universities. How were they different from today's universities? How was the development of the universities directly related to the Church?

Answer: Schools that had been attached to cathedrals grew in number and in the range of the subjects offered. Their structure was at first very informal. Students hired a teacher; or a teacher would offer a course, and if students took it, he was in business. Eventually teachers formed themselves into faculties like guilds and were granted licenses to teach. There were no campuses as such. Students and teachers used their apartments as meeting places—usually near a cathedral. Degrees were signs of attainment, but the requirements were very informally set. To attain a degree one had to pass an oral examination. Students lived on their own; there were no dormitories as we know them. The Church aided the universities by encouraging theological studies there by men hoping to be priests. Also, the universities were protected from civil authorities by the pope and bishops.

Question 14: What materials did the medieval scholars depend on to do their research?

Answer: Up to this time the best sources of books were the monasteries, but now books came from the Middle East—brought back by Crusaders and other travelers. The medieval universities listened carefully to those who had learned from Muslim scholars.

Question 15: Saint Thomas Aquinas contributed a whole new method to theology. What did he do differently? How did people react during his lifetime to these changes? How was Thomas Aquinas more than just a scholar?

Answer: Thomas used the logical principles of the Greek philosopher Aristotle to order his theological investigations. He wanted to show that revelation was not contrary to reason. This method came up against stiff opposition, and Thomas, like many other innovative thinkers, argued with those who refused change. In addition, Aquinas was a prayerful religious who took time to write poems and hymns.

Question 16: The Third and Fourth Lateran Councils brought several changes to the Church as Institution. What were these changes? Why were they so important?

Answer: At the Third Lateran Council, the College of Cardinals was created to elect the pope. Many of the offices of the Vatican were also established. The Fourth Lateran Council decreed that priests were conclusively forbidden to marry, could not

10

have a secular occupation, and had to receive training. The election of the pope by cardinals was an attempt to free the elections from the control of kings, emperors, and noble Roman families.

Other Questions and Activities for Discussion

1) To discuss the development of the university, ask your students these queries:
- What advantages did the medieval university have over the type of university system we have now?
- What are some disadvantages?
- If you look at a university or college newspaper today, what sort of headlines will you find?
- Imagine that there was a University of Paris newspaper in medieval times. What sort of headlines would there have been then?

2) Ask some students to find pictures of Oxford or Cambridge. They could prepare reports about each of these universities to answer these and other questions:
- When was the university founded?
- How was the university organized?
- What tuition was charged by the teachers?
- What was the social and economic background of most of the students?

3) Have the students review Thomas Aquinas's argument for the possibility of a just war (see pp. 174–175 of the student text). Notice that Augustine is his point of reference—not the Christian Scriptures. His reasoning is based on justice as the chief virtue, not on love. This just-war theory has been used for centuries to approve of certain wars, but it seems inadequate in the face of atomic destruction. If you want to examine Thomas's thinking about war further, pose these questions:
- What part do the Christian Scriptures play in Thomas's argument for a just war?
- In Thomas's argument, where does the principle of love of neighbor and doing good to your enemies come in?
- If instead of saying, "in order for war to be just," Aquinas had said, "in order for war to be loving," what three conditions would Aquinas have made to create a "loving-war theory"? Is it possible to have a loving war? [Note: You may want to structure a debate on this point.]

Then describe the following case to the students:

Two radical Islamic countries refuse to sell oil to our country because we are Judeo-Christian and have supported the right of Israel to exist. These countries have persuaded their neighboring Islamic countries to go along with them. The price of oil goes up drastically. Our ally Japan is in bad shape due to its dependence on foreign oil. Over a period of months the situation becomes critical to many Western nations. Unless the embargo ends, the Western economies will be in extreme trouble. In addition, one of the two Islamic countries has shot down one of our Air Force planes that was caught spying in its air space. We must decide among several courses of action, one of which is to declare war on the two countries, invade, and take the oil.
- If we decide to declare war, would it be a just war, based on Aquinas's three criteria?

Summary Activities for the Chapter

1) In writing their reflections about how they have been Servant, Sacrament, Body of Christ, and Herald, ask the students to reflect on and write about how they have also been peacemakers this week.

2) If you have not already used these questions for daily quizzes, distribute to the class Student Handout 10-D, "Quiz on Chapter 10" (found at the end of this chapter). The answers to the quiz are as follows:

1) c	9) a	17) d	25) d
2) b	10) d	18) a	26) a
3) d	11) c	19) b	27) b
4) a	12) b	20) d	28) a
5) d	13) d	21) c	29) b
6) c	14) b	22) b	
7) d	15) b	23) b	
8) b	16) c	24) b	

3) Student Handout 10-E, "Prayer Service: For Peace and a Simple Lifestyle" (found at the end of this chapter), is provided for closing this unit. Appropriate hymns to use with it include "Peace Prayer" (based on Saint Francis's prayer) and "Come to the Water" both by John Foley, *Glory and Praise* (Phoenix: North American Liturgy Resources, 1977, 1980), in vols. 1 and 3 respectively. As additional choices, two songs that represent the period and were written by Thomas Aquinas are "Sing My Tongue, The Savior's Glory" and, for those who remember the days of chant, "Pange Lingua."

10

Noah's Flood

The following segment is from a medieval miracle play that portrays Noah and his family as they prepare to board the finished ark. The play would have been acted out in a cathedral, on its front steps, or in an open space near the cathedral.

Characters: Noah; Noah's Wife; Noah's sons—Shem, Ham, Japhet; Gossips; God

All stop work. The ark is finished.

Noah: Wife, in this ship we all must keep
And float upon the waters deep.

Wife: I would as soon that thou did'st sleep!
　　To all that thou doest say
I will not pay the slightest heed.

Noah: Do as I bid, good wife, I plead.

Wife: No! Not unless I see more need,
　　Though thou stand and stare all day.

Noah: Lord, that women be so sour,
And strive always to show their power!
But all that you have seen this hour
　　Will not make me lose heart.
Good wife, I pray thee, do not jeer,
For everyone will think, I fear,
That thou, not I, art master here
　　—And, by St. John, thou art! . . .

Noah goes into the ark. His family carry to him food, stores, and pictures of the animals and birds. When they have done this, they go aboard themselves. Noah's Wife stays outside and joins a group of Gossips at some distance from the ark.

Shem: Sir, here are lions, strong and fine,
Leopards, horses, oxen, swine;
Camels, asses, sheep and kine
　　Now at this ship do meet. . . .

[*Other animals enter in pairs.*]

Noah: Wife, come in! Why stand'st thou there?
Thou art headstrong, that I dare swear.
Come in! For we are in God's care,
　　And surely shall not drown.

Wife: Yea, sir, go on! Set up your sail,
And then row forth into the gale.
But I stay here, for, without fail,
　　I will not leave this town.

Unless thou tak'st my gossips on,
Not one more foot will I be gone.
If they must drown, then, by St. John,
　　I will not save my life.

They love me well. I do not jest.
Take them with me into thy chest,
Or else row forth and do thy best
    To get thee a new wife. . . .

Gossip: (*Singing*)
The flood comes flowing in so fast,
    On every side it doth appear;
For fear of drowning I am aghast.
    Good gossip, now let us draw near.
Or let us drink ere we be caught,
    For often have we all done so;
And at a draught thou drinkest a quart,
    And that would I do ere I go.

[*Noah's sons—Shem, Ham, and Japhet—try to persuade their mother to come aboard.*]

Japhet: We come to thee, brother and brother,
And after us shall come no other.
Enter the ship we pray, good Mother,
    For we be waiting still.

Wife: That will I not, for all your call,
Unless I have my gossips all.

Shem: Thy drowning, then, we must forestall,
    Even against thy will.

Shem, Ham, and Japhet bundle the protesting Noah's Wife into the ark. Now all the family is aboard.

Noah: Welcome, wife! Now naught's forgot!

Wife: Then add thou this unto thy lot!

She gives him a slap.

Noah: Ha! Ha! Marry, this is hot!
    Still, she's aboard the boat.
This waste of time makes me to grieve,
For long ago I meant to leave.
The water spreads, and I believe
    My ship begins to float. . . .

[*After the forty days of flooding are done*]

God: Thy task for me, good Noah, is done.
Thy wife and children, every one,
Shall go with thee into the sun,
    And great contentment know.
Also the beasts, and birds that fly,
Shall leave the ship, now it is dry,
To live on Earth and multiply;
    I will that it be so.

Becket; or, The Honour of God

Excerpt from the Play by Jean Anouilh

Characters: King Henry II, Thomas à Becket

[*King Henry and Becket have just received word that the Archbishop of Canterbury is dead.*]

Becket: (*In a murmur*) That little old man. How could that feeble body contain so much strength?

King: Now, now, now! Don't squander your sorrow, my son. I personally consider this an excellent piece of news.

Becket: He was the first Norman who took an interest in me. He was a true father to me. God rest his soul. . . .

King: Becket! . . . An extraordinary idea is just creeping into my mind. . . . A master-stroke. . . . Listen, Thomas. Tradition prevents me from touching the privileges of the Primacy. You follow me so far?

Becket: Yes, my prince.

King: But what if the Primate is my man? If the Archbishop of Canterbury is for the King, how can his power possibly incommodate me?

Becket: That's an ingenious idea, my prince, but you forget that his election is a free one.

King: No. You're forgetting the Royal Veto. It's fully a hundred years since the Conclave of Bishops has voted contrary to the wishes of the King.

Becket: I don't doubt it, my Lord. But we know all your Bishops. Which of them could you rely on? Once the Primate's mitre is on their heads, they grow dizzy with power.

King: Are you asking me, Becket? I'll tell you. Someone who doesn't know what dizziness means. Someone who isn't even afraid of God. Thomas, my son, . . . you are going over to England.

Becket: I am at your service, my prince. . . .

King: You are going to deliver a personal letter from me to every Bishop in the land. And do you know what those letters will contain, my Thomas, my little brother? My royal wish to have you elected Primate of England.

Becket is deathly white.

Becket: (*With forced laugh*) You're joking of course, my Lord. (*He opens his fine coat to display his even finer doublet.*) Just look at the edifying man, the saintly man whom you would be trusting with these holy functions. . . . A fine Archbishop I'd have made. Look at my new shoes. They're the latest fashion in Paris. Attractive, that little upturned toe, don't you think? Quite full of unction and compunction, isn't it, Sire? [Why, my prince—you really fooled me for a second.]

King: . . . I'm in deadly earnest. . . .

Becket: (*Stammering*) But, my Lord, I'm not even a priest.

King: You're a deacon. You can take your final vows on Monday and be ordained within a month. . . .

Becket: My Lord, I see now that you weren't joking. Don't do this.

King: Why not?

Becket: It frightens me.

King: Becket, this is an order.

Becket: (*Gravely*) If I become Archbishop, I can no longer be your friend. . . . This is madness, my Lord. Don't do it. I could not serve both God and you.

King: You've never disappointed me, Thomas. And you are the only man I trust. You will leave tonight.

An Inquisition by Bernard Gui

Bernard Gui (1261–1331) was one of the most famous inquisitors. He wrote a treatise about how to conduct an interrogation of suspected heretics. The interrogation below is adapted from a model that Gui used to instruct future inquisitors. The heretic in this scene is suspected to be a member of the Waldenses, who would take no oaths and obey no authority but God, whose authority they claimed to receive directly as the only holy and perfected Christians.

Characters: Inquisitor, Heretic, Narrator

Inqui: [What is your faith?]

Heret: I believe all that a good Christian ought to believe.

Inqui: And what do you consider a good Christian?

Heret: He who believes as the Holy Church teaches to believe and hold.

Inqui: What do you call the Holy Church?

Heret: Lord, what you say and believe to be the Holy Church.

Inqui: I believe the Holy Church to be the Roman Church, over which the Pope presides as lord, and other prelates under him.

Heret: And I believe it.

Narra: [The heretic means] "*I* believe that *you* believe it. . . ."

Inqui: [Do you] believe that the bread and wine are changed in the Mass, at the words of the priest, into the body and blood of Our Lord?

Heret: Ought I not indeed to believe that?

Inqui: I do not ask whether you *ought* to believe it, but *do* you believe it?

Heret: I believe whatever you and other good doctors order me to believe. . . .

Inqui: If you are a simple man, reply and act simply, without any cloak of words.

Heret: Willingly.

Inqui: Then you are willing to *swear* that you have never taught anything against faith . . . ?

Heret: (*Trembling a little*) If I ought to swear, I will swear willingly.

Inqui: You are not asked whether you *ought*, but whether you are *willing* to swear.

Heret: If you order me to swear, I will swear.

Inqui: I don't compel you to swear, because since you believe an oath to be unlawful, you will try to shift the blame to me for compelling you; but if you swear, I will hear. . . .

Heret: How ought I to speak when I swear?

Inqui: Swear as you know.

Heret: Lord, I don't know unless you teach me! . . .

Inqui: If I had to swear, then, I would raise my hand and touch the holy Gospel of God, and say, "I swear by this holy Gospel of God that I have never taught and believed anything that might be against the true faith that the holy Roman Church believes and holds."

Narra: The heretic . . . mumbles something rather verbose which he intends to have sound like an oath, but not to have the form of an oath. . . .

Inqui: Well, will you swear?

Heret: Didn't you hear me swear?

Narra: Finally, when the heretic is straitened by questions, and at the end of his resources of evasion, he pretends to weep, or flatters the Inquisitor, saying that he will perform any penance to free himself from the infamous charge of which he, a simple man, is wholly innocent.

Quiz on Chapter 10

_____ 1) Medieval unions were called (a) societies (b) clubs (c) guilds (d) none of the above.

_____ 2) This invention, which was brought back from China in medieval times, helped increase the trade done by sea: (a) canvas (b) the compass (c) the steering wheel (d) metal rudders.

_____ 3) The excessive charging of interest on loans is called (a) simony (b) parsimony (c) embezzlement (d) usury.

_____ 4) One reason Jews became bankers was that (a) they were forbidden to own land (b) they were ordered to by the Frankish kings (c) most had practiced this trade in Israel (d) it paid better than winemaking.

_____ 5) The main room of a cathedral used for public Mass is called the (a) chancel (b) choir (c) sanctuary (d) nave.

_____ 6) Which of these was _not_ one of the common uses of the cathedrals? (a) a hiring hall for workers (b) a place for travelers to sleep (c) a royal audience hall (d) a place for religious plays

_____ 7) Pope Gregory VII and Emperor Henry IV argued over (a) more papal lands in Sicily (b) Henry's desire for a divorce (c) Henry's murder of his chancellor (d) the appointment of bishops.

_____ 8) In the eleventh century, the real issue that divided the Eastern and Western Church was (a) funding from the emperor (b) the power of the patriarch versus the power of the pope (c) the nature of the Blessed Mother (d) images.

_____ 9) The pope called for the First Crusade because (a) Christians could not make pilgrimages to Jerusalem in peace (b) the Arabs had struck oil in Yemen (c) he wanted to convert the Muslims (d) Muslims had kidnapped Christian diplomats.

_____ 10) Which of these was _not_ a reward for going on a Crusade? (a) indulgences (b) loot (c) immunity from taxes (d) an allotment of land in one's country of origin

_____ 11) The Third Crusade was a failure in large part because (a) there were too few soldiers (b) booty was scarce (c) the Crusaders fought among themselves (d) the Muslims used "Greek fire."

_____ 12) The Crusaders of the Fourth Crusade attacked Constantinople because (a) the Muslims were vulnerable there (b) they were paid to help a deposed emperor regain his throne (c) heretics ruled it (d) the pope ordered them to.

_____ 13) This Crusade made the split between the Eastern and Western Church almost complete: (a) First (b) Second (c) Third (d) Fourth.

_____ 14) The Children's Crusade (a) was a collection of money for the Second Crusade (b) ended when the children were sold into slavery (c) never was organized (d) touched the heart of the Muslim leader Saladin.

_____ 15) This thing was *not* brought back from China by merchants: **(a)** silk **(b)** aluminum **(c)** spaghetti **(d)** new spices.

_____ 16) *Friar* means **(a)** monk **(b)** friend **(c)** brother **(d)** deacon.

_____ 17) The real name for the Dominicans is the Order of **(a)** Jesus **(b)** Saint Dominic **(c)** Teachers **(d)** Preachers.

_____ 18) The Franciscans were "mendicants," meaning **(a)** beggars **(b)** travelers **(c)** wanderers **(d)** workers.

_____ 19) Saint Francis stressed that his followers should embrace a life of **(a)** teaching **(b)** poverty **(c)** priesthood **(d)** silence.

_____ 20) This friend of Saint Francis began an order of nuns who depended completely on the gifts of people for their livelihood: **(a)** Teresa **(b)** Joan **(c)** Catherine **(d)** Clare.

_____ 21) Heretics scared civil rulers because rulers considered heresy to be **(a)** an attempt to gain power **(b)** antimonarchy **(c)** treason **(d)** a cause of crop failure.

_____ 22) The Albigensians were heretics because they believed that **(a)** the pope was to be deposed **(b)** all material things were bad **(c)** Jesus was just a human **(d)** all people were going to heaven.

_____ 23) A crusade was led against the Albigensians when they **(a)** kidnapped the king of France **(b)** killed the papal legate **(c)** attacked Avignon **(d)** burned two Dominicans at the stake.

_____ 24) This number of witnesses was required to make a charge of heresy against someone: **(a)** one **(b)** two **(c)** three **(d)** four.

_____ 25) The actual execution of heretics was carried out by **(a)** Franciscans **(b)** Cathari **(c)** papal troops **(d)** civil authorities.

_____ 26) The universities originated from **(a)** cathedral schools **(b)** monasteries **(c)** royal charters **(d)** papal decrees.

_____ 27) Probably the most famous university of the High Middle Ages was **(a)** Oxford **(b)** Paris **(c)** Milan **(d)** Rome.

_____ 28) Many of the resources and books used by scholars in European universities actually came through the work of scholars from **(a)** Muslim countries **(b)** Germany **(c)** China **(d)** Ireland.

_____ 29) Thomas Aquinas's nickname was **(a)** Thomas the Wise **(b)** Dumb Ox **(c)** Tom the Good **(d)** Slow Tom.

Prayer Service: For Peace and a Simple Lifestyle

Opening Hymn

Prayer from "Canticle to the Sun" by Saint Francis of Assisi

Left: Praised be thou, my Lord, with all thy creatures,
Especially the honored Brother Sun,
Who makes the day and illumines us through thee. . . .

Right: Praised be thou, my Lord, for Sister Moon and the stars,
Thou hast formed them in heaven clear and precious and beautiful.

Left: Praised be thou, my Lord, for Brother Wind,
And for the air and cloudy and clear and every weather,
by which thou givest sustenance to thy creatures.

Right: Praised be thou, my Lord, for Sister Water,
Who is very useful and humble and precious and chaste.

Left: Praised be thou, my Lord, for Brother Fire,
By whom thou lightest the night,
And he is beautiful and jocund and robust and strong.

Right: Praised be thou, my Lord, for our sister Mother Earth,
Who sustains and directs us,
And produces various fruits with colored flowers and herbage.

All: Praise and bless my Lord and give him thanks
And serve him with great humility.

(Pause for a moment's reflection.)

Reading of Matthew 19:16–26

(Pause for reflection.)

Prayer Adapted from Matthew 25:34–40

Left: At the Last Judgment, the Lord will say: Come, you whom my Father has blessed, take for your heritage the kingdom prepared for you.

Right: For I was hungry and you gave me food;

Left: I was thirsty and you gave me drink;

Right: I was a stranger and you made me welcome;

Left: naked and you clothed me,

Right: sick and you visited me,

Left: in prison and you came to see me.

Right: Lord, when did we do these things for you?

Left: In so far as you did these to one of the least of these brothers and sisters of mine, you did it to me.

Closing Hymn

CHAPTER 11

Public Turmoil, Personal Piety: 1300–1500

Major Concepts

A. More and more the papacy was being controlled by political factions. Political influence was at its height when the French king forced the removal of the papacy to Avignon. As the Black Death raged through Europe and the Hundred Years' War dragged on and the Church grew more corrupt, calls for a return of the papacy to Rome were finally heeded. Eventually, one pope led the Church again.

B. Even though much of Europe was picked apart by intrigues, the Renaissance—the rebirth of classical culture—began, first in Italy and then spreading throughout Europe. Many of the popes of this period were much better patrons of the arts than spiritual leaders. One of the most important moments of the Renaissance was the printing of the Bible by Johannes Gutenberg. And as more people read the Bible, calls for reforms increased.

C. A bedrock of faith in Jesus persisted among the common people, but this faithfulness was abused by the selling of indulgences and other corrupt practices.

D. The Ottoman Turks, who had been slowly biting off chunks of the Eastern empire, finally eradicated the Byzantine world when they conquered Constantinople. Moscow then became the center of Orthodox Christianity.

E. At the end of the 1400s, an era of explorations began that led to the Europeans' discovery of new worlds for trade and settlement and of new peoples to whom the missionaries would preach the Word of God.

Activities for Concept A

More and more the papacy was being controlled by political factions. Political influence was at its height when the French king forced the removal of the papacy to Avignon. As the Black Death raged through Europe and the Hundred Years' War dragged on and the Church grew more corrupt, calls for a return of the papacy to Rome were finally heeded. Eventually, one pope led the Church again. (Pages 190–193 of the student text.)

11

Review Questions and Exercises from the Student Text

Question 1: How did the popes' removal to Avignon signal a change in the status of the papacy?

Answer: Clearly the removal of the papacy to Avignon signaled that the power of earlier popes over kings was gone. The popes no longer had the power to protect their own rights to direct the Church.

Question 2: The Hundred Years' War had implications for the Church. What were some of these?

Answer: Seeing the pope under the domination of the French seemed to signal the complete politicization of the Church. The English, who were at war with France, were most concerned; would a French pope be a tool for the French king against the

169

English? In addition, the Church could hardly mediate between France and England when there were two popes or when the sole pope was French.

Question 3: In what ways was the Avignon papacy difficult for the whole Church at this time?

Answer: The Church had been one of the few sources of unity in Europe. When there were two popes, loyalties were split along national lines. People did not know whom to follow for spiritual leadership. In addition, the Avignon papacy caused church taxes to rise.

Question 4: The Black Death killed one-third of Europe's population. What effect did this have on religious practice?

Answer: Many priests and monks died in the plague while serving the people. Therefore, areas were left without the sacramental life of the Church. Later replacements were frequently hastily selected and poorly trained. Thus, the credibility of the Church suffered.

Question 5: Explain why Saint Catherine of Siena was such an unusual person for her era—maybe for any era. Why was the religious order to which she belonged different from most of the other religious orders for women?

Answer: Catherine was a woman who had great moral authority among those in power. She influenced the pope to return to Rome. She mediated disputes between states. In an era when few men could read or write, she did both admirably well, even though she was thirty before she could write (remember that Charlemagne never got the hang of writing). The order of lay women to which she belonged went about actively serving the needy. Strictly speaking they were not religious sisters because at this time nuns, by definition, lived in cloistered convents.

Question 6: What were the causes and effects of the elections of two and then three popes at the same time? How was the situation resolved?

Answer: After the papacy moved from Avignon back to Rome, the Romans demanded that a Roman be elected pope. In a compromise, an Italian (but non-Roman) was elected; while trying to impose reforms, this pope made enemies. Thus, the French cardinals declared his election invalid and elected a French pope of their own. This divided the loyalties of Catholics for about thirty years. In 1400 a council at Pisa elected another pope, in hopes that the other two would resign or that they could be deposed. When this failed to solve the problem, another council was held from 1414 to 1418, eventually electing Martin V as the sole pope. All this confusion badly weakened the Church.

Other Questions and Activities for Discussion

1) On a large wall map, point out the places that are important to this chapter: Avignon, Pisa, Constance.

2) Until the election of Pope John Paul II, the popes that people commonly remember were all Italians. The nationality of the pope has always been an issue for some Christians. To explore the implications of the pope's nationality, here are some discussion questions:
- Most of the popes were Italians. Given what you've read so far, why do you think that has been the case?
- Should the nationality of the pope make any real difference in his ability to lead the Church?
- Has the nationality of Pope John Paul II been a negative factor in his leadership?

11

- What are the positive aspects of breaking the tradition of all Italian popes?
- Do you think that a U.S. or Canadian pope would act different from a European, especially Italian, pope?
- How do you think people would respond to an Asian pope or an African pope or a South American pope?
- During the period from 1300 to 1500, travel was very dangerous, even for a pope. Today the popes can and have traveled extensively. What kind of effect does limited and extensive travel have on peoples' perception of the pope's nationality?

Then, consider with your students the possibility of changing the pope's residency.
- Is it conceivable that the pope could move church headquarters to another city? Why has the Church maintained its center in Rome?
- In your lifetime most Catholics will live in developing nations. Would the Church be a better sign of service, hope, and identification with the poor of God if the pope lived in Manila or Rio de Janeiro or Kinshasa?

3) Student Handout 11–A, "The Black Death" (found at the end of this chapter), describes the terror and some of the consequences of the plague. Either duplicate this handout for the students or read sections of it out loud to your class. The psychological effects of the plague were devastating too; needless to say, people had a strong sense of their own mortality. There are still occasional outbreaks of bubonic plague, but it is controlled quite readily now. To help your students understand the horror of the plague, ask these questions:
- One-third of Europe was wiped out by the plague. Is there anything of equal or worse destructive capability that exists in nature today?
- Are there any other sources of mass death that exist today? [nerve gas, biological weapons, nuclear bombs]
- What is the key difference between the Black Death and the sources of mass death we have today? [human control]

Divide the class into groups of four of five students. Then ask the groups to analyze this case and respond to the questions below:

Having been warned of an attack by the enemy of your country, you and some others from your small town managed to escape to the nearby mountains where you hid in a cave that had been prepared for just such an attack. The enemy has used biological weapons. Your group has to abandon the hideout because you have run out of food and water. Knowing that there is no use in waiting any longer, you walk back to town.
- As you enter the outskirts of town, you see . . . [Have the groups compose a scenario about what they would face on entering the town.]
- What problems would your group face? What fears would you have to live with?
- Presuming that you manage to survive, how would this experience affect your view of life?

4) Even before the Black Death had killed a third of Europe, medieval people had a fatalistic view of life. They saw themselves ruled by Fortune, the Empress of the World. While theologians maintained that humans had free will, the common people were not so sure. In 1937, the composer Carl Orff brought out *Carmina Burana*, a collection of songs based on poetry written by "goliards"—wandering writers of the late thirteenth and early fourteenth centuries. Orff called his work "profane songs for singers and vocal chorus with instruments and magical pictures." Student Handout 11–B, "Fortune, Empress of the World" (found at the end of this chapter), contains the words to the first song, "Fortuna Imperatrix Mundi." If you can find a recording of *Carmina Burana* (many public libraries would have it), play this piece for your students after they have read the words in English. If no recording is available, you might have a small group of students do a choral reading of the poem. Then discuss the poem.

11

- Why is Fortune called variable?
- Does the poet see fortune as always bad?
- Why is the image of the "wheel" of fortune used?
- How is the term *wheel of fortune* used today?
- Do people still believe in fate or fortune or luck today? How do you see this manifest?
- Do you think that the poet believed that people are free?
- If people believed that they were merely the tools of their fates, how would they act?
- Why would medieval people believe very strongly in Fortune?
- Why would medieval people turn to fortune-tellers? astrologers?
- One of the popular methods of fortune-telling in medieval times was the use of tarot cards. One of the cards is the Wheel of Fortune. If someone has tarot cards, perhaps they can explain the meaning of the Wheel of Fortune.
- Do people today believe in fate as strongly as medieval people did?
- What happens to trust in God if people believe that their fates are sealed?

5) Death was frequently personified as a skeleton. In medieval times people would do what came to be known as the "dance of death." The dance was done to illustrate people's fear of death. In some places people did dances or had pageants in which death was banished or driven away. These folk ceremonies often originated in medieval times, sometimes as a result of the Black Death. Many other customs that surround death and funerals are ways of forgetting death or at least of temporarily making death seem less terrible. Assign some students to find out more about the medieval dance of death and other students to bring in art works from books or other sources that have representations of death. Students might also do some additional reports about Irish wakes, funerals in New Orleans and the use of blues bands in these, and other images of death such as an old man with a scythe. Many of these customs and representations have their roots in medieval times.

6) One great figure who emerged out of the Hundred Years' War is Saint Joan of Arc. All too little is really known about her, but she is credited with changing the course of the war in France's favor. According to Joan and affirmed at her canonization, she was inspired by God to act as she did. Student Handout 11–C, "Saint Joan of Arc (1412–31): A Brief Biography" (found at the end of this chapter), summarizes Joan's life.

If you have time and wish to continue the discussion of Joan, have the students do further research on her life. You might want them to treat such issues as the following: Why would Joan be declared a saint? How was she a good example of Christian living? Was she more than just a French heroine? Also, George Bernard Shaw wrote a most intriguing play about Joan of Arc; perhaps some students could perform a section of her trial by the British. Movies have been made about her; rent one and discuss Joan after showing it. The Learning Corporation of America produced a film starring Sandy Dennis, called *Joan of Arc: A Profile in Power* (25 min., color). Joan of Arc is interviewed and explains her position about helping in the liberation of France. (Note: This film was not reviewed by the author.)

7) *The Middle Ages: A Wanderer's Guide to Life and Letters* (Learning Corporation of America, 27 min., color) is a journey through the culture of the Middle Ages as seen through the eyes of a wandering poet. Segments of the morality play *Everyman*, selections from Dante's *Love Sonnets*, and the prologue to Chaucer's "Wife of Bath's Tale" are performed. The wanderer comments on village life, the great Gothic cathedrals, romance, pilgrimages, and so on. If you have time in your lesson plan, the film is a nice synopsis of the Middle Ages. A study guide comes with the film.

11

Activities for Concept B

Even though much of Europe was picked apart by intrigues, the Renaissance—the rebirth of classical culture—began, first in Italy and then spreading throughout Europe. Many of the popes of this period were much better patrons of the arts than spiritual leaders. One of the most important moments of the Renaissance was the printing of the Bible by Johannes Gutenberg. And as more people read the Bible, calls for reforms increased. (Pages 194–197 of the student text.)

Review Questions and Exercises from the Student Text

Question 7: What was the political situation of Italy at this time, and how did it influence the Church?

Answer: Italy was being torn apart by wars between city-states. The Church found itself mediating some conflicts but involved in others. Again, wars divided loyalties.

Question 8: After his death, Savonarola became somewhat of a hero to people trying to reform the Church. Why might this be so?

Answer: Savonarola spoke against corruption in the Church and enacted governmental and religious reforms in Florence. [*Teacher's note:* For a short time Florence's government was a democracy trying to rule by following Christian values.]

Question 9: What is an interdict? Could it be used today by the pope? What would be the results if he tried to use it?

Answer: An interdict is an order from the pope that priests are not to administer the sacraments to a certain group until this group comes to terms with the Church. Using it today would be very difficult because people might not fear the spiritual power of the pope as much as they used to. If people, en masse, disobeyed, it would cause great harm to the credibility of the papacy. A partial interdict has been used in some areas of Guatemala because of the murder of catechists, religious, and priests by right-wing death squads. The efficacy of the interdict is hard to measure.

Question 10: How did the political situation in Germany pose problems for the Church?

Answer: The German emperor was elected by seven "electors." And, Germany itself was really a very loose confederation of small states. Considerable tension and intrigue existed between these states, and sometimes, the Church was caught up in these problems.

Question 11: What was the Renaissance, and how was the Church a patron of this movement?

Answer: The Renaissance was a period of rebirth of interest in Greek and Roman culture. With printing presses operating, copies of the Greek and Roman writings were more readily available. Europeans tended to glamorize Greek and Roman culture; it seemed to offer them much more interest, reason, and joy in living than medieval culture and orthodox Christianity. People were in a mood to enjoy the fruits of humanity and to not worry quite as much about a seemingly abstract afterlife. The Church sponsored architects to build neo-Roman churches, painters to decorate these churches, musicians to write hymns, and libraries to preserve the best that had been thought and said.

Question 12: In 1456 the Bible was printed by Gutenberg. How did this event hasten the demands for reform in the Church?

Answer: The first book off Gutenberg's press was the Bible. Naturally, more people were able to read the Bible. [*Teacher's note:* These people saw that many practices of church people did not correspond with the Word of God. Critics of corruption now had fuel for their arguments.]

11

Question 13: The popes of the Renaissance seemed to lead double lives. What does this mean?

Answer: The popes were supposed to lead upright Christian lives; they were to be the Vicars of Christ on earth. In reality, however, many of them were immoral, incompetent, and much more interested in art, literature, music, and buildings than in holy lives.

Personal Reflection Exercise

The events of this chapter may seem surprising to some people. However, most institutions go through periods when they need to be reformed; the Church is no exception. Many of the popes led double lives—at one level as leaders of the Church while on another level as greedy, pleasure-seeking men. Before all of this causes us to be too discouraged or critical of the institutional Church, maybe it would be useful to reflect on how we all sometimes live double lives. Here are some questions to guide your reflections:

- Have I ever knowingly done something that I knew was wrong?
- Have I ever disapproved of something that others did—but that I have done myself?
- Have there been times when I wanted to do one thing but ended up doing the opposite?
- How do I feel when I have been forgiven for my wrongdoing?
- If I have a hard time changing my ways, can I condemn the Church for not being perfect?
- Have I ever tried to make something good happen when I knew the way I was doing it was wrong?
- How can I help the Church strive to be what it is really intended to be?

Other Questions and Activities for Discussion

1) Savonarola was certainly one of the most intriguing figures of the period before the Reformation. On the one hand, condemned as a disobedient scoundrel, for many years he was used as an object lesson against those who would criticize the Church. On the other hand, many reformers looked to him as a hero. Student Handout 11–D, "Savonarola" (found at the end of this chapter), contains sections of the play *Savonarola: The Flame of Florence* by Urban Nagle, OP. The document of excommunication that is read in the play is from the original text, which was sent not to Savonarola directly, but to the superior of the rival Franciscans.

The second section of the play pictures Savonarola after he has been tortured. The civil authorities who assumed control of Florence after wresting it from Savonarola and his followers tortured him, demanding a confession. Savonarola's hands were tied behind his back; using ropes hung from a pulley on the ceiling, he was lifted up by ropes tied around his wrists. Suspended twenty feet in the air he would then be dropped to within a short distance from the floor. This happened four times in an hour. Savonarola was tortured for about six days during fourteen sessions. By the time they were through with him, his major joints were dislocated, his body was completely bruised, and he could barely maintain consciousness. Through it all, he never truly confessed, but maintained an eerie control. Nevertheless, Savonarola worried that in a delirium he would say something like a confession. He also had hallucinations, like his conversation with Pope Alexander in the play.

The execution of Savonarola and two other Dominican friars loyal to him was a long affair. They were stripped of their religious vestments and habits. Their fingernails were scraped with glass to show that they had been stripped of their priesthood.

11

Their heads were shaved too, thus ruining their tonsures. The entire transcripts of their trials were read publicly. Oddly, on the way to their hanging and burning, a Bishop Romolino read to them a document from Pope Alexander granting them a plenary indulgence releasing them from all papal penalties and the excommunication. In short, Alexander, their enemy, had freed them from sin, "back into your original state of sinlessness." In turn, the two friars and Savonarola were first hanged and then burned. This was a tragic chapter in church affairs, but it was a harbinger of the larger revolt that was to come.

2) The Renaissance movement had a dramatic effect on art, literature, music, and thought. However, only in the revolutions of the eighteenth century did the Renaissance profoundly influence the lives of the common people. The stress on, as Protagoras says, "man as the measure of all things" resulted in a sense of the value of the individual person. As individuals were recognized for their worth, they began to expect better treatment—and certain rights. Eventually, therefore, the Renaissance's emphasis on humanity did have practical results for common people, but these were three centuries away for the people who lived during the early Renaissance.

In medieval art, human figures were represented as static and saints as very ethereal. But in Renaissance art, human figures were heroically proportioned. Male figures, even of saints or Jesus, were muscular, ideally proportioned, vibrant, even sensual; in short, they were modeled after sculptures of the Greek and Roman times. From this point until the late nineteenth century, all figures in art took on the dimensions and aspects of Greek gods and goddesses. The differences between Renaissance madonnas and Greek goddesses, other than the amount of clothing they wore, were few.

Michelangelo's statue of David presented an ideal for Renaissance people to follow; he is portrayed as intelligent, strong, proportioned perfectly, defiant, confident, heroic, and nude. Interestingly, the statue of David was commissioned in Florence by the officials of the republic that Savonarola had inspired. David was the slayer of a tyrant; the people of Florence had thrown out the tyrannical Medici family. In effect, David is a symbol of the heroic individual rising out of obscurity—the well-rounded person of the Renaissance. Every library has a picture of Michelangelo's David; discuss this statue with your class as a representation of the Renaissance ideal. (For an excellent discussion of the Renaissance, see chapter 4 in Kenneth Clark's *Civilisation*.)

3) You may wish to invite an art teacher to talk to your students about Renaissance art and architecture, especially about representations of religious figures.

4) To get some idea of the revolutionary effects that the printing press had on humankind, examine with your students the effects of something like the transistor or microchips.
- What new inventions were made possible with the invention of the microchip? [List these.]
- How has each one of these inventions influenced the way we live our lives, communicate with one another, make other technological discoveries?
- How do technological inventions affect all of life, like the ripple effect from a rock thrown into a pond?
- Gutenberg's invention made it possible for many more people to read the Bible, trade important medical and scientific information, publish widely great literature, and so on. But, there were negative effects too: heretical ideas were spread more easily, people became very discontented with their status—there were religious and peasant revolts. What cautions must be applied to the development of inventions? Or, should inventors freely advance any discovery no matter what?

5) A student may have a small hand-set printing press at home or a model of Gutenberg's press. If so, it might be enjoyable to have a student demonstrate this first method of typesetting and printing.

11

Activities for Concept C

A bedrock of faith in Jesus persisted among the common people, but this faithfulness was abused by the selling of indulgences and other corrupt practices. (Pages 197–200 of the student text.)

Review Questions and Exercises from the Student Text

Question 14: What were some of the ordinary religious practices of the common people during the fourteenth and fifteenth centuries? Particularly, how did the practice of granting indulgences begin, and what distortions resulted?

Answer: At noon and 6:00 P.M., many people said special prayers; they went to Sunday Mass and enjoyed the feast days. Religious plays were performed in public; they were not only instructive but often amusing. Frequently people made pilgrimages to the shrines where the relics of certain saints were preserved. Many people believed that these relics had curative powers.

Penances for sins were often seen as reparation for an offense against God and the community. Some people were granted indulgences—remission of sins—for building a church or contributing to the support of a convent; these were good acts that made reparation. The corruption of this practice came when people believed that they could buy their way into heaven, or when people forgot that God's forgiveness has already been given and that we must repent humbly and mend our ways; a sincere heart is essential—money is not.

Other Questions and Activities for Discussion

1) All during medieval times, there was great veneration of Jesus' mother, Mary. To the knights she was the model of pure womanhood. To peasants she was an intermediary with their Lord, a gentle mother who cared for them. To women she was a model of motherhood: strong, courageous, suffering, noble. Stories about Mary abound from these times. Student Handout 11–E, "Medieval Tales of Mary and Saint Martin" (found at the end of this chapter), contains two such stories. These might be read in sermon form to the students, as indeed they were taken from sermons. Or, the students can read them silently. This handout also includes a story about a miracle at the tomb of Saint Martin. Since Mary and the saints have played such a large part in the common devotional life of the Church, after the students have read the passages, discuss the role of devotions using questions like these:

- What are your reactions to these stories about Mary and the miracle?
- Do people have a harder time believing in saints and miracles now than in the past? If so, why? If not, why not?
- Do people pray to Mary now as much as they used to? [To answer this, you may need to assign students to interview their parents or grandparents about this question and to prepare written or oral reports.]
- Are there any special saints to whom people pray for certain favors today?
- Why is Mary worth imitating? What are some reasons that she should be a subject of veneration?

2) In this chapter, Chaucer's description of a poor parish priest is included (see p. 198 of the student text). Chaucer, at the end of "The Pardoner's Tale," has the avaricious pardoner sermonize to his fellow travelers in an attempt to sell them relics and indulgences. The host of the pilgrims becomes furious at the pardoner and, illustrating Chaucer's antipathy to this character, threatens severe bodily damage to the pardoner if he so much as opens his mouth again. Clearly the pardoner's speech is a caricature of medieval indulgence sellers, but it is instructive because many people shared Chaucer's antipathy. Student Handout 11–F, "Chaucer's Pardoner Tries

11

to Sell His Indulgences" (found at the end of this chapter), gives the pardoner's speech. Have one of your students read the speech to the class with great vigor, strong emphasis, and greedy intent. Then, discuss the speech and the host's reaction.

- If you heard a speech like this today, what would you think?
- If you really believed that simply buying a pardon from this fellow would give you remission of all sins, how would that be a distortion of the Gospels?
- How would the poor feel if they thought that indulgences were necessary, but they were too poor to buy them?
- Why does the host say, "Then I would be under Christ's curse"?

3) Some students could be assigned to trace the route of and estimate mileage for pilgrimages from Rome to Canterbury and from Paris to Santiago de Compostela in Spain, which is the alleged site of the tomb of Saint James and one of the principal places of pilgrimage in Europe since the eleventh century.

4) Pose this issue about penance to your students:
- Would we be better people if at the end of the rite of Reconciliation we had to make some sort of reparation for our sins like donating to Catholic Relief or some other charity, or having to work at a fund-raiser for a home for the handicapped run by the Church? Is simply meditating or praying enough to remind us of our need to build community?

You may even wish to set up a debate on this issue.

Activities for Concept D
The Ottoman Turks, who had been slowly biting off chunks of the Eastern empire, finally eradicated the Byzantine world when they conquered Constantinople. Moscow then became the center of Orthodox Christianity. (Pages 200–201 of the student text.)

Review Questions and Exercises from the Student Text

Question 15: How did Moscow come to be called the "third Rome"? What relationship became established between the Roman Catholic Church and the Orthodox Church?

Answer: With the fall of Constantinople (which was called the "second Rome") to the Ottoman Turks, Ivan the Great declared Moscow the "third Rome" because it became the haven for Orthodox religion. The separation of the Roman Church and the Orthodox Church became rigid.

11

Other Questions and Activities for Discussion

1) Here are some brief research projects on which your students could report:
a) a short history of the Ottoman Turks, whose empire lasted for several centuries
b) the layout of Constantinople at the time of the assault
c) the essential differences between Orthodox beliefs and practices, and Roman Catholic beliefs and practices
d) the extent of the Mongol Empire under Genghis Khan and Kublai Khan
e) the boundaries of Russia in the fifteenth century

2) Ask your class to imagine what it would be like to be in a fort under siege. Establish a list of all the problems with which you would have to contend, especially if you were under siege for a few months.

Activities for Concept E

At the end of the 1400s, an era of explorations began that led to the Europeans' discovery of new worlds for trade and settlement and of new peoples to whom the missionaries would preach the Word of God. (Pages 201–202 of the student text.)

Review Questions and Exercises from the Student Text

Question 16: Why would people of this period look with such hope at the explorations of da Gama, Columbus, and Cabot? How did the Church view these discoveries?

Answer: Europe had been suffering through terrible wars and the Black Death. Treasuries were stretched; horizons were limited. The discovery of new territories promised riches, land, adventure, and for the Church, the chance to spread the Word of God.

Question 17: During the fourteenth and fifteenth centuries, how did the Church act as Sacrament? Herald? Servant?

Answer: The Church was the sign of Jesus present through the work of simple people like Chaucer's parish priest and great spiritual leaders like Catherine of Siena. With the invention of the printing press, the Bible and other important religious books found larger audiences. And, with new explorations came new listeners to the Word of God. As Servant, again, many simple people—lay and religious—served the needy; Catherine of Genoa is a good example.

Other Questions and Activities for Discussion

1) Ask some students to research the exploratory trips of Columbus, da Gama, and Cabot; and, on a large wall map of the world, have them trace these trips for the class.

2) It is easy to understand the Europeans' interest in gold and jewels, but why were they so interested in spices? Again, have one or two students prepare brief explanations about what spices Europeans wanted, where the spices were found, and to what lengths they went to get them.

3) Pose these questions about exploration to your class:
- What is it about the human spirit that demands exploration and new discoveries?
- Why do people receive a thrill from space shuttle journeys, moon missions, deep sea explorations?
- How can these explorations deepen our appreciation of God?

Summary Activities for the Chapter

1) As usual the students should be asked to write down their reflections about how they have been Servant, Herald, Sacrament, and Body of Christ. In addition, they might be asked to record their reflections on the chapter, especially about how, even during this time of problems, the Church still managed to do good and be Church.

11

178

2) If you have not already used these questions for daily quizzes, distribute to the class Student Handout 11-G, "Quiz on Chapter 11" (found at the end of this chapter). The answers to the quiz are as follows:

1) a	8) c	15) c	22) d
2) c	9) d	16) a	23) d
3) b	10) b	17) c	24) d
4) d	11) b	18) b	25) d
5) b	12) a	19) a	
6) b	13) a	20) a	
7) a	14) d	21) b	

3) Student Handout 11-H, "Prayer Service: Forgiveness" (found at the end of this chapter), is provided as a way of closing the study of this unit. Select hymns to be sung at the beginning and at the end of the service. Some contemporary hymns that fit are "Turn to Me" by John Foley, in *Glory and Praise*, vol. 1 (Phoenix: North American Liturgy Resources, 1977), and "Create in Me a Clean Heart" by John Michael Talbot. Hymns from the period of this chapter are the Resurrection hymn "Jesus Christ Is Risen Today," which is based on a fourteenth-century song "Surrexit Christus Hodie," and "O Sons and Daughters" by Jean Tisserand of the fifteenth century; both of these hymns stress Jesus' saving power, and many students should know them. Before the prayer service, have the students review their responses to the personal reflection exercise in this chapter. Being a sinner and being forgiven is the subject of the prayer service reflection.

11

The Black Death

1) A Description of the Disease from *A Distant Mirror* by Barbara W. Tuchman

. . . The diseased . . . showed strange black swellings about the size of an egg or an apple in the armpits and groin. The swellings oozed blood and pus and were followed by spreading boils and black blotches on the skin from internal bleeding. The sick suffered severe pain and died quickly within five days of the first symptoms. As the disease spread, other symptoms of continuous fever and spitting of blood appeared instead of the swellings or buboes. These victims coughed and sweated heavily and died even more quickly, within three days or less, sometimes in 24 hours. In both types everything that issued from the body . . . smelled foul. Depression and despair accompanied the physical symptoms, and before the end "death is seen seated on the face."

2) The Plague in England from an Eyewitness Account by Thomas Walsingham

In the year of grace 1349, . . . a great mortality of mankind advanced over the world; beginning in the regions of the north and east, and ending with so great a destruction that scarcely half of the people remained. Then towns once full of men became destitute of inhabitants; and so violently did the pestilence increase that the living were scarce able to bury the dead. Indeed, in certain houses of men of religion, scarcely two out of twenty men survived. It was estimated by many that hardly a tenth part of mankind had been left alive. A murrain [pestilence] among animals followed immediately upon this pestilence; then rents ceased; then the land, because of the lack of tenants, who were nowhere to be found, remained uncultivated. So great misery followed from these evils that the world was never afterward able to return to its former state.

Fortune, Empress of the World

Written by a Wandering Medieval Poet

O Fortune,
   variable
as the moon,
   always dost thou
   wax and wane.
Detestable life,
   first dost thou mistreat us,
   and then, whimsically,
thou heedest our desires.
   As the sun melts the ice,
   so dost thou dissolve
both poverty and power.

   Monstrous
   and empty fate,
thou, turning wheel,
   art mean,
   voiding
good health at thy will.
   Veiled
   in obscurity,
thou dost attack
   me also.
   To thy cruel pleasure
I bare my back.

   Thou dost
   withdraw
my health and virtue,
   thou dost
   threaten
my emotion and weakness with torture.
   At this hour,
   therefore, let us
pluck the strings without delay.
   Let us mourn
   together,
for fate crushes the brave.

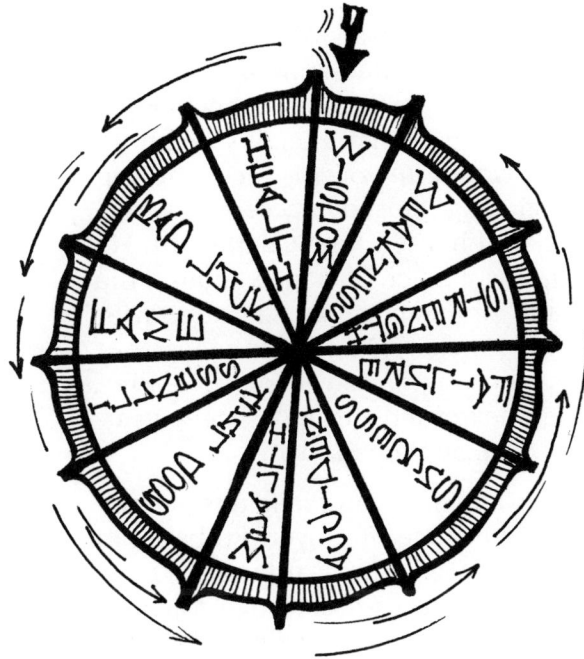

I lament Fortune's blows
   with weeping eyes,
for she extorts from me
   her gifts,
now pregnant
   and prodigal,
now lean
   and sear.

Once was I seated
   on Fortune's throne,
crowned with a garland
   of prosperity.
In the bloom
   of my felicity
I was struck down
   and robbed of all my glory.

At the turn of Fortune's wheel,
   one is deposed,
another is lifted on high
   to enjoy a brief felicity.
Uneasy sits the king—
   let him beware his ruin,
for beneath the axle of the wheel
   we read the name of Hecuba.

Saint Joan of Arc (1412–31): A Brief Biography

During the Hundred Years' War, the English invaded Normandy. After some decisive victories, the English forced the French king, Charles VI, to agree that after his death an English king would rule over France. The son of the French king refused to accept this treaty and declared himself King Charles VII. He had the loyalty of much of France, though the Burgundians for the most part still sided with the English. However, Charles' army was not strong, and he was not an inspiring leader. Help came unexpectedly from a sixteen-year-old countrywoman named Joan.

Joan was intelligent and religious, spending much of her time in prayer. Probably in answer to her prayers, she heard the voices of several saints, including the archangel Michael. They told her to go to the new king of France and to have him crowned in the cathedral of Rheims; in this way, the French people would be united. Joan went to an army camp near her home and succeeded in convincing an officer that although she was a teenager without political experience, she was talking sense. He gave her a bodyguard of knights to take her safely to the king. Discouraged by the odds against him, Charles gave Joan armor and a horse, and put her in charge of a unit of soldiers. When she arrived at Orléans, she amazingly led the troops, and they drove off the English who were attacking the city.

Her success seemed so impossible that the French soldiers were sure she was sent from heaven, while the English, equally impressed, said she was a witch working with the power of the devil. Meanwhile, Joan succeeded in persuading Charles to come to Rheims with her.

His coronation was the sign to the people that Charles was really king of France. A short time after the crowning, Joan was betrayed by a group of Burgundians who captured her and turned her over to the English. At a local inquisition composed of a French bishop and his court—all of them on the side of the English—she was condemned as a witch. At nineteen years of age, Joan suffered the fate of witches; she was burned at the stake.

The execution of Joan brought new courage to the French king and his people. After twenty years, they drove out the English. In 1456, the pope reviewed Joan's trial and declared her innocent of all charges. She was canonized a saint in 1920 and made patron saint of France.

Savonarola

Segments from a Play by Urban Nagle

Characters: Benedetto, Savonarola, Umberto, Ricardo, Pope Alexander

[*The city of Florence is being pressured to turn against Savonarola; nevertheless, he has just finished collecting jewels and other luxuries from the people of the city in order to feed the hungry. Now two other Dominicans and he receive a message.*]

Bened: (*Suddenly*) Oh, I almost forgot. A messenger from the convent of Santissima Annunziata gave me this. (*He holds up a scroll.*)

Savon: (*Opening it*) Nothing is important now. Oh! A copy of a brief from [Pope] Alexander. And why did he send it to [the Franciscans]? (*Beginning to read*) "We have heard from many persons worthy of belief that a *certain* Fra Girolamo Savonarola, *said to be vicar of* St. Mark's, hath disseminated pernicious doctrines to the scandal and great grief of souls." I can't read it very well. Try it, Umberto.

Umber: (*Picking up the thread from there, as the rest of the community stands by tensely*) "We had already commanded him by his vows of holy obedience to suspend his sermons and come to Us to seek pardon for his errors; but he refused to obey and alleged various excuses which We too graciously accepted, hoping to convert him by Our clemency."

Savon: That's a lie.

Umber: You couldn't possibly have gone to Rome.

Savon: Go on.

Umber: "But on the contrary he persisted still more in his obstinacy; wherefore by a second brief We commanded him under pain of excommunication to unite the Convent of St. Mark to the Tusco-Roman congregation recently created by Us."

Savon: That brief was not addressed to me.

Umber: And by vote we all appealed.

Bened: It would have been impossible.

Savon: So? . . .

Umber: "Therefore We now command ye on all festivals and in the presence of the people, to declare the said Fra Girolamo excommunicate . . .

Savon: (*Walking across the room*) I knew it. I knew it. (*Turning to Umberto*) Can there be more?

Umber: ". . . and to be held as such by all men for his failure to obey Our apostolic admonitions and commands."

Ricar: There's apostolic irony. The one thing you tried not to do.

Umber: "And under pain of the same penalty all are forbidden to assist him . . . or approve him either by word or deed inasmuch as he is an excommunicated person and suspected of heresy." (*Pause.*) That's all. . . .

Savon: Well, do I look the same? Has my skin turned black? Shall I seek a cave in the woods lest some be contaminated? Shall I walk through the streets crying "Unclean"? (*Picking up [a donated] necklace*) Excommunicated. (*Looking at the necklace*) A woman wept and laughed and wept and gave the children this as a token of a new life. And thousands of men and thousands of women throughout the city have swept and garnished their souls. (*Pause.*) He doesn't know those things, does he? . . .

[*The civil authorities have arrested Savonarola and have been torturing him for several days to force a confession. In this prison cell, he is lying partially delirious.*]

Savon: They turned the rack . . . and when I said . . . it was all for God's glory . . . they wrote down "human glory" . . . and I think I signed a paper.

Ricar: Yes, Fra Girolamo. But a forced confession doesn't mean anything. . . . I came to tell you that our appeal isn't going very well.

Savon: I don't care about the appeal. I only want them . . . to write the truth. They wrote down that I wanted to depose the Pope . . . to reform the clergy . . .

Ricar: Didn't you?

Savon: Not by myself. I wanted the proper authorities . . . to act. Then I signed a confession saying that I was a false prophet . . . that I perverted the people. They won't believe that . . . will they?

Ricar: Not if they lived with you. . . .

Ricardo leaves. Savonarola tries to rise and falls back unconscious. In his delirium, Pope Alexander appears to him.

Savon: (*Bitterly*) Why have you done this to me?

Alex: Come, my son. You speak as though you were the one aggrieved.

Savon: . . . Are you not guilty of simony? Confess!

Alex: I came to discuss your case—not mine. This is *your* day of confession.

Savon: I have nothing to confess. I have ever done as I thought right.

Alex: Then hear my side, lest you die in bitterness—because I think you are going to die. When a friar decides to reform the Church, he does not begin by assuming dictatorship of a city, because the temporal interest of the Church may clash with the spiritual ones. Then he does not defy the orders of his spiritual superiors. Nor does he call a general council to depose those who disagree with him. It is presumption enough to pass judgment on your superiors without destroying the machinery of government. If I were convinced of your innocence, I could hardly save you because your democracy of Florence has [turned against] you. As it is, I am convinced only of your stupidity.

Savon: Let me explain. I am innocent. I can prove . . .

[*Alexander's image fades.*]

184

Medieval Tales of Mary and Saint Martin

1) The Horrible Death of a Blasphemer of the Virgin

Also near Cluny, as I have heard from many, it happened recently, namely, in the year of our Lord 1246, when I was there, that a certain tavern keeper on the Saturday before Advent, in selling wine and taking his pay, blasphemed Christ during the whole day. But when about the ninth hour, in the presence of a multitude of men, he had sworn by the tongue of the blessed Virgin, by blaspheming her he lost the use of his tongue, and by speaking basely of her, suddenly stricken in the presence of the multitude, he fell dead.

2) A Robber Delivered from Hanging Because of His Prayers to the Virgin

Also we read that a certain robber had this much of good in him, that he always fasted on bread and water on the vigils of the blessed Mary, and, when he went forth to steal, he always said, "*Ave Maria,*" asking her not to permit him to die in that sin. When moreover he was captured and hung, he remained there three days and could not die. When he called out to the passers by, that they should summon a priest to him, and when the priest had come and the prefect and others, he was removed from the gallows, and said that a most beautiful virgin had held him up by the feet during the three days. Promising reform, he was let go free.

3) The Relics of St. Martin Healed Two Beggars Against Their Will

Moreover, although poverty and other tribulations are advantageous, yet certain ones abuse them. Accordingly we read that when the body of St. Martin was borne in procession it healed all the infirm who met it. Now there were near the church two wandering beggars, one blind, the other lame, who began to converse together and said, "See, the body of St. Martin is now being borne in procession, and if it catches us we shall be healed immediately, and no one in the future will give us any alms, but we shall have to work and labor with our own hands." Then the blind man said to the lame, "Get up on my shoulders because I am strong, and you who see well can guide me." They did this; but when they wished to escape, the procession overtook them; and since, on account of the throng, they were not able to get away, they were healed against their will.

Chaucer's Pardoner Tries to Sell His Indulgences

Excerpt from *The Canterbury Tales* by Geoffrey Chaucer

Oh, cursed sin of all evil! Oh treacherous murder, oh, wickedness! Oh, gluttony, luxury, and gambling! You blasphemer of Christ with vulgarity and large oaths, born of habit and pride! Alas, mankind, how can it be that you are so false and so unkind to your Creator, who made you and redeemed you with His precious heart's blood?

Now, good men, may God forgive you your trespasses and keep you from the sin of avarice! My holy pardon can cure you all, so long as you offer nobles [gold coins], or silver pennies, or else silver brooches, spoons, or rings. Bow your head before this holy document! Come on up, you wives, offer some of your wool! I will at once enter your names here on my roll, and you shall go into the bliss of heaven. I absolve you by my great power—you who will offer—as clean and as white as you were born. And there, ladies and gentlemen, that's the way I preach. And may Jesus Christ, who is our soul's physician, grant that you receive His pardon, for that is the best; I will not deceive you.

But, sirs, I forgot one word in my tale: I have relics and pardons in my bag, as fine as any man's in England, which were given to me by the Pope's own hand. If any of you wish, out of piety, to make an offering and to receive my absolution, come up at once, kneel down here, and humbly receive my pardon. Or else you can accept pardon as you travel, fresh and new at the end of every mile, just so you make another offering each time of nobles or pennies which are good and genuine. It is an honor to everyone here that you have available a pardoner with sufficient power to absolve you as you ride through the country, in case of accidents which might happen. Perhaps one or two of you will fall off your horses and break your necks. See what security it is to all of you that I happen to be in your group and can absolve you, both high and low, when the soul passes from the body. I suggest that our Host, here, shall be first; for he is most enveloped in sin. Come on, Sir Host, make the first offering right now, and you can kiss each one of the relics. Yes, for just a groat [large coin]! Unbuckle your purse at once.

"No, no!" said the Host. "Then I would be under Christ's curse! Stop this, it won't do, as I hope to prosper!"

Quiz on Chapter 11

_____ 1) A French pope caused the center of the Church to move from Rome to **(a)** Avignon **(b)** Toulouse **(c)** Lyons **(d)** Innsbruck.

_____ 2) At the time of the pope's removal from Rome, the French were at war with the English; this war was called the **(a)** War of Succession **(b)** Cathari Crusade **(c)** Hundred Years' War **(d)** War of Clement.

_____ 3) One of many reasons people objected to the pope's living away from Rome was that **(a)** construction stopped on Saint Peter's **(b)** taxes went up **(c)** Rome was more centrally located **(d)** they preferred Italian food.

_____ 4) The Black Death was transmitted by **(a)** dogs **(b)** lice **(c)** cats **(d)** fleas.

_____ 5) It is estimated that this percentage of Europe was killed by the plague: **(a)** one-fourth **(b)** one-third **(c)** one-half **(d)** five-eighths.

_____ 6) The Church was severely damaged by the plague because **(a)** people stopped attending church **(b)** many priests were killed **(c)** people blamed God and burned down churches **(d)** priests and monks were somehow spared.

_____ 7) This person applied pressure on the pope to return to Rome: **(a)** Catherine of Siena **(b)** Thérèse de Lisieux **(c)** Francis of Assisi **(d)** Francis Borgia.

_____ 8) Right before the selection of Pope Martin V, there were this many people claiming to be pope: **(a)** one **(b)** two **(c)** three **(d)** four.

_____ 9) The council that finally settled the issue about who was pope was the Council of **(a)** Pisa **(b)** Milan **(c)** Nante **(d)** Constance.

_____ 10) This family controlled Florence for years and was finally driven out by Savonarola and his followers: **(a)** Borgias **(b)** Medici **(c)** Colonnas **(d)** Sartos.

_____ 11) When the pope commands that priests are not to administer the sacraments to people of a certain place, the place is under **(a)** excommunication **(b)** interdict **(c)** anathema **(d)** interrogation.

_____ 12) The fate of Savonarola was that he **(a)** was burned at the stake **(b)** died as a cardinal **(c)** retired to a monastery **(d)** became Pope Innocent VI.

_____ 13) Germany at this time was **(a)** split into small states **(b)** united under the Austrian flag **(c)** an enemy of the British **(d)** the most powerful country in Europe.

_____ 14) The movement or rebirth of interest in Greek and Roman culture is called **(a)** Aristotelianism **(b)** Reformation **(c)** Reichstag **(d)** Renaissance.

_____ 15) The first book printed by Gutenberg was **(a)** _The Canterbury Tales_ **(b)** _Doctor Faustus_ **(c)** the Bible **(d)** _Imitation of Christ_.

_____ 16) The rebirth of Greek and Roman culture focused interest on **(a)** humankind more than religion **(b)** religion more than humankind **(c)** contemporary culture **(d)** heaven.

_____ 17) This pope had six children before he assumed the papacy and has gone down in history as one of the most scandalous popes: **(a)** Nicholas V **(b)** Martin V **(c)** Alexander VI **(d)** Celestine I.

_____ 18) This practice began as a way of people doing penance for their sins: **(a)** buying relics **(b)** granting indulgences **(c)** persecuting Jews **(d)** the Inquisition.

_____ 19) These were boys taken from their Christian families by the Turks and raised as Muslim soldiers: **(a)** janissaries **(b)** mercenaries **(c)** caravansaries **(d)** hara-kiries.

_____ 20) The Eastern and Western Church were temporarily reunited when **(a)** John VIII sought aid from the West to fight the Turks **(b)** the patriarch of Constantinople initiated a secret reconciliation **(c)** Nicholas V called a council at Antioch **(d)** Rome was under attack by the French.

_____ 21) Constantinople is now known as **(a)** Islamabad **(b)** Istanbul **(c)** Beirut **(d)** Nicosia.

_____ 22) This city was called the "third Rome": **(a)** Kiev **(b)** Belgrade **(c)** Alexandria **(d)** Moscow.

_____ 23) Ivan the Great freed Russia from the **(a)** Cossacks **(b)** Magyars **(c)** Vikings **(d)** Mongols.

_____ 24) One commodity that the Portuguese were especially interested in obtaining in the East was **(a)** silk **(b)** the abacus **(c)** the clock **(d)** spices.

_____ 25) John Cabot sailed across the Atlantic and landed at **(a)** Hudson Bay **(b)** Greenland **(c)** Maine **(d)** Newfoundland.

Prayer Service: Forgiveness

Opening Hymn

Leader: Let us remember that God is present here. Jesus Christ died for our sins, and we are forgiven if we will have faith and seek to reform our lives.

Reading of Mark 2:15–17

Reflection

Leader: Let us reflect silently on our experiences of being sinners and of being forgiven.

Prayer Adapted from Luke 17:3–4

Leader: If your brother or sister does something wrong,

All: reprove him or her,

Leader: and if he or she is sorry,

All: forgive.

Leader: And if someone wrongs you seven times a day and seven times comes back to you and says, "I am sorry,"

All: you must forgive.

Leader: Let us each ask for forgiveness. And, let us pray that our Church continually reforms itself into the People of God, the Body of Christ.

All: Amen.

Closing Hymn

CHAPTER 12

A Reforming Church: 1500–1600

Major Concepts

A. Martin Luther initiated the Reformation by calling on Christians to believe in Jesus, not rely on indulgences; he also stressed a return to the Bible, preaching the Word, and the priesthood of all believers. His excommunication split Germany between Catholics and Protestants.

B. John Calvin moved further away than Luther from Roman Catholic beliefs, especially by articulating predestination and the sole authority of the Bible as freely interpreted by the individual.

C. Henry VIII, in his desire for a male successor, demanded a divorce. When the pope refused, he declared himself head of the Church in England. Henry rejected Protestantism and maintained many Roman traditions, but he demanded absolute loyalty to the Church of England and to himself.

D. The Council of Trent managed to cleanse the Church of some corrupt practices and to clearly state church teachings, but it failed to reunite the whole Christian community. Restoration of the Church was aided by new orders like the Jesuits and by holy people like Teresa of Ávila.

E. Despite the religious turmoil in Europe, Catholic Christianity was being spread by intrepid missionaries working in Asia, South America, and, to a lesser degree, Africa.

Activities for Concept A
Martin Luther initiated the Reformation by calling on Christians to believe in Jesus, not rely on indulgences; he also stressed a return to the Bible, preaching the Word, and the priesthood of all believers. His excommunication split Germany between Catholics and Protestants. (Pages 206–215 of the student text.)

Review Questions and Exercises from the Student Text

Question 1: What were the Ninety-five Theses and why were they so important?
Answer: The Ninety-five Theses were statements made by Martin Luther about a whole range of topics—indulgences, sin and the forgiveness of sins, papal power—that he wished to discuss and debate with anyone who was interested. These theses were published all over Germany and caused a real stir among theologians and many other people. Luther's theses were the beginnings of the Reformation movement.

Question 2: What were the main reforms that Luther thought the Church should make?
Answer: Luther insisted that the practice of selling indulgences should be eliminated. Stress should be placed on faith rather than on indulgences or even on good works done solely to gain heaven. Practices not explicitly approved by the Bible should be considered superfluous.

Question 3: Why were people so concerned about gaining indulgences? How did this lead to a corruption of the original meaning associated with indulgences?
Answer: Many people had a real fear of purgatory, a state of purifying punish-

ment before one was permitted into heaven. Indulgences were a way around purgatory; they were reparation for sins. After a while, some people forgot that even if they bought indulgences, unless they had pure hearts and sincere faith, the indulgences meant nothing.

Question 4: Why was Luther excommunicated? Why was the situation more complicated due to political factors? What made excommunication such a terrible penalty?

Answer: Luther was excommunicated because he would not retract his criticisms of indulgences, because he placed the Bible as the sole source of authority for Christians, and because he would not go to Rome to answer charges against him. The situation became complicated because some of the lesser rulers in German lands, in following Luther, could throw off the authority of Rome and of the Holy Roman emperor. [*Teacher's note:* These rulers were irritated by taxes paid to Rome and to the emperor.] Excommunication was terrible because the civil rulers were bound to carry out its execution. Thus, an excommunicated person became an outlaw.

Question 5: What rather unexpected effects did Luther's teaching have on German society? Was he pleased with the results?

Answer: Luther's emphasis on the priesthood of all believers was understood as an encouragement of all people to exert their rights. To some extent, the Peasants' Revolt was a result of Luther's views (although later Luther would condemn the excesses of this rebellion). Luther's teachings split the German states into two groups. Luther never intended so much divisiveness.

Question 6: What were the three main emphases that Luther made in religious belief that differed from Catholic tradition?

Answer: Luther maintained that the Bible was the sole authority in a Christian's life, that humans were saved by faith alone, and that all believers shared in priesthood.

Question 7: Why are followers of Luther called Protestants?

Answer: In 1525 the German assembly and Charles V gave Catholics the freedom to practice their religion in any German state, but Luther's followers were restricted to areas where they were already organized. Luther's partisans protested and thus were called Protestants.

Question 8: How did Erasmus criticize both war and the selling of indulgences? How was his criticism different from that of Luther?

Answer: In his public lectures and many writings, Erasmus called for changes. In his dialogue on military affairs, the only reason given for going off to war is to gain booty, but even this is squandered away. Also, the swaggering soldier is not worried about even the most heinous crimes because he can buy indulgences that he thinks will remit his sins. Erasmus's "Military Affairs" makes much the same point about the abuse of indulgences as did Luther, but Erasmus couches his message in humorous dialogue.

12

Question 9: How was the religion of a region of Germany decided? Do you think this process would be acceptable today?

Answer: The ruler of each German state could decide what religion he would allow. The decree of 1525 said that Catholics could practice anywhere; in effect though, local rulers, who were often motivated by political concerns, controlled the choices of all the people in their areas.

Question 10: On a map, trace the movement of the Reformation through Europe.

Answer: Sweden, Denmark, Iceland, Holland, Scotland, Finland, Switzerland, Moravia, and northern Germany came to be Protestant centers. Italy, France, Spain, southern Germany, and Poland stayed with Rome. Russia, Greece, and other Eastern European countries maintained ties with Orthodoxy.

Other Questions and Activities for Discussion

1) Inviting a Lutheran minister into class to discuss Martin Luther, the person and the reformer, and his contribution to Roman Catholicism is highly encouraged. Ask him to describe reforms that Luther pointed out that are now accepted by the Roman Catholic Church.

2) The film *Protest and Reform* from the series The Christians (ROA Films, 40 min., color) summarizes the main currents of the Reformation: Martin Luther and the Reformation, the publication of the Bible for common people, the formation of the Church of England. The photography is excellent; it shows many of the sites and portraits of the important figures of this period. Some students might find the film slow moving, but it is quite a good summary.

3) Student Handout 12-A, "The Sale of Indulgences" (found at the end of this chapter), contains two readings: (*a*) portions of a letter written by German Archbishop Albert to his subordinates giving them instructions about contributions for indulgences, from which the proceeds would go to building Saint Peter's Basilica in Rome, and (*b*) a section from a sermon about indulgences by Tetzel, the opponent of Luther. Either assign students to read the articles to the class—delivering each speech with the appropriate drama—or, give the students copies of the handout to read.

After the students have heard or read the sections, discuss them; you might ask the following:
- Was the building of Saint Peter's Basilica important enough to justify the selling of indulgences as a common practice?
- To what in Archbishop Albert's letter would Luther object?
- If Catholics want to build a church today, how do they go about it?
- What is your reaction to Tetzel's speech?
- What fears in his audience does Tetzel use to convince them to buy indulgences?
- Tetzel was quite effective in his day. Would this sermon be effective today? If so, why? If not, why not?
- Why would Luther and Erasmus object to Tetzel's approach to sin and forgiveness?
- If you were a poor person listening to Tetzel, how would you feel?
- Why do you think the Church stopped people like Tetzel and Archbishop Albert?

4) Luther's loyalty to the Church and to the pope early on in his life cannot be overemphasized to students. To illustrate this, read aloud to the students the following passages from his letter to Pope Leo X; Luther wanted to reform the Church, not break from it.

An Open Letter to Pope Leo X

To Leo X, Pope at Rome, Martin Luther wishes salvation in Christ Jesus our Lord. Amen.

Living among the monsters of this age with whom I am now for the third year waging war, I am compelled occasionally to look up to you, Leo, most blessed father, and to think of you. Indeed, since you are occasionally regarded as the sole cause of my warfare, I cannot help thinking of you. . . .

I freely vow that I have, to my knowledge, spoken only good and honorable words concerning you whenever I have thought of you. If I had ever done otherwise, I myself could by no means condone it, but should agree entirely with the

12

judgment which others have formed of me; and I should do nothing more gladly than recant such indiscretion and impiety. . . .

I have, to be sure, sharply attacked ungodly doctrines in general, and I have snapped at my opponents, not because of their bad morals, but because of their ungodliness. Rather than repent this in the least, I have determined to persist in that fervent zeal and to despise the judgment of men, following the example of Christ who in his zeal called his opponents "a brood of vipers." . . .

. . . I never intended to attack the Roman Curia or to raise any controversy concerning it. But when I saw all efforts to save it were hopeless, I despised it. . . . Then I turned to the quiet and peaceful study of the Holy Scriptures so that I might be helpful to my brothers around me. When I had made some progress in these studies, Satan opened his eyes and then filled his servant Johann Eck [a priest who challenged Luther to a public debate], a notable enemy of Christ, with an insatiable lust for glory and thus aroused him to drag me unawares to a debate, seizing me by means of one little word which I had let slip concerning the primacy of the Roman church. Then that boastful braggart, frothing and gnashing his teeth, declared that he would risk everything for the glory of God and the honor of the Apostolic See. Puffed up with the prospect of abusing your authority, he looked forward with great confidence to a victory over me. . . . When the debate ended badly for the sophist, an unbelievable madness overcame the man, for he believed that it was his fault alone which was responsible for my disclosing all the infamy of Rome.

. . . I do not consider it absurd if I now forget your exalted office and do what brotherly love demands. I have no desire to flatter you in so serious and dangerous a matter. If men do not perceive that I am your friend and your most humble subject in this matter, there is One who understands and judges (John 8:50).

From this letter, Luther's intent to reform is clear. Also obvious is Luther's forceful personality, which would allow little opposition to stand firm against his views.

5) Student Handout 12-B, "Luther" (found at the end of this chapter), contains two scenes from John Osborne's play *Luther*. The play was highly praised, not only as a work of art but also as a balanced picture of Luther. Select a student to play Luther and another to play Cajetan. In the first scene Luther preaches against indulgences and enunciates his belief in salvation through faith alone. In the second scene he answers Cajetan's questions. When the scenes have been acted out, ask your students these questions:
- Why would Luther's arguments make sense to poor people especially?
- How would people react today if priests used such fiery language in homilies?
- What is your reaction to his sermon?
- In the second scene, how is Cajetan portrayed?
- What main point about Luther's beliefs is highlighted in the second scene?

6) Here is a hands-on project that your students might enjoy doing—Reformation bumper stickers or T-shirts. The instructions follow:

If you were Luther and you wanted to get the word out about your proposed reforms and if you lived in this century, one method you might use is bumper stickers, another might be monogrammed T-shirts. Considering what you know of Luther's main beliefs, design a Reformation bumper sticker or T-shirt logo.

When the class is finished, let each student display his or her design. The class should select the best three, four, or five designs for display on the bulletin board.

7) Assign one or two students to go through the hymnals used in their parishes and find hymns by Luther.

12

Activities for Concept B
John Calvin moved further away than Luther from Roman Catholic beliefs, especially by articulating predestination and the sole authority of the Bible as freely interpreted by the individual. (Pages 215–216 of the student text.)

Review Questions and Exercises from the Student Text

Question 11: How did Calvin take the Reformation many steps further than Luther? What relationship did Calvin see between church and state?

Answer: Calvin rejected the sacraments as Catholics understand them, including the real presence of Jesus in the Eucharist. Complete reliance on the authority of the Bible was one of his main teachings. He also taught predestination. Calvin believed in a sort of theocracy in which people conformed to a Christian lifestyle, by law.

Question 12: What is predestination? Why is this notion so different from Catholic belief?

Answer: Predestination means that God has marked certain people for salvation. Our fates are predestined. Catholics believe that salvation is given to those who accept it in faith and action and that people have free will by which they accept or reject God.

Other Questions and Activities for Discussion

1) Three religious groups that are rooted in the Calvinistic tradition are Methodists, Presbyterians, and the United Church of Christ. Each church has its own particular interpretation of Calvin; for example, most Methodists do not believe in absolute predestination. You might want to invite a minister from one of these churches to discuss the ways in which Calvin influenced the development of their religious tradition. If necessary, students could be assigned to outline for class members the essential beliefs of each of these religious bodies.

2) In order to discuss a very narrow, literal interpretation of the Bible, you might do the following: Tell the students to find one passage each from the Christian Scriptures that, if taken literally, would lead to very harsh results, for example, the passages about gouging out one's eyes if they are a source of evil. After the students have found their passages, call on a student to read a selection out loud. Then ask these questions:
- What would be the result if you took this passage literally and did or believed what it says?
- What does the passage really mean?

Remind your students that the Bible is an infinite source of divine wisdom, a place to encounter Jesus. However, reading the Scriptures knowledgeably takes study.

3) Over the years terrible prejudices have developed between Catholics and Protestants. While efforts are being made toward reaching common understandings and appreciations between religious groups, much more progress is needed. To help your students understand earlier, pre–Vatican II, attitudes toward Protestants, assign the students to interview people who would have been in their twenties or thirties before Vatican II. The interviews should focus on answering these two questions:
- What were common beliefs about and practices toward Protestants in the days before Vatican II?
- What were people taught to think about relationships with non-Catholics, especially Protestants?

12

194

4) Assign some students to prepare brief reports about these different denominations: Baptists, Methodists, Presbyterians, United Church of Christ, Mennonites, Dutch Reformed, Congregationalists. The reports should answer questions such as who started them, why they were started, where they began, and what their present status is.

5) Finally, discuss ecumenism with your students.
- Why should Catholics want to stay in dialogue with Protestant denominations?
- How would the world be a different place if there were fewer misunderstandings between religious groups?

Activities for Concept C

Henry VIII, in his desire for a male successor, demanded a divorce. When the pope refused, he declared himself head of the Church in England. Henry rejected Protestantism and maintained many Roman traditions, but he demanded absolute loyalty to the Church of England and to himself. (Pages 217–219 of the student text.)

Review Questions and Exercises from the Student Text

Question 13: Why did Henry VIII break from the Catholic Church? Why would the people of England generally understand, if not support, this separation?

Answer: The pope would not allow Henry to divorce his wife, Catherine of Aragon. Henry needed a son to succeed him; Catherine did not give him one. People would understand his desire to have a son; every time a king did not have a clear-cut successor there were wars among factions, which was disastrous for the country. The debacle of the Avignon papacy strained the relationship between the Roman Church and the English. Furthermore, the pope who refused Henry's request for a divorce was under the power of the Spanish king [*teacher's note:* the enemy of England]. To refuse to support Henry became an act of treason.

Personal Reflection Exercise

> Loyalty to one's country is certainly a value that is important. But how far can one go in loyalty to one's country? In this chapter, whole countries left the Catholic Church because of their leaders' commands. Would this be the proper motivation for a change in religious belief? List as many ways as possible in which government policy or power does or might conflict with personal moral choice. How do governmental decisions influence morality? Describe the dilemmas created for Christians. When religious convictions and governmental demands conflict, which should take precedence?

Other Questions and Activities for Discussion

1) Especially if you have not had a guest speaker so far, invite an Episcopalian priest to discuss the Church of England. Ask her or him to stress the similarities between the Roman Catholic and Episcopalian beliefs and practices.

2) Student Handout 12-C, "Thomas More and Henry VIII" (found at the end of this chapter), consists of two cuttings from the play *A Man for All Seasons* by Robert Bolt. In the first section of the handout, Henry VIII confronts More, asking for More's support in the divorce proceedings. More wants to be loyal to both his king and his God. Later, when on trial before the parliament, More has been framed by several perjuring witnesses who say that he rejected the king as head of the Church of England.

12

More, in fact, had never either denied or accepted Henry as head of the Church; he had maintained strict silence. In the last scene, More finally professes his faith in the Catholic Church.

Select four students to take the roles on the handout and ask them to perform the cuttings in readers' theater style. This play might well be done before the students complete the personal reflection exercise.

3) The film *A Matter of Conscience: Henry VIII and Thomas More* (Learning Corporation of America, 31 min., color) contains cuttings, including the ones in Student Handout 12-C, from the movie version of *A Man for All Seasons*. It highlights More's standing alone for what he believes. The full-length movie of *A Man for All Seasons* could probably be rented in videocassette.

4) Student Handout 12-D, "Thomas More Sends Greetings to His Friend Master Erasmus" (found at the end of this chapter), contains part of a letter to More's very close friend, Erasmus. To guard against the students' receiving the impression that Thomas More was uncritical of some of the Church's ills, point out that the two men agreed on many issues, including the necessity of church reform, but they both opposed Luther and Henry. The excerpt from his letter also illustrates More's sense of humor.

Activities for Concept D

The Council of Trent managed to cleanse the Church of some corrupt practices and to clearly state church teachings, but it failed to reunite the whole Christian community. Restoration of the Church was aided by new orders like the Jesuits and by holy people like Teresa of Ávila. (Pages 219–223 of the student text.)

Review Questions and Exercises from the Student Text

Question 14: The results of the Council of Trent were mixed. Why? Give examples of successes and failures of the council.

Answer: There were political pressures on the members of the Council of Trent. Attendance varied, both in numbers and in nationalities represented. Successes included reaffirming and defining Catholic teachings, cleaning up some of the corrupt practices like bishops living outside their dioceses, and establishing more seminaries. The great failure was the unhealed split between Catholics and Protestants.

Question 15: How were politics involved even in the Council of Trent? Is it possible to completely separate religion and politics?

Answer: Charles V and King Francis I of France had been at war, thus making travel to a council practically impossible. Once the war was over, to get these rulers to agree on a place for the council was difficult. The second session was sparsely attended because France and Germany were at war once again. To completely separate politics and religion seems impossible.

Question 16: Who are the Jesuits? Why did they play an important role in the Catholic Restoration?

Answer: Founded by Saint Ignatius of Loyola, the Jesuit order of priests and brothers is especially dedicated to service to the pope. The Jesuits have been well known for their work in schools and universities and in missionary areas. The rigorous academic training that was required of the Jesuits produced very well-educated teachers who, in turn, gave their students a solid Catholic education. The Jesuits also trained seminarians very well. Thus, they aided the Catholic Restoration.

Question 17: Teresa of Ávila was very influential in monastic reform in Spain. Why was she such an influential person? Why did the Carmelites oppose her?

Answer: Saint Teresa had tremendous zeal in opening houses of nuns that were devoted to the contemplative life—a life of silence, prayer, work, meditation. She was also very holy, living in faith, hope, and love. Her correspondence was voluminous and reflects a keen intelligence and an eye for the practical details needed to found convents. Unreformed Carmelites opposed her because they did not approve of the reforms she was making and because they did not like being confronted with their own lack of commitment.

Other Questions and Activities for Discussion

1) Discuss these issues about reform with your students:
- Why are institutions always difficult to change?
- Why would some people in the Church at the time of the Reformation oppose any reforms?
- To get an understanding of the difficulty of making reforms, list a number of aspects of the national government that people seem constantly to say need changing. Why has so little been done to reform these matters?
- Are there any problems around school that need reform? What would complicate reforming these matters?

2) On a large wall map, point out Trent to your students. Then ask them these queries:
- If France and Germany were at war, bishops coming from what countries would have a hard time getting to Trent?
- What natural obstacles confronted travelers to Trent?

3) Students could be assigned to report on various aspects of Saint Ignatius of Loyola's life. Invite a Jesuit brother or priest to discuss the dynamism of Ignatius and his contributions to the Catholic Restoration.

4) So that your students can comprehend the amount of traveling over terrible roads that was undertaken by Saint Teresa, trace on a wall map some of the Spanish towns in which she established convents: Ávila, Málagon, Valladolid, Toledo, Pastrana, Salamanca, and Alba de Tormes.

Activities for Concept E

Despite the religious turmoil in Europe, Catholic Christianity was being spread by intrepid missionaries working in Asia, South America, and, to a lesser degree, Africa. (Pages 223–227 of the student text.)

12

Review Questions and Exercises from the Student Text

Question 18: On a map, trace the spread of Christianity through Asia and South America. What problems arose because of the relationship between missionaries and Western governments?

Answer: Asian countries that you may wish to point out are India (especially Goa and Kerala), Sri Lanka, Burma, Thailand, Indonesia, Malaysia (especially Malacca where Francis Xavier stayed), the Philippines, Japan (especially Nagasaki), Macau. In South America, point out that Central America was actually conquered first.

The Western explorers were more interested in becoming rich than in bringing souls to Jesus. Especially in the Philippines and in South America, the native peoples were made into virtual slaves of the Spaniards. While missionaries could preach to the people, they frequently were viewed as agents of foreign governments. Inevitably, acceptance of Christianity was part of being a conquered people.

Question 19: Why did the missionaries experience so little success in China and Japan?

Answer: The missionaries to China and Japan were considered barbarians who came from countries with vastly inferior cultures. Moreover, religious traditions in these two countries were centuries old and very well established. To accept Christianity was seen as accepting Western culture and power.

Question 20: How did the friars often have to protect the local people from the Spaniards?

Answer: The Spanish conquerors needed labor for the plantations they wished to start. Largely through the efforts of the friars, the Spaniards were prevented from completely enslaving the local people. Religious orders even began training programs for native people, but these were frequently hampered by Spaniards who wanted to keep the local population in ignorance.

Question 21: Why did the Indians of Central and South America become Christian?

Answer: Some of the Central and South American Indians really believed in Jesus. Some Indians felt that the Spanish god must be stronger than their gods because the Spaniards conquered them. Thus, these Indians believed because of a show of strength. Some converted just to be on the side of the Spanish rulers. [*Teacher's note:* The mixed motives for conversion left the missionaries with a lot of uncertainty about the commitments of their congregations. Also, some Indians continued with their previous religious practices, some of which were repugnant to the missionaries.]

Question 22: How were the Indians really second-class members of the Church for many years?

Answer: In many places Indians could not receive the Eucharist because it was feared that they would not understand it. For many more years Indians could not be ordained as priests. The Spanish crown forbade the ordination of native clergy. [*Teacher's note:* It was feared that a native clergy would lead rebellion against Spanish rule. Indeed this is what eventually happened in many places, notably Mexico and the Philippines.]

Question 23: Why is the division that splits Christians into many groups such a scandal to non-Christians?

Answer: Jesus came to teach people to love one another. The divisions in the Christian Church have caused hate to grow instead. It is a scandal to preach love and yet be divided.

Other Questions and Activities for Discussion

1) To explain further to your students the difficulties that missionaries faced in converting Japan, show them parts of the made-for-TV movie *Shogun*, based on the novel about feudal Japan by James Clavell. The entire production is far too long to show, but some segments picturing the seeming barbarity of the Dutch sailors when compared to the Japanese would illustrate why the Japanese generally rejected Western religion.

2) By the sixteenth century, China's Imperial Palace, or the Forbidden City, had been in existence for a century. The size and grandeur of the Forbidden City dwarf even Versailles. If slides or a movie about the Imperial Palace are available, you might

show these to your class. They can imagine Matteo Ricci's amazement at such splendor. Or, one or more students could prepare a report about the Forbidden City, discussing the number of rooms, the splendor of its decoration, the residents, the number of servants, the customs practiced there, the system for selecting civil servants, the religious customs, and so on.

Student Handout 12-E, "Letters About China from Saint Francis Xavier" (found at the end of this chapter), describes his attempts to enter this large forbidding country. These letters give us a sense of his awe at the greatness of China and of his tremendous courage.

3) If a slide series or a picture book about the collection of the National Palace Museum in Taipei is available, show your students the fabulous art treasures, many of which were created during the sixteenth century for the imperial families.

4) Discuss the whole notion of colonization with your students; here are some issues to raise:
- Colonization has a bad image today, but obviously from the sixteenth to the nineteenth centuries, European powers thought that it was their right to rule over other areas of the world. How would the colonizers affect your life if, let's say, you were an Inca in Peru? In what most basic ways would your life be different? [Groups may be formed to brainstorm on this question before general discussion.]
- Why do you think the Europeans thought that they could conquer any place they wanted and rule in the manner they thought best?
- Although the Church often protected the native people from abuses by colonizers, the Church accompanied the conquistadores and accepted converts among conquered people. How could the Church justify such a position? Would Jesus approve of supposedly Christian countries oppressing groups of non-Christians?
- If you were a native of a land conquered by a European power, how would you feel toward the foreign power and the Church associated with that power?

5) For additional research projects, students could prepare reports on the following topics: the conquest of the Aztecs or Incas; how Central American colonies were governed under the Spaniards; products that Central and South America gave the world; rebellions by native people against colonizers in Central and South America and in Asia, and how these rebellions affected the Church; how missionaries set up mission stations.

6) If your students do not know much about the geography of Central and South America, review important locations, using a large wall map.

7) Perhaps for a week, students could be assigned the task of bringing in articles that appear in the newspapers about Central and South American countries that were first colonized during the sixteenth century. Then discuss these questions:
- What is the situation of these countries now?
- What role does the Church play in these countries after four centuries?
- Is the Church on the side of the people or the oppressors?
The position of the Church in countries like Guatemala, Nicaragua, El Salvador, Peru, and the Philippines would be worth examining with your students.

Summary Activities for the Chapter

1) Once again, ask your students to write down their reflections about this week's service, community building, sacramental life, and spreading of the Word. In addition, you might ask them to record their reflections about how the Church and they need to reform themselves constantly. And/or, ask them to reflect on how, as citizens of developed countries and as Christians, they are part of a global society with interlocking dependencies with less developed countries.

2) If you have not already used these questions for daily quizzes, distribute Student Handout 12-F, "Quiz on Chapter 12" (found at the end of this chapter). The answers to the quiz are as follows:

1) b	9) c	17) b	25) b
2) a	10) c	18) d	26) a
3) d	11) a	19) b	27) c
4) b	12) d	20) c	28) a
5) c	13) a	21) b	29) d
6) c	14) a	22) c	30) b
7) d	15) d	23) c	31) a
8) a	16) c	24) d	32) d

3) Student Handout 12-G, "Prayer Service: For Christian Unity" (found at the end of this chapter), contains the Church's prayer for unity. Hymns you might use are "Turn to Me" by John Foley, in *Glory and Praise*, vol. 1 (Phoenix: North American Liturgy Resources, 1977), and "A Mighty Fortress Is Our God" by Martin Luther.

12

The Sale of Indulgences

1) The following excerpt is part of the instructions that Archbishop Albert of Mainz, Germany, gave to his subcommissioners. They were to sell indulgences to the people. Half of the income was for building Saint Peter's Basilica in Rome, and half was for Archbishop Albert.

The first grace [a person receives from the indulgence] is the complete remission of all sins; . . . moreover, through this remission of sins the punishment which one is obliged to undergo in Purgatory on account of the affront to the divine Majesty, is all remitted, and the pains of Purgatory completely blotted out. And although nothing is precious enough to be given in exchange for such a grace,—since it is the free gift of God and a grace beyond price,—yet in order that Christian believers may be more easily induced to procure the same, we establish the following rules, to wit: [What followed were the prayers and visits to churches that people must make in order to gain the indulgences.]

Respecting, now, the contribution to the chest, for the building of the said church of the chief of the apostles, the penitentiaries and confessors, after they have explained to those making confession the full remission and privileges, shall ask of them, for how much money or other temporal goods they would conscientiously go without the said most complete remission and privileges; and this shall be done in order that hereafter they may be brought the more easily to contribute. And because the conditions and occupations of men are so manifold and diverse that we cannot consider them individually, and impose specific rates accordingly, we have therefore concluded that the rates should be determined according to the recognized classes of persons.

2) Luther especially opposed the methods of Tetzel. Below is an extract from a sermon that Tetzel used to sell indulgences.

. . . In sin we are conceived,—alas! what bonds of sin encompass us, and how difficult and almost impossible it is to attain to the gate of salvation without divine aid; since He causes us to be saved, not by virtue of the good works which we accomplish, but through His divine mercy; it is necessary then to put on the armor of God.

You may obtain letters of safe conduct from the vicar of our Lord Jesus Christ, by means of which you are able to liberate your soul from the hands of the enemy, and convey it by means of contrition and confession, safe and secure from all pains of Purgatory, into the happy kingdom. For know that in these letters are stamped and engraven all the merits of Christ's passion there laid bare. Consider, that for each and every mortal sin it is necessary to undergo seven years of penitence after confession and contrition, either in this life or in Purgatory.

But with these confessional letters you will be able at any time in life to obtain full indulgence for all penalties imposed upon you. . . . Therefore throughout your whole life, whenever you wish to make confession, you may receive the same remission, . . . and afterwards, at the hour of death, a full indulgence as to all penalties and sins, and your share of all spiritual blessings that exists in the church militant and all it members.

. . . Are you not willing, then, for the fourth part of a florin, to obtain these letters, by virtue of which you may bring, not your money, but your divine and immortal soul safe and sound into the land of Paradise?

Wherefore I counsel, order, and by virtue of my authority as shepherd, I command that they shall receive together with me and other priests, this precious treasure. . . .

Luther

Excerpts from Two Scenes of a Play by John Osborne

Characters: Martin Luther, Cardinal Cajetan

The Castle Church, Wittenberg, October 31, 1517. Martin Luther walks swiftly to the pulpit and ascends it.

Martin: We are living in a dangerous time. We Christians seem to be wise outwardly and mad inwardly, and in this Jerusalem we have built there are blasphemies flourishing. . . . Today is the eve of All Saints, and the holy relics will be on show to you all; to the hungry ones whose lives are made satisfied by trinkets, by an imposing procession and the dressings up of all kinds of dismal things. You'll mumble for magic with lighted candles to St. Anthony for your erysipelas [a disease of the skin]; to St. Valentine for your epilepsy; to St. Sebastian for the pestilence. . . . And tomorrow the deacons will have to link hands to hold you back while you struggle to gawp at four hairs from Our Lady's head. . . . You'll sleep outside with the garbage in the streets all night so you can stuff your eyes like roasting birds on a scrap of swaddling clothes, eleven pieces from the original crib, one wisp of straw from the manger and a gold piece specially minted by three wise men for the occasion. . . . Shells for shells, empty things for empty men. You must be made to know that there's no security, there's no security at all, either in indulgences, holy busywork or anywhere in this world. It came to me. . . . I thought of the righteousness of God, and wished his gospel had never been put to paper for men to read, who demanded my love and made it impossible to return it. And I sat in my heap of pain until the words emerged and opened out. "The just shall live by faith." My pain vanished. . . . I could see the life I'd lost. No man is just because he does just works. The works are just if the man is just. If a man doesn't believe in Christ, not only are his sins mortal, but his good works. This I know; reason is the devil's whore, born of one stinking goat called Aristotle, which believes that good works make a good man. But the truth is that the just shall live by faith alone.

In Augsburg, a year later, [Cardinal Cajetan], the Pope's hightest representative in Germany, is questioning Luther about his sermons and writings.

Cajetan: (*Impatient*) My son, you have upset all Germany with your dispute about indulgences. I know you're a very learned doctor of the Holy Scriptures, and that you've already aroused some supporters. However, if you wish to remain a member of the Church, and to find a gracious father in the Pope, you'd better listen. I have here, in front of me, three propositions which, by the command of our holy father, Pope Leo the Tenth, I shall put to you now. First, you must admit your faults, and retract all your errors and sermons. Secondly, you must promise to abstain from propagating your opinions at any time in the future. And, thirdly, you must behave generally with greater moderation, and avoid anything which might cause offense or grieve and disturb the Church.

Martin: May I be allowed to see the Pope's instruction?

Cajetan: No, my dear son, you may not. All you are required to do is confess your errors, keep a strict watch on your words and not go back like a dog to his vomit. Then, once you have done that, I have been authorized by our most holy father to put everything to rights again.

Martin: I understand all that. But I'm asking you to tell me where I have erred.

Cajetan: If you insist. (*Rattling off, very fast*) Just to begin with, here are two propositions you have advanced, and which you will have to retract before anything else. First, "the treasure of indulgences does not consist of the sufferings and torments of our Lord Jesus Christ." Second, "the man who received the holy sacrament must have faith in the grace that is presented to him." Enough?

Martin: I rest my case entirely on Holy Scriptures.

Thomas More and Henry VIII

Excerpts from *A Man for All Seasons* by Robert Bolt

Characters: King Henry VIII, Thomas More, Thomas Cromwell, Norfolk

[*King Henry VIII has come to persuade Thomas More, his chancellor, to support his divorce of the queen.*]

Henry: (*Offhand*) Touching this matter of my divorce, Thomas; have you thought of it since we last talked?

More: Of little else.

Henry: Then you see your way clear to me?

More: That you should put away Queen Catherine, Sire? Oh, alas (*He thumps the chair in distress.*) as I think of it I see so clearly that I can *not* come with Your Grace that my endeavor is not to think of it at all.

Henry: Then you have not thought enough! . . . (*With real appeal*) Great God, Thomas, why do you hold out against me in the desire of my heart— the very wick of my heart?

More: (*Draws up his sleeve, baring his arm*) There is my right arm. (*A practical proposition*) Take your dagger and saw it from my shoulder, and I will laugh and be thankful, if by that means I can come with Your Grace with a clear conscience.

Henry: (*Uncomfortably pulls at the sleeve*) I know it, Thomas, I know. . . . (*Reasonable, pleasant*) You must consider, Thomas, that I stand in peril of my soul. It was no marriage; she was my brother's widow. Leviticus: "Thou shalt not uncover the nakedness of thy brother's wife. . . ."

More: (*Bursting out*) Your Grace, I'm not fit to meddle in these matters—to me it seems a matter for the Holy See—

Henry: (*Reprovingly*) Thomas, Thomas, does a man need a Pope to tell him when he's sinned? It was a sin, Thomas; I admit it; I repent. And God has punished me; I have no son . . . Son after son she's borne me, Thomas, all dead at birth, or dead within the month; I never saw the hand of God so clear in anything . . . I have a daughter, she's a good child, a well-set child—But I have no son. (*He flares up.*) It is my bounden *duty* to put away the Queen, and all the Popes back to St. Peter shall not come between me and my duty! How is it that you cannot see? Everyone else does.

More: (*Eagerly*) Then why does Your Grace need my poor support?

Henry: Because you are honest. What's more to the purpose, you're known to be honest . . . There are those like Norfolk who follow me because I wear the crown, and there are those like Master Cromwell who follow me because they are jackals with sharp teeth and I am their lion, and there is a mass that follows me because it follows anything that moves— and there is you.

More: I am sick to think how much I must displease Your Grace.

[*Much later More, who has refused to take the Oath of Supremacy and suffered seemingly endless interrogations and attempts to persuade him into compliance, has been condemned by parliament. He now addresses parliament before the sentence is read.*]

More: . . . (*He rises; all others sit.*) To avoid this I have taken every path my winding wits would find. Now that the Court has determined to condemn me, God knoweth how, I will discharge my mind . . . concerning my indictment and the King's title. The indictment is grounded in an Act of Parliament which is directly repugnant to the Law of God. The King in Parliament cannot bestow the Supremacy of the Church because it is a Spiritual Supremacy! And more to this the immunity of the Church is promised both in Magna Carta and the King's own Coronation Oath!

Crom: Now we plainly see that you *are* malicious!

More: Not so, Master Secretary! (*He pauses, and launches, very quietly, ruminatively, into his final stock-taking.*) I am the King's true subject, and pray for him and all the realm . . . I do none harm, I say none harm, I think none harm. And if this be not enough to keep a man alive, in good faith I long not to live . . . I have, since I came into prison, been several times in such a case that I thought to die within the hour, and I thank Our Lord I was never sorry for it, but rather sorry when it passed. And therefore, my poor body is at the King's pleasure. Would God my death might do him some good . . . (*With a great flash of scorn and anger*) Nevertheless, it is not for the Supremacy that you sought my blood—but because I would not bend to the marriage!

Norf: Prisoner at the bar, you have been found guilty on the charge of High Treason. The sentence of the Court is that you shall be taken from this Court to the Tower, thence to the place of execution, and there your head shall be stricken from your body, and may God have mercy on your soul!

Thomas More Sends Greetings to His Friend Master Erasmus

London, 31 October [1516]

My answer, dear Erasmus, is a little tardy, because I was anxious to get some definite information to send on to you from Urswick about that horse for you; but that has been impossible, since he is gone on a business trip several miles from London and has not as yet returned. . . .

Our two letters encouraging Latimer to spend a month or two with the Bishop of Rochester reached him too late; he had already made up his mind to go to Oxford and could not possibly be persuaded to postpone his trip for the time being. You know how these philosophers regard their own decisions as immutable laws; I suppose from a love of consistency. He does like your rendering of the New Testament very much, although you are too punctilious to suit him. . . .

. . . I am reluctant, of course, to mention any names. . . . However, I shall tell you anyhow, to put you more on your guard. The top-ranking Franciscan theologian, whom you know and to whom you gave honorable mention in your edition of [Saint] Jerome, has picked a group of men who are of the same Order and made of the same stuff, and has hatched a plot with them, aimed at refuting any errors of yours he can find. To make this opera-tion easier and more effective, they devised a scheme whereby they would divide up your works among themselves, read through each one with a critical eye, and then understand absolutely nothing of it all. So you see what a crisis is hanging over your head! You have got to work hard to condition your troops for facing this monstrous peril. You can be sure, Erasmus, this decision was reached at a council meeting of the elders, late at night, when they were well soaked. But the morning after, as I am told, with the effects of the wine slept off, they forgot, I guess, all about their resolution; since the decree was written in wine, it was now blotted out of their memory, and so they abandoned their proposal, and instead of reading, they went back to their begging, which experience had taught them to be a far more profitable enterprise. . . .

Farewell, dearest Erasmus, more precious to me than my own eyes! . . .

Hurriedly, from London, before dawn, All Hallows Eve.

Letters About China from Saint Francis Xavier

1) In the extract below, Francis Xavier describes his impressions of this great, forbidding country.

To Ignatius of Loyola:

China is a huge country, very peaceful and governed by great laws. There is only one king and all render him the strictest obedience. It is an extremely wealthy country, only a short distance from Japan, and abounds in all manner of produce. The Chinese are very clever people, desirous of knowledge, and much given to study, especially of the human laws by which the empire is governed. . . . War is unknown among them. . . . I am in great hope that by the labours of the Society of the name of Jesus both Chinese and Japanese will abandon their idolatries and adore God and Jesus Christ, the Saviour of all peoples.

2) Francis had traveled to the island of Sancian, about thirty miles from Canton, China, but had difficulty finding passage to Canton. This letter makes plain the danger he was in.

To Father Perez at Malacca:

I tried hard to persuade one of [the Cantonese merchants] to take me to Canton, but [at first] they all begged to be excused, saying that their lives and fortunes would be put in jeopardy if the governor of Canton discovered my presence. Nothing I could offer would induce them to give me a passage on one of their ships. By the good pleasure of God our Lord, however, an honourable citizen of Canton eventually agreed to take me for two hundred *cruzados* in a little junk. . . . More than that, he volunteered to keep me hidden in his house for three or four days, after which he would escort me before dawn . . . to a gate of the city whence I could at once proceed to the governor's palace to tell him that we had come in

order to make our way to the court of the King of China. . . . According to other Chinamen this course involves two risks, first, that the man taking us, when paid his money, may cast us adrift on some desert island or dump us in the sea to make himself safe against discovery by the governor, and secondly, that, even if we reached Canton and appeared before the governor, he might order us to be tortured or consigned to a dungeon . . . , since the King of China had so stringently forbidden foreigners entrance into his territories without his express written permission. . . . We are therefore determined to make our way into China at all costs, and I hope in God that the upshot of our journey will be the increase of our holy faith. . . .

[Francis Xavier died on the island of Sancian still hoping to bring Christ to China.]

Quiz on Chapter 12

_____ 1) Martin Luther began the Reformation with his posting of (a) the Eighty-five Theses (b) the Ninety-five Theses (c) the Augsburg Confession (d) the Diet of Worms.

_____ 2) Luther was (a) an Augustinian priest (b) a Jesuit (c) a Dominican (d) a layperson.

_____ 3) Luther strongly objected to (a) prayers to the Blessed Mother (b) the Eucharist (c) an ordained clergy (d) the selling of indulgences.

_____ 4) Indulgences were believed to (a) keep one out of hell (b) shorten the time in purgatory (c) placate a vengeful God (d) ensure the favor of the local prince.

_____ 5) Luther never really intended to (a) reform the Church (b) give central importance to the Bible (c) split the Church (d) stir up debate.

_____ 6) This person was sent to Augsburg as the pope's representative to talk with Luther: (a) Tetzel (b) Cardinal Cerularius (c) Cardinal Cajetan (d) Doppelganger.

_____ 7) Luther lived under the protection of (a) Duke Maximilian (b) Emperor Charles V (c) King Henry VIII (d) Duke Frederick.

_____ 8) Luther was kidnapped in order to (a) protect him from the emperor (b) take him to Rome for trial (c) extort money from the king (d) force him to be scholar-in-residence at Wartburg.

_____ 9) Which of the following did Luther consider the only valid sacraments? (a) Reconciliation and Eucharist (b) Eucharist and Confirmation (c) Baptism and Eucharist (d) Baptism and Marriage

_____ 10) Which of the following was _not_ one of Luther's teachings? (a) the sole authority of the Bible (b) salvation by faith alone (c) the belief in clerical celibacy (d) the priesthood of all believers

_____ 11) One unexpected result of Luther's teachings was (a) the Peasants' Revolt (b) translations of the Bible into German (c) tension with the Vatican (d) conflict with indulgence sellers.

_____ 12) This document summarizes the teachings of the Reformers: (a) the Diet of Worms (b) the Wittenberg Legacy (c) the Edict of Nantes (d) the Augsburg Confession.

_____ 13) The religion of a region of Germany was decided by (a) the local duke (b) individuals (c) Rome (d) an assembly of electors.

_____ 14) Which of these countries was not part of the Protestant Reformation? (a) France (b) Denmark (c) Scotland (d) Holland

_____ 15) Calvin initiated reforms and made his home here: (a) Zurich (b) Wartburg (c) Basel (d) Geneva.

_____ 16) One of Calvin's key teachings that made him different from Luther was (a) the sole authority of the Bible (b) the priesthood of all believers (c) predestination (d) the importance of preaching.

_____ 17) Henry VIII wanted to divorce Catherine of Aragon because **(a)** she was caught in adultery **(b)** he needed a son to succeed him **(c)** she was Spanish **(d)** she was Catholic.

_____ 18) How many times was Henry married? **(a)** three **(b)** four **(c)** five **(d)** six

_____ 19) The Act of Supremacy says that **(a)** the Eucharist is invalid **(b)** the king of England is head of the Church there **(c)** the pope is head of the Church **(d)** the people select the head of the Church.

_____ 20) This man wrote the book *Utopia* and was beheaded because he refused to assent to the Act of Supremacy: **(a)** John Fisher **(b)** Thomas Cromwell **(c)** Thomas More **(d)** Richard Rich.

_____ 21) The Council of Trent intended to state clearly the principal teachings of the Church and to **(a)** condemn the Protestant Reformation **(b)** bring Protestants and Catholics back together **(c)** reunite Rome and Canterbury **(d)** exert the power of the patriarchies.

_____ 22) One problem in holding the Council of Trent was **(a)** an earthquake in Italy **(b)** the Spanish bishops did not want to come to France **(c)** Charles V and Francis I were at war **(d)** England invaded Rome.

_____ 23) The founder of the Jesuits was **(a)** Francis Gonzaga **(b)** Francis Xavier **(c)** Ignatius of Loyola **(d)** Camillus Dufresne.

_____ 24) The Jesuits take a special vow of **(a)** teaching the poor **(b)** association **(c)** scholarship **(d)** absolute obedience to the pope.

_____ 25) Saint Teresa did much to reform the monasteries of this country: **(a)** Germany **(b)** Spain **(c)** France **(d)** Italy.

_____ 26) "Discalced" means **(a)** without shoes **(b)** penniless **(c)** disowned **(d)** disgraced.

_____ 27) This Jesuit lived and worked in China: **(a)** Aloysius Gonzaga **(b)** Robert Bellarmine **(c)** Matteo Ricci **(d)** Semper Fidelis.

_____ 28) The Jesuit missionaries thought it best to **(a)** harmonize with the dress and customs of the local people as much as possible **(b)** bring European customs to non-Christians first **(c)** teach natives Latin **(d)** only use European missionaries.

_____ 29) The only Christian country in Asia is **(a)** Taiwan **(b)** Malaysia **(c)** Burma **(d)** the Philippines.

_____ 30) Cortés conquered **(a)** the Mayas **(b)** the Aztecs **(c)** the Incas **(d)** the Toltecs.

_____ 31) One reason that the Indians became Christian was **(a)** to be on the winning side **(b)** they had no previous religion **(c)** they wanted to imitate their welcome new rulers **(d)** they were bribed.

_____ 32) One of the friars who protected the Indians from abuse by the Spaniards was **(a)** Francisco Martin **(b)** Miguel Campos **(c)** Andrew González **(d)** Bishop de Las Casas.

Prayer Service: For Christian Unity

Leader: Save us, O Lord our God.

All: And gather us from among the nations.

Leader: That we may give thanks to thy holy name.

All: And glory in Thy praise.

Opening Hymn

The Church's Prayer for Unity

Leader: Let us pray. Sovereign Lord, Ruler of the universe, look down from heaven upon your Church, upon all your people, and upon your little flock, and save all of us, your unworthy servants, the creatures of your flock, and give us your peace, your love, and your assistance. Send down upon us the free gift of your Holy Spirit so that with a clean heart and a good conscience we may kiss one another with holy love, not deceitfully nor hypocritically, nor to control each other's freedom, but blamelessly and purely in the bonds of peace and of love. For there is only one Body, and one Spirit and one Faith as we have been called in one hope of our calling so that we might all come to you and to your infinite love in Jesus Christ our Lord, with whom you are blessed with your all-holy, good, and life-giving Spirit, now and through endless ages.

All: Amen.

Readings from the Christian Scriptures

Read one or two of the following: Luke 1:68–79; Acts 10:34–48; Romans 15:7–13; 1 Corinthians 10:1–13; Ephesians 6:10–20; Hebrews 2:10–18; 1 Peter 2:9–12. (Pause for reflection.)

Closing Hymn

CHAPTER 13

The Liberation of the Church: 1600–1900

Major Concepts

A. The countries of Europe were clearly divided between Catholic and Protestant. Even while baroque churches were being built to overwhelm the devout with the power of God and the Church, new religious congregations of men and women were bringing Jesus' love to the poor.

B. Work in the missions continued unabated, with new efforts in Africa. Two different styles of evangelizing came into conflict: the Jesuits' approach of adapting Christian practice to local customs and the approach of the friars who wanted native people to accept European culture with the Christian faith.

C. The eighteenth century is known as the Age of Reason because thinkers at that time sought truth through reason and sensory experience—not through faith and divine revelation. One political offshoot of the elevation of reason was the push for democracy.

D. Religious nationalism became a divisive movement in the Church.

E. The period roughly from 1780 to 1900 was a time of national revolutions both in Europe and in the New World. In many instances overthrow of monarchies was coupled with rejection of the Church. While the Church lost temporal power, it began assuming spiritual leadership.

F. Despite turmoil in Europe, a new surge of missionary effort was made in the nineteenth century.

G. One sign of the Church's spiritual freedom was Pope Leo XIII's efforts on the side of the oppressed, especially laborers in the Industrial Revolution.

Activities for Concept A
The countries of Europe were clearly divided between Catholic and Protestant. Even while baroque churches were being built to overwhelm the devout with the power of God and the Church, new religious congregations of men and women were bringing Jesus' love to the poor. (Pages 232–237, 238 of the student text.)

Review Questions and Exercises from the Student Text

Question 1: What was the religious alignment of Europe by the mid-1600s? Had peace really been achieved?

Answer: Scandinavia, Prussia, and parts of southern Germany were Lutheran. Switzerland, Holland, and Scotland were primarily Calvinist. England's Church was ruled by the king or queen. The rest of Europe was mostly Catholic, although there were pockets of Protestants in many countries. Many violent incidents still occurred, especially the wars against the Huguenots in France.

13

Question 2: How did the baroque cathedrals symbolize the status of the Church during the seventeenth century?

Answer: Baroque churches were meant to overwhelm people with the power of God and the Church; they also emphasized Catholic beliefs by focusing attention on the tabernacle or by representing lives of saints in the paintings.

Question 3: What revolutionary changes were begun by Vincent de Paul, Louise de Marillac, and John Baptist de La Salle? How are their works continuing today?

Answer: Vincent de Paul and Louise de Marillac began the Daughters of Charity, a religious congregation of women devoted to active service of the poor. This new order was revolutionary because women who wanted to join a religious order, up to this point, had to become cloistered nuns. Women religious, it was thought, should not be out in the world. The Daughters of Charity acted out their faith by serving the poor. Today they are the largest institute of religious sisters in the world.

De La Salle founded the Brothers of the Christian Schools to provide Christian education for the poor; before him, schooling was almost the exclusive preserve of the rich. De La Salle created many of the classroom educational practices we now take for granted. Today the Christian Brothers are the largest order of brothers in the Church.

Other Questions and Activities for Discussion

1) To consider the reasons used for persecuting people of other religious beliefs, here are some issues for discussion:
   - In the 1600s, the Catholic French persecuted the Huguenots and the English persecuted Catholics. What reasons did the French and English use to justify their actions? In what ways are these reasons similar to the reasons that the Romans used in persecuting Christians and that Ferdinand and Isabella used to justify the Inquisition that was directed at Jews and Muslims?
   - Why were people so afraid of the religious beliefs of others?
   - What evidence of intolerance of other people's religions do you find today?
   - Historically, persecution of a religious group has only served to strengthen the resolve of that group. Is this principle still true of persecuted religious minorities today? What are some examples that support your view?
   - How does persecution of people for their religion have far-reaching effects? For example, in chapter 5 of the student text, we read that the Jews tended to expel Christians from the Jewish communities; this caused anger and distrust to grow between Christians and Jews. How has this distrust continued today? Religious wars between Catholics and Protestants are still having effects. Can you think of any of these effects?
   - Can you think of any evidence from the Christian Scriptures to support religious wars?

2) If you did not point out on a map the Lutheran, Calvinist, and Catholic parts of Europe as part of your discussion in the last chapter, you may wish to do so now.

3) Ask the students to reflect on the faith of the brothers and priests who were executed after the Gunpowder Plot (see pp. 232 and 233 of the student text).
   - Imagine that you were Brother Ralph or Brother John, Father Garnet or Father Oldcorne. You have been jailed, tortured, examined; what sort of prayers would you direct to God during your imprisonment? Write a prayer that you would address to God in this situation.
   - Next, write an imaginary interview with one of the four men. First, write a question from you, as interviewer, and then write what you think he would answer. You might want to find out about his motives for being in England and what his life was like before and during this time.

13

After the students have had time to respond to these assignments, invite volunteers to read their prayers and interviews. Discuss each prayer and interview, inquiring as to why each student wrote what he or she did.

4) Some enterprising students might build a model of an English house or room in a house that contained a hiding place for Catholic priests.

5) Three types of church architecture have been discussed in the student text: the Romanesque, the Gothic, and the baroque. Have the students look at pictures of each of these types of church building. Then, take an informal poll about their favorite church architecture.
- Which type of church building do you prefer? Why?

Then, divide the students according to which parishes they are from. Tell the groups to classify their parish churches as Romanesque, Gothic, baroque, or some other style. Each group should explain why their church fits into the classification they select. Also ask them to summarize the effects that the church building has on them when they worship there. Finally, your students might be instructed to interview some parishioners about their reactions to the church to which they belong. How does the place of worship affect worship?—this is an important question to address. Here are some other questions that you might raise with your students and that they might raise with those they interview:
- When you go into your church, where is your attention pointed? toward the altar? the tabernacle? the cross? the Bible?
- Why do you think the church designer wants your attention focused in this place or on this object?
- Where should your focus of attention be in a church? Why?
- Is your church intended to be mostly a place of quiet prayer, of celebration of the Eucharist, or of celebration of the community listening to the Word and celebrating the Eucharist together?

6) The founding of the Daughters of Charity was an important breakthrough in the development of ministry by women in the Church. But, how do people really feel about the role of women in ministry? Here are some questions for discussion:
- Why did people think that religious sisters should stay only in cloisters, away from the world?
- Do people still feel that way about women religious?
- What are some common reactions that people have when they see pictures or stories in the newspaper about women religious who are part of public protests or who are working with people in developing countries?
- Do women religious get respect, as professionals, from others? Do they, for instance, receive as much respect as do priests or permanent deacons? What do you think of this situation?

7) Invite a Daughter of Charity or a member of another active religious order of women to speak to your class about the changing nature of religious life, especially as it pertains to women.

8) Invite a religious brother, especially from a congregation composed only of brothers, to speak to your class about how orders of all brothers came into being and what their ministry is in the Church.

9) The meditation in the student text written by Saint John Baptist de La Salle (see p. 238) makes very clear that our salvation is to be found in meeting Jesus in others:

13

other people are a source of the presence of God. Ask your students to write their reflections about this meditation in their journals.

- How do you make Jesus present to other people?
- In what way are your relationships with others part of your ministry?

Activities for Concept B

Work in the missions continued unabated, with new efforts in Africa. Two different styles of evangelizing came into conflict: the Jesuits' approach of adapting Christian practice to local customs and the approach of the friars who wanted native people to accept European culture with the Christian faith. (Pages 237 and 239 of the student text.)

Review Questions and Exercises from the Student Text

Question 4: On a map, trace the spread of missionaries throughout the world during the 1600s. What conflict between the Jesuits and the Spanish friars caused a change in missionary policy?

Answer: On the map, point out the Kerala state in southern India, Sri Lanka, Thailand (Ayutthaya), Vietnam, Macau, Zaire, Senegal, and Madagascar. The Jesuits tried to adapt Christian practice to local customs; for example, Matteo Ricci dressed like a mandarin, spoke fluent Chinese, and said the Mass in Chinese. The friars used Latin, dressed as they did in Europe, and emphasized that native populations should act like Europeans. Eventually, the friars' position gained sway with the Congregation for the Propagation of the Faith at the Vatican.

Other Questions and Activities for Discussion

1) Stage a debate with two students on each side of the issue of adopting the Jesuits' approach or the friars' approach to missionary activity. As much as possible, encourage the teams to use the Christian Scriptures and appeals to logic in their arguments. The class can decide which case is strongest.

2) Have the students research and prepare short reports on the religious practices and local customs that the missionaries would have had to face when they first came to the following countries: Zaire, Madagascar, Thailand, Vietnam, India, and Sri Lanka.

Activities for Concept C

The eighteenth century is known as the Age of Reason because thinkers at that time sought truth through reason and sensory experience—not through faith and divine revelation. One political offshoot of the elevation of reason was the push for democracy. (Pages 240–242 of the student text.)

13

Review Questions and Exercises from the Student Text

Question 5: How did the Age of Reason challenge traditional thinking about God? Who were the deists, and how did they lead the way for the formation of the Freemasons? How did the rationalists and empiricists give an intellectual basis for the French (and American) Revolution?

Answer: Rationalists and empiricists challenged the notion of revealed truth. They believed that truth can only be verified through reason and/or sensory experience. Therefore, the laws by which humans are to behave should be arrived at by studying natural laws, not by following the Scriptures.

The deists were rationalists who reasoned to the existence of God, using the argument from causality; however, the deists' God was not a personal being who intervenes in human affairs. Most deists opposed the Catholic Church and monarchies, especially since most monarchies were based on the idea of the divine right of kings. Deistic thinking was the basis of the movement of Freemasons.

Since each individual could reason and come to his or her own conclusions, rationalists believed that each person had dignity and rights equal to all others. Since persons had rights and since monarchies denied these individual rights, rationalists argued that monarchies should be overthrown.

Other Questions and Activities for Discussion

1) There are many people today who might be considered deists, people who believe in God but do not conceive of a personal being who has much to do with their lives. Exploring the deists' philosophy might help your students appreciate the role of revealed religion in their own lives. Here are some questions to use:
- Why would some people find deism an appealing philosophy?
- If a person lived according to a rationalistic philosophy like the deists did, how might his or her life be different from a Christian's life?

Then, divide the class into small groups (or have them work as individuals) and tell them the following:

Imagine that you are a deist. You must construct a set of guidelines for your lifestyle—without the use of the Scriptures or tradition—solely based on what is reasonable. List reasonable guidelines for living, that is, construct a deist's ten commandments.

After the students have finished their ten commandments, discuss them in class; push the students to give reasons totally devoid of faith or religious language. Once you have a fairly extensive list of guidelines, compare their laws to the morality of the Christian Scriptures and the Ten Commandments. Point out differences and discuss the ways in which revealed religion supports morality.

2) Empiricism was of course not all bad. Ask your students these questions:
- In what way is the empirical method essential for scientific research?
- If one rejected empirical methods in doing medical research, what problems could arise? Give some examples.
- Why is it valuable to approach even some human issues by using an empirical method of gathering sensory data in order to come to conclusions? Give examples.
- The Age of Reason was also the age when modern science really came into being. Why was that?

3) Voltaire was very influential during the Age of Reason. Typical of his approach to questions is the short article contained in Student Handout 13–A, "Voltaire on Democracy" (found at the end of this chapter). Have the students read through his argument for democracy, and then, compare it to the typical arguments proposed today for why democracy is better than other forms of government. (You might select a few students to present Voltaire's argument for democracy in readers' theater style, with different paragraphs being read by different students as in a public discussion.)

13

4) Today, Catholics may belong to the Freemasons. You might wish to invite a Catholic Freemason into your class to talk about the history of the Masons and to answer questions (such as, Why were the Freemasons so anti-Catholic? What changed their attitude toward Catholics? and so on).

Activities for Concept D
Religious nationalism became a divisive movement in the Church. (Pages 242–243 of the student text.)

Review Questions and Exercises from the Student Text

Question 6: What were Gallicanism and Febronianism? Why did these movements begin?

Answer: Gallicanism was a movement in France for more autonomy from Rome for the French Church. The French king believed that he should have more authority over the Church in France than a foreign pope. Febronianism was a movement among some German bishops for more independence from Rome. Primarily these movements began as nationalism increased.

Other Questions and Activities for Discussion

1) The subject of church-state relations has come up over and over again in the history of the Church because there is a constant tension between the two. The suppression of the Jesuits was an especially unfortunate offshoot of the power of national governments over the Church. Discuss this suppression with your students:
- Could governments today force Rome to suppress a religious order like the Jesuits? If so, why; if not, why not?
- What is the proper role of nationalism in church affairs?

Activities for Concept E
The period roughly from 1780 to 1900 was a time of national revolutions both in Europe and in the New World. In many instances overthrow of monarchies was coupled with rejection of the Church. While the Church lost temporal power, it began assuming spiritual leadership. (Pages 243–249 of the student text.)

Review Questions and Exercises from the Student Text

Question 7: During the French Revolution the Catholic Church was persecuted and replaced by a philosophy of reason. Why was the Revolution directed against the Church as well as the monarchy?

Answer: The common French people saw the Church as part of the monarchy. Priests and bishops were appointed by the king and/or local nobles and thus were under the control of the government. [*Teacher's note:* Special privileges had been granted to monasteries and convents; consequently, they owned huge tracts of land and were often quite well-off. In contrast, the masses of French people were poor, landless peasants in virtual enslavement to the nobility.]

Question 8: What was Napoleon's attitude toward the Church? How was this attitude demonstrated?

13

Answer: Napoleon had contempt for the Church, although he tried to use it to give prestige to his coronation as emperor. He reneged on the concordat he signed with the pope, imprisoned the pope, and in other ways repressed the Church.

Question 9: How did the Italian Revolution, in effect, free the Church from worldly power? What was the initial reaction (by church officials) to Italy's unification? How has the loss of the Papal States actually been a positive thing?

Answer: When Italy was unified, the new government stripped the Papal States from the Church. Thus, the Vatican had almost no territory under its rule. For many years the popes considered themselves prisoners in the Vatican. Without having to be a temporal ruler, the pope can now be a strictly spiritual leader; this has been a positive result. (In addition, the Church is free from the obligations of having an army, demanding taxes, and so on—all part of being a temporal power.)

Question 10: Describe the changing status of the Church in Spain, Germany, England, and Ireland.

Answer: Napoleon established a puppet regime in Spain after he conquered it. However, he destroyed the monarchy. When Napoleon was defeated, republican governments occasionally took power. When the republics were declared, monasteries, seminaries, and convents were suppressed; the Church was harassed. In Germany, under the leadership of Bismarck, the Church was put under pressure to be more German, and some repressive restrictions were placed on the Church. The Church was legalized in England during the nineteenth century. In Ireland the Church has always been the mainstay of the Irish, but during the nineteenth century it was given more freedom from English rule.

Question 11: What were the important declarations made by Pius IX before Vatican Council I? by the council itself?

Answer: Pius IX proclaimed the doctrine of the Immaculate Conception and published a list of errors that Catholics should reject. In 1870 (the same year in which the Church was stripped of the Papal States, its temporal power), the key dogma of Vatican Council I declared that the popes were infallible on matters of faith and morals.

Personal Reflection Exercise

> Sometimes God does indeed work in strange ways. In this chapter, the Church was stripped of the Papal States—land it had ruled for twelve hundred years. And yet, this loss actually freed the Church from governmental power and allowed the Church to be the spiritual community that Jesus called it to be. In other words, God does act in history—that is, in the life of the Church and the lives of persons. Have you ever had something happen to you that at first seemed bad but turned out to be quite good? Think about this for a while. Think about yourself between the ages of one and six, then seven and thirteen, and finally during the years since then: Were there bad events that turned out well? How much of "being happy" is really a matter of the way we see and understand events and not just the events themselves?

13

Other Questions and Activities for Discussion

1) During the French Revolution the Church was attacked because of its seeming alliance with the aristocracy who oppressed the masses of poor people. Discuss with your students the place of the poor in the Christian Scriptures. Assign the students to find at least one passage each from the Christian Scriptures that talks about the poor. Have the students read out loud the passages that they found, and then discuss these passages in relation to the French Revolution:

- If the Church had clearly lived according to the principles of the Christian Scriptures, would the Church have been persecuted during the French Revolution?
- Why is it tempting for the Church or individuals in the Church to identify with the rich and powerful?
- Where do we see the Church of today taking the side of the poor?
- What are some instances today where the Church seems to be taking the side of the rich and powerful?

2) The French revolutionaries tried to enthrone reason as a goddess for the people. Of course the act was symbolic, but it illustrated the attempt to direct the people away from Christianity. Here are some questions to guide the discussion of this event:
- Why would the revolutionaries try to enthrone reason as a goddess?
- Considering our discussion of rationalism and the violent anticlericalism during the French Revolution, why didn't the people accept this new goddess of reason?
- Why is reason less satisfying than religion?

3) Like most violent revolutions, the French Revolution got completely out of hand during the Reign of Terror. Here are a few questions to ask the students:
- Why do almost all revolutions end in tremendous bloodshed?
- Consider what you know of the French, Russian, Cuban, Vietnamese, Chinese, Iranian, and Nicaraguan revolutions. What are the effects on the lives of people after revolutions? Is the immediate aftermath more liberating or more oppressing? [You may need to assign some students to research the aftermaths of each of these revolutions.]
- Should the Church support violent revolutions? [You may wish to construct a debate on this issue, with two students saying that the Church should support revolutions and two other students opposing this idea.]

4) Napoleon is an ironic figure in history. On the one hand, he was a lowborn soldier who supported the revolution in France and fought the enemies of the revolution. On the other hand, he led French troops to conquer other lands, killing the common soldiers; and he crowned himself emperor. This pattern of going from revolutionary leader to absolute ruler is not uncommon when one considers Lenin, Mao, Castro, Hitler. Talk about this phenomenon with your students:
- Why is it that many revolutionary leaders who have risen from poverty and obscurity, instead of becoming democratic leaders actually become absolute rulers?
- As part of his rise to power, Napoleon tried to humiliate the pope. Why would he do this?

5) Most of us forget that Italy has only been a unified country for a little over a century.
- Why would the pope oppose Italian unification and the loss of the Papal States?
- In what ways would being a temporal power interfere with the Church's role as a spiritual leader to people? [List these on the chalkboard.]

6) Some students could be directed to prepare very brief reports about the liberation movements in Colombia, Ecuador, Bolivia, and Chile that freed these countries from Spain: What role did the Church play in these revolutions?

13

Activities for Concept F
Despite turmoil in Europe, a new surge of missionary effort was made in the nineteenth century. (Pages 249–251 of the student text.)

Other Questions and Activities for Discussion

1) On a large wall map, point out the African countries where missionary work started in the nineteenth century: Tanzania, Uganda, Zaire, Zambia, Kenya, and Malawi.

2) The Boxer Rebellion was crushed by foreign troops because the colonial powers wanted to keep pillaging China. Assign a student or two to prepare short reports on the fate of Catholic missionaries in the Boxer Rebellion.

3) If possible, invite a missionary from the White Fathers, the Society of the Divine Word, Mill Hill, or the Congregation of the Immaculate Heart of Mary to talk about the work of his congregation in the nineteenth century and about what they are doing now.

Activities for Concept G
One sign of the Church's spiritual freedom was Pope Leo XIII's efforts on the side of the oppressed, especially laborers in the Industrial Revolution. (Pages 251–253 of the student text.)

Review Questions and Exercises from the Student Text

Question 12: What problems did Marx and Darwin raise for the Church?
Answer: Marx rejected religion. He claimed that religion was just a tool used by capitalists to oppress the working class. Darwin's theory of evolution caused some people to doubt the existence of God and the validity of Christian morality. After all, if one accepts survival of the fittest as a natural law, what happens to love of neighbor, concern for the poor and sick, and so on?

Question 13: How was the Industrial Revolution a challenge to the Church and all Christian people? Why was it truly a revolution?
Answer: During the age of the Industrial Revolution, people crowded urban slums, workers were exploited by greedy factory owners, and all sorts of other problems spun off the industrialization of Europe and the Western world. The Church was faced with the problem of how to help its people. The Industrial Revolution was truly a revolution because the agrarian economy and culture that had been a way of life for almost all people in these parts of the world was suddenly gone for the masses.

Question 14: What were Pope Leo XIII's attitudes toward unions, the rights of laborers, and Christian political parties?
Answer: Leo encouraged gradual social reforms. He supported unions because they protected the rights of laborers. He also backed Christian political parties.

13

Other Questions and Activities for Discussion

1) Pope Leo XIII's statements about the rights of workers are as relevant today as when they were written. Strikingly, he sees respect for each person's dignity as an

absolute obligation, not just a right. Have your students compare these statements by Leo to the U.S. Declaration of Independence. How are the two statements similar in their recognition of the rights of humans?

2) Assign your students to scour the newspapers and recent magazines to find instances of the Church taking the side of workers in disputes with employers. In the last several years there have been noteworthy examples: the Church's support of the United Farm Workers, the Lutheran minister who used his church as an organizing place for unemployed steelworkers, and so on. After the students have brought in some clippings, discuss their findings.

Summary Activities for the Chapter

1) In their journals, as usual, students should write their reflections about how they have been heralds, sacraments of God's presence, servants, and members of the Christian community this week. Also, you might want them to write their reactions to how they have given away some of the dignity that God gives them as persons, and how they need to reestablish their individual dignity.

2) If you have not already used these questions for daily quizzes, distribute to the class Student Handout 13-B, "Quiz on Chapter 13" (found at the end of this chapter). The answers to the quiz are as follows:

1) a	9) b	17) a	25) a
2) b	10) a	18) c	26) b
3) d	11) c	19) a	27) c
4) b	12) a	20) b	28) c
5) d	13) d	21) b	29) b
6) b	14) a	22) c	30) b
7) d	15) d	23) a	31) d
8) a	16) b	24) c	32) a

3) Student Handout 13-C, "Prayer Service: Experiencing the Presence of God" (found at the end of this chapter), can be used to close the study of this unit. Hymns that might be sung are "You Are Near" by Dan Schutte, in *Glory and Praise,* vol. 1 (Phoenix: North American Liturgy Resources, 1977), and "Lead Kindly Light" by John Henry Newman. Any of the great Masses written by Renaissance composers would be good to play during the period of meditation, especially perhaps a Kyrie or Sanctus.

13

Voltaire on Democracy

As a rule there is no comparison between the crimes of great men, who are always ambitious, and the crimes of the people, who always want, and can only want, liberty and equality. These two sentiments, Liberty and Equality, do not lead straight to calumny, rapine, assassination, poisoning, the devastation of one's neighbors' lands, etc. But ambitious might and the mania for power plunge men into all these crimes, whatever the time, whatever the place.

Popular government is in itself, therefore, less iniquitous, less abominable than despotic power.

The great vice of democracy is certainly not tyranny and cruelty. There have been mountain-dwelling republicans who were savage and ferocious; but it was not the republican spirit that made them so, it was nature.

The real vice of a civilized republic is expressed in the Turkish fable of the dragon with many heads and the dragon with many tails. The many heads injured one another, and the many tails obeyed a single head which sought to devour everything.

Democracy seems suitable only to a very little country, and one that is happily situated. However small it may be, it will make many mistakes, because it will be composed of men. Discord will reign there as in a monastery; but there will be no St. Bartholomew [Massacre], no Irish massacres, no Sicilian vespers, no Inquisition, no condemnation to the galleys for having taken some water from the sea without paying for it—unless one assumes that this republic is composed of devils in a corner of hell.

Which is better—runs the endless question—a republic or a monarchy? The dispute always resolves itself into an agreement that it is a very difficult business to govern men. The Jews had God Himself for their master, and see what has happened to them as a result: nearly always have they been oppressed and enslaved and even today they do not appear to cut a very pretty figure.

Quiz on Chapter 13

_____ 1) Which of these was *not* a Protestant country? **(a)** England **(b)** Sweden **(c)** Holland **(d)** Switzerland

_____ 2) This group of French Calvinists was persecuted by French Catholics: **(a)** Dervishes **(b)** Huguenots **(c)** Mennonites **(d)** Seventh Day Adventists.

_____ 3) Many English Catholics were persecuted as a result of **(a)** the Saint Valentine's Day Incident **(b)** Guy Fawkes's Day **(c)** the Act of Insurgency **(d)** the Gunpowder Plot.

_____ 4) The new type of architecture that flourished in this period was called **(a)** arabesque **(b)** baroque **(c)** Gothic **(d)** Novatian.

_____ 5) The purpose of this new style of church was to **(a)** give people a quiet place to pray **(b)** focus attention on the preaching from the pulpit **(c)** not distract people with lots of decoration **(d)** overpower the devout with its scenes.

_____ 6) The first congregation of women to serve the poor in the world actively and not to live in cloisters was the **(a)** Carmelites **(b)** Daughters of Charity **(c)** Sisters of Mercy **(d)** Poor Clares.

_____ 7) The first order of all teaching brothers was the **(a)** Society of Mary **(b)** Brothers of Mercy **(c)** Marists **(d)** Brothers of the Christian Schools.

_____ 8) Much of modern classroom methodology was created by **(a)** John Baptist de La Salle **(b)** Louise de Marillac **(c)** Francis de Sales **(d)** Vincent de Paul.

_____ 9) The Vietnamese language was systematized and put into western alphabet by **(a)** Nguyen Thach **(b)** Alexander de Rhodes **(c)** Francis Xavier **(d)** Hop Dao.

_____ 10) One thing that severely hurt the efforts of missionaries in Africa was **(a)** the slave trade **(b)** Islam **(c)** British explorers **(d)** diphtheria.

_____ 11) There were almost no native priests in Spanish colonies because **(a)** the natives refused to enter seminaries **(b)** the natives could not learn Latin **(c)** the Spanish kings forbade ordination of natives **(d)** the friars and Jesuits did not allow native vocations.

_____ 12) The Jesuits believed that missionaries should **(a)** adapt to local cultures as much as possible **(b)** make local people accept European ways before conversion **(c)** only convert the rich **(d)** only convert the poor.

_____ 13) Philosophers who believe that truth can only be arrived at through the evidence of the senses are called **(a)** rationalists **(b)** realists **(c)** romanists **(d)** empiricists.

_____ 14) David Hume dismissed the miracles of Jesus because **(a)** they went against the laws of nature **(b)** he claimed that Jesus was just a good physician **(c)** Jesus did not exist **(d)** they were not important for faith.

_____ 15) This political system was promoted during the Age of Reason: **(a)** socialism **(b)** aristocracy **(c)** oligarchy **(d)** democracy.

_____ 16) Many deists banded together into a secret brotherhood called the **(a)** Knights of Malta **(b)** Freemasons **(c)** Squires of the Temple **(d)** Knights of Labor.

_____ 17) The attempt of the French king to dominate the Church in France was called **(a)** Gallicanism **(b)** Iberianism **(c)** Francophilia **(d)** Agoraphobia.

_____ 18) The movement of some German bishops to be independent of Rome was called **(a)** Kulturkampf **(b)** Modernism **(c)** Febronianism **(d)** Melanchtonism.

_____ 19) The Jesuits were dissolved in part because of **(a)** the greed of the French king **(b)** their heretical practices **(c)** their rebellion against the popes **(d)** their support for the deists.

_____ 20) The French Revolution really began with the attack on the **(a)** Louvre **(b)** Bastille **(c)** Tuileries **(d)** Place de la Concorde.

_____ 21) The Church was persecuted during the French Revolution, in part, because **(a)** the revolution was inspired by Protestants **(b)** the Church was identified with the monarchy **(c)** the Church fielded an army against the peasants **(d)** the French had been forced to convert by Clovis.

_____ 22) The new religion of France centered on **(a)** Gallicanism **(b)** Albigensianism **(c)** Reason **(d)** Bonapartism.

_____ 23) Napoleon brought Pope Pius VII to Paris in order **(a)** for the pope to crown him emperor **(b)** to execute him **(c)** to sign a concordat with him **(d)** to submit to his rule.

_____ 24) One of Pius VII's last acts was to **(a)** excommunicate Napoleon **(b)** put France under interdict **(c)** restore the Jesuits **(d)** institute the Inquisition in France.

_____ 25) To unify Italy, the revolutionaries had to **(a)** take the Papal States **(b)** fight the English **(c)** execute all Freemasons **(d)** drive the Mafia out of Sicily.

_____ 26) After the unification of Italy, Pope Pius IX called himself **(a)** father of Italy **(b)** prisoner of the Vatican **(c)** bishop of Italy **(d)** guardian of the State.

_____ 27) Which one of these South American countries did not gain its independence from Spain in the 1820s? **(a)** Chile **(b)** Bolivia **(c)** Brazil **(d)** Ecuador

_____ 28) This person made Germany a world power: **(a)** Franz Jägerstätter **(b)** Dietrich Bonhoeffer **(c)** Otto von Bismarck **(d)** King Ludwig I.

_____ 29) John Cardinal Newman was part of this group of students who tried to move Anglicanism closer to Catholicism; the group was called **(a)** the Papist Plotters **(b)** the Oxford Movement **(c)** the Cambridge Circle **(d)** the Westminster Ministry.

_____ 30) Before Vatican Council I started, Pope Pius IX declared this dogma: **(a)** papal infallibility **(b)** the Immaculate Conception **(c)** the Assumption **(d)** *Rerum Novarum.*

_____ 31) This philosopher claimed that capitalism oppressed the workers, religion was a means of oppression, and class struggle would lead to a workers' state: **(a)** Hume **(b)** Voltaire **(c)** Huxley **(d)** Marx.

_____ 32) This scientific theory caused many people to question the truth of the Bible: **(a)** evolution **(b)** gravity **(c)** spontaneous combustion **(d)** genetic multiplication.

Prayer Service:
Experiencing the Presence of God

Opening Hymn

Leader: Let us remember that we are in the presence of God.

God's Presence in Beauty, in Our Hearts, and in Others

Reader: "Pied Beauty" by Gerard Manley Hopkins, SJ
        Glory be to God for dappled things—
            For skies of couple-colour as a brinded cow;
                For rose-moles all in stipple upon trout that swim;
        Fresh-firecoal chestnut-falls; finches' wings;
            Landscape plotted and pieced—fold, fallow, and plough;
                And all trades, their gear and tackle and trim.
        All things counter, original, spare, strange;
            Whatever is fickle, freckled (who knows how?)
                With swift, slow; sweet, sour; adazzle, dim;
        He fathers-forth whose beauty is past change:
                    Praise him.

All: To be with God it is not necessary to be always in church. We may make
        a chapel of our heart whereto we may escape from time to time to talk
        with Him quietly, humbly and lovingly. Everyone is capable of such close
        communion with God, some more, some less; He knows what we can
        do. Begin then; perhaps He is waiting for a single generous resolution.
        [From *The Practice of the Presence of God* by Brother Lawrence of the
        Resurrection, 1666]

(Pause for reflection.)

Reader: The words of Saint Vincent de Paul:

Friendliness . . . is the outward effect of charity in the heart. It springs
from the heart and shows how very glad you are to be with a particular
poor person. . . . It is the joy you feel when you see a person you love
and it shows in your face; for when someone has joy in her heart she
cannot hide it; you see it clearly on her face.

Prayer: "God's Grandeur" by Gerard Manley Hopkins, SJ

Leader: The world is charged with the grandeur of God.
　　　　It will flame out, like shining from shook foil;
　　　　It gathers to a greatness, like the ooze of oil
　　　Crushed. Why do men then now not reck his rod?
　　　Generations have trod, have trod, have trod;
　　　　And all is seared with trade; bleared, smeared with oil;
　　　　And wears man's smudge and shares man's smell: the soil
　　　Is bare now, nor can foot feel, being shod.

All:　　And for all this, nature is never spent;
　　　　There lives the dearest freshness deep down things;
　　　And though the last lights off the black West went
　　　　Oh, morning, at the brown brink eastward,
　　　　　springs—
　　　Because the Holy Ghost over the bent
　　　　World broods with warm breast and with ah!
　　　　　bright wings.

Closing Hymn

CHAPTER 14

The Church in North America

Major Concepts

A. Spanish missionaries accompanied the conquistadores into what is now the U.S. Southwest. They established missions and converted Native Americans. At the same time, French missionaries were working in eastern Canada.

B. When Canada became a British colony, French Catholics were granted the freedom to practice their religion. English religious dissidents also found refuge in the New World. Even though Catholics were given Maryland, they suffered from the religious intolerance of their neighbors.

C. Catholics played prominent roles in the war of U.S. independence. Bishop John Carroll was elected to lead the small, poor U.S. Church. He also had to prepare priests for the new flow of immigrants.

D. To provide a Catholic education, the Church established its own school system. In the face of this separate school system and the immigrant makeup of the Catholic Church, and due to religious bigotry, an anti-Catholic movement of nativists attacked the Church in the United States.

E. Even as the Church was spreading west with the flood of immigrants, the Church, like the nation, was embroiled in the devastating Civil War and the issue of slavery, which triggered it.

F. The tide of Catholic immigration swelled after 1850, and with it came the establishment of ethnic parishes. Also influencing church order was the democratization of the church institutions.

G. Ethnic divisions affected the growing Church in Canada too. Particularly numerous were the Irish immigrants who had been driven from their country by the Potato Famine.

H. In the twentieth century, the Catholic Church became the largest church in the United States, but it was still looked upon with suspicion and as being foreign. The election of John F. Kennedy as president proved that a Catholic president could lead the country and remain free from a foreign pope.

Activities for Concept A

Spanish missionaries accompanied the conquistadores into what is now the U.S. Southwest. They established missions and converted Native Americans. At the same time, French missionaries were working in eastern Canada. (Pages 258–265, 266 of the student text.)

Review Questions and Exercises from the Student Text

Question 1: On a map, locate the places where Spanish missionaries worked in what is now the United States. What problems did these missionaries encounter? Why were the efforts of Father Junípero Serra so remarkable?

Answer: These are just a few of the many Spanish mission stations: Saint

Augustine, Florida; Santa Fe, New Mexico; San Antonio, Texas; San Diego, Santa Barbara, Santa Clara, San Francisco, California. The Spanish missionaries encountered some of the same hostility that the Native Americans showed the Spanish soldiers. Life was also difficult for the friars because they were very far away from home and the amenities of Spanish life. Finally, much frustration must have plagued them because of the resistance of the Indians to the new religion. Junípero Serra was extraordinary because he built so many missions despite physical handicaps. His plan of building missions worked well and firmly planted Christianity in California.

Question 2: Using a map showing Canada and the United States, locate the spots identified in this chapter as places where the French missionaries worked.

Answer: Important areas where the missionaries worked include Nova Scotia; the Saint Lawrence River valley; Montreal; upstate New York and Vermont; Quebec City; Sault Sainte Marie, Ontario; Saint Ignace, Michigan.

Question 3: Why was the French approach to dealing with Native Americans so different from those of the English and Spanish settlers?

Answer: The French came to the New World to trade with the Indians. Trading requires that good relationships be built. So the French treated Native Americans with some level of respect, even adopting some of their ways. The Spanish and English settlers, however, came to conquer a new land. The Indians were looked upon as savages because they were not Europeans. Therefore, the Spanish and English justified, in their own minds, the violent suppression of the Indians; the Native Americans were forced to relinquish their lands to the new colonizers.

Question 4: Why were the explorations of Marquette and La Salle not only important for France but for the Catholic Church?

Answer: Marquette and La Salle mapped out new territories for the French: the Ohio and Mississippi valleys and the Great Lakes area. La Salle explored as far as what is now New Orleans. Thus, the French claimed a huge new area. Naturally, Father Marquette claimed these territories as missionary areas for the Church.

Question 5: What sort of moral problems confronted the French missionaries in their frontier congregations?

Answer: The Indian converts had many customs and values that were radically different from the French and with which the missionaries were unaccustomed. The French traders sometimes tried to take advantage of the Native Americans. There were questions of intermarriage, the sale of liquor, just prices for goods, restitution, and so on.

Other Questions and Activities for Discussion

1) Some students might be assigned to do research about Native American religions. The focus should be on understanding the religious beliefs of Native Americans and how these beliefs might have come into conflict with the missionaries who were preaching Christianity.

2) Bring in additional pictures that show the layout of Spanish missions; they usually included a monastery, a garden, barns, and a fortress-like construction. Discuss the practicality of their design.

14

3) Assign a student to point out all of the missions established by Junípero Serra and to estimate the distance he traveled from the bottom of California to the northernmost mission. Considering that he walked the whole way, how long might one trip take?

4) The Serra Club of the United States is an organization committed to encouraging religious and priestly vocations. One of the club's members might be invited to speak about the club and about Junípero Serra.

5) This is a journal-writing assignment designed to have the students reflect on the life of a missionary in the New World; here are the instructions:

> Imagine that you are a Franciscan named Friar Benildo. Your parents live in Barcelona, Spain. You are writing them on a warm May Sunday afternoon in Santa Barbara. The mission church is in the process of construction (see p. 259 of the student text for a picture of the finished Santa Barbara church). You are sitting under a tree at a small, somewhat shaky table looking at the foundations that have just been built. Since it is Sunday, the workers and you are having a day of rest. The other friars have headed north to build other missions with Father Junípero.
>
> What will you tell your parents about the new mission and your feelings? Write the letter home. On a separate piece of paper, write down the thoughts and feelings that you (as Friar Benildo) have about your life here in the mission but that you don't tell your parents because they might be too disturbed by them— or just would not understand.

After all the letters have been written and the private thoughts and feelings recorded, select one or more of the letters and journal entries to read and discuss with the class (you might want to keep the authors' names a secret). Here are some questions to ask:

- Why would Friar Benildo say these things?
- Is there any aspect of the letter that betrays a twentieth-century mentality and would not be accurate for a Franciscan of the sixteenth or seventeenth centuries?
- Why would Friar Benildo not tell his parents the things he put in his private journal?

6) Here are some other research projects that students could be assigned to report on: the life of a voyageur; the beaver-pelt business; the lives of Marquette, Joliet, La Salle, Catherine Tekakwitha, Isaac Jogues, Bishop Laval (what sort of people were they? what motivated them?); the locations of French forts and trading posts in the midcontinental region.

7) Ask your students to imagine that they are Native Americans who are seeing Caucasians for the first time. Have each student list five questions that he or she would ask first of these odd-looking people. Then, discuss what the Indians might have thought about the foreign colonizers.

Activities for Concept B

When Canada became a British colony, French Catholics were granted the freedom to practice their religion. English religious dissidents also found refuge in the New World. Even though Catholics were given Maryland, they suffered from the religious intolerance of their neighbors. (Pages 265, 267–269 of the student text.)

Review Questions and Exercises from the Student Text

14

Question 6: What was the Quebec Act of 1774, and why was it so important to Canadian Catholics?

Answer: [*Teacher's note:* After the English had won Canada from the French, many Canadian Catholics were afraid that Catholicism would be forbidden just as it was in England at that time.] The Quebec Act legalized Catholicism for the French Canadians.

Question 7: The Puritans and many of the other religious groups who first came to America were escaping religious persecution in their homeland. Why then were they so intolerant of Catholicism?

Answer: Most of the religious groups who left England had been in trouble there because they objected to how Catholic the Church of England was. Many of them were Calvinists who believed in a narrow interpretation of the Bible and in predestination and who opposed the celebration of the Eucharist, the ordained hierarchy of ministers, and the role of tradition in church order. [*Teacher's note:* They felt that they had not escaped from persecution in order to allow their enemies, the Catholics, to practice in the New World too.]

Other Questions and Activities for Discussion

1) Have some students prepare reports on Puritan beliefs that were in conflict with Catholicism and on the Society of Friends, or Quakers (they might focus on the American Friends Service Committee).

2) Here is a case that your students might discuss first in small groups and then as a class:

You are in the Maryland legislature in 1720. Before the group is a proposal that all Indians be driven out of the western portion of the state. To do this, the legislature must raise money to put together a militia. The Pennsylvania people have made treaties with the Indians, but this has taken time and money. The Puritans have forced the Indians out of their forest homes, believing them to be savages. As a member of the legislature, you must decide what Maryland is to do. As a Catholic, you must consider what is Christian. Here are some questions to answer:
- Who owns the land?
- What is proper treatment of non-Christians?
- How would you like to be treated if you were an Indian?
- What would be the effects if the militia defeated the Native Americans?
After your group has answered these questions, it should decide how you will vote on the issue.

If there is disagreement among the groups, organize a debate. Discuss the pressures on the colonizers—their motivations for wanting new land—and the moral implications of the colonizers' treatment of Native Americans.

Activities for Concept C

Catholics played prominent roles in the war of U.S. independence. Bishop John Carroll was elected to lead the small, poor U.S. Church. He also had to prepare priests for the new flow of immigrants. (Pages 269–271 of the student text.)

Review Questions and Exercises from the Student Text

Question 8: Why would American Catholics support the Revolution so staunchly?

Answer: In the 1700s, England still forbade the practice of Catholicism. Freedom from England meant freedom from the Church of England. In the colonies, only two areas—Maryland and Pennsylvania—were relatively open to the practice of Catholicism. Catholics would have supported the early founders of the United States who promised separation of church and state.

14

Question 9: Describe the many difficulties facing Bishop John Carroll as he took office in 1790.

Answer: When John Carroll became the first U.S. bishop, there were very few priests; the small number of Catholics were spread out all over the country; U.S. Catholics did not want foreigners to run the Church; the U.S. legislature had put all churches under lay trustees, who sometimes proved uncooperative; and immigrants wanted their own native priests.

Other Questions and Activities for Discussion

1) The election of Bishop Carroll by U.S. priests was an unusual event. To discuss the election and other issues related to the selection of bishops, here are some questions to use:
   - Why was the election of Bishop Carroll so unusual?
   - Why would U.S. Catholics demand a U.S. bishop?
   - Would Americans have tolerated a foreign bishop at this point in their history?
   - What are the advantages and disadvantages of diocesan priests electing their bishop?
   - In the early Church, communities elected their own bishop. Would this method still work well for the election of the bishop in our diocese?
   - Should it make any difference where a bishop comes from?

2) The lay trustee boards were established for all churches by the U.S. legislature. Carroll did not approve of this law; indeed, the Church had not been so controlled by laypersons since the earliest days. Discuss lay boards with your students:
   - Why would Bishop Carroll and, in fact, the institutional Church object to the establishment of lay trustee boards?
   - What would be some advantages to having lay trustees?
   - How did the system of lay trustees fit in with the spirit of the times in the United States?
   - Today we have parish councils. Do the powers of the parish councils match those of the lay trustee boards? [You may wish to invite a member of a local parish council to talk about his or her role in parish leadership.]
   - Would the Church be better off if laypersons could hire and fire pastors and other church officials?
   - What are the reasons for the present hierarchical system of governance in the Church?

3) On a large wall map, outline the diocese that came under the jurisdiction of Bishop Flaget. Have some students use a modern road map to figure out the distances from Bardstown to Chicago, Fort Wayne, Madison, and Cleveland. Then let the students figure out how long a trip by horseback would take between any two of these cities.

4) Here is a case you might pose to your students to simulate the conditions among frontier Catholics:

> You are homesteading in Illinois in 1820. You have come from southern Germany where Catholicism is very strong. Unfortunately the priest only comes to the nearest town about once every three months. You want to raise your children so that they know about the Church, and you want to continue to keep Sundays holy.
>   - How will you maintain your relationship with God and the Church under these circumstances?

After the students have had time to reflect on what they would do, let them share their thoughts and discuss these ideas with the class.

14

Activities for Concept D

To provide a Catholic education, the Church established its own school system. In the face of this separate school system and the immigrant makeup of the Catholic Church, and due to religious bigotry, an anti-Catholic movement of nativists attacked the Church in the United States. (Pages 272–273, 276 of the student text.)

Review Questions and Exercises from the Student Text

Question 10: Why did U.S. Catholics establish their own school system? Why were these schools the source of such violent controversy?

Answer: Catholics wanted to ensure that their children received instruction in their faith. The public schools were, to all intents and purposes, Protestant schools. The Protestant influence could be seen in the use of the King James Version of the Bible, school prayers, and, in some instances, the heavy involvement of Protestant ministers in the management of the public schools. When U.S. Catholics decided to start their own schools, some Americans feared that this was a sign that Catholics wanted to remain foreign, un-American.

Question 11: Who were the nativists and why did they object to immigrants and Catholics in particular? Can you think of any examples of similar kinds of anti-Catholic groups active today?

Answer: The nativists were a group claiming to be "real" Americans—native-born, true-blue Americans. They objected to all the immigrants flooding into the cities, taking jobs, speaking foreign languages, and having different customs. Catholics were especially feared because Protestants were becoming outnumbered in some places and feared that the Catholics would force them to conform to the Church of Rome, turn the public schools into Catholic schools, and suppress Protestant religions. Some of this fear still motivates members of the Ku Klux Klan and some right-wing non-Catholic sects.

Other Questions and Activities for Discussion

1) The development of women's religious orders in the United States and Canada is an interesting story in itself. Many congregations were founded by courageous women who came from Europe, and others were diocesan congregations founded to work in specific dioceses. Invite a member of the Sisters of Charity to talk about Mother Seton, or a sister of the Sacred Heart order to discuss Philippine Duchesne, or a member of any order of sisters that was founded to serve in the United States or Canada. Ask the sister to focus her remarks on the roots of their apostolate in the new land; what obstacles faced the early sisters?

2) Some students might be assigned to interview elderly sisters about what the lives of women religious were like during the early days of this century. What sort of payment did they get from pastors? What sort of restrictions in terms of lifestyle did they live under? What was their place in the Church? What was their workload like? It would be interesting to tape-record the interviews and then play to the class parts of the responses.

3) Assign some students to find out about the history of their parish grade schools, if they have them. The students can prepare brief written histories of the schools and display pictures of the schools now and from their early days (perhaps using old yearbook pictures or class pictures from the archives of the parish) for their classmates to view.

14

Other students might be charged with writing a brief history and doing a display of your high school from the founding to the present.

4) Presently there is much talk about prayer in schools. Instruct some students to examine *Time, Newsweek, U.S. News and World Report,* or other magazines to find out the sources of this drive to reinstate prayer and even Bible readings in public schools. Discuss this issue of prayer in public schools with your students.

5) Archbishop Ireland proposed that the state help Catholic schools or at least release Catholic students for religious instruction. Here are some related issues about Catholic schools to raise with your students:
- In what ways does our state now help Catholic schools?
- Could the state legally do more than it is doing?
- The Supreme Court declared that the tuition tax credit plan is constitutional. This plan allows the states to give tax credits to parents of students who attend parochial schools. What do you think of this plan? What advantages and disadvantages might it create for the parochial schools? for the public schools?
- Today students can be released from the public schools for attendance at religious instruction. Would this be a good substitute for Catholic schools?
- Can parish religious education programs be just as effective as Catholic schools?
- Should we maintain Catholic schools as an alternative to public schools? What value do they have?
- Will you send your children to Catholic schools? Why or why not?
- The public school systems are now really public and not Protestant; thus, the old reason for the Catholic school system is gone. Are there new reasons for maintaining the system?

6) How do your students and their parents feel about immigrants now? Here are some questions to ask:
- How do people feel about the new immigrants to the United States?
- Do you detect any hostility to recent immigrants, for example, Vietnamese, Cambodians, Ethiopians, and so on?
- Are people afraid of immigrants?

Encourage your students to interview their parents and then write brief reports about their parents' attitudes toward the United States' accepting refugees or immigrants: What objections do they raise? Do they see any benefits in accepting these people?

7) Your students might also construct a survey of attitudes toward immigrants to use with a sampling of the student body outside their class. Some items on the survey might be like the following, with responses ranging from strongly agree (SA) to strongly disagree (SD):

1. Our country should have even freer rules about admitting immigrants.   SA   A   D   SD
2. Admitting immigrants is generally good for the country.   SA   A   D   SD

All items on the survey should try to determine the students' attitudes about admitting immigrants. Your class can tabulate and then discuss the results. The conclusions might be written up for an article in the school newspaper. Finally, discuss this issue:
- What should the Christian attitude be toward accepting immigrants and refugees into a developed country?

14

233

Activities for Concept E
Even as the Church was spreading west with the flood of immigrants, the Church, like the nation, was embroiled in the devastating Civil War and the issue of slavery, which triggered it. (Pages 274–275, 276–277 of the student text.)

Questions and Activities for Discussion

1) There are many passages from *Death Comes to the Archbishop* that demonstrate the trials of being a priest in the Old West. You might select some passages to read to your students.

2) Sister Blandina's description of the opening of a school in the Colorado Territory (see p. 274 of the student text) may surprise readers today. After your students have read this story, ask the following questions:
   - What does this story tell about the strength and faith of this sister?
   - Why would she move to Trinidad if the school was such a temporary and inadequate building?
   - How is this picture of a religious sister different from the picture we got of women religious at the time of Saint Teresa of Ávila?
   - What do you imagine a small Colorado frontier town would be like in 1876?

3) Fr. P. N. O'Brien's letter (see p. 275 of the student text) is also interesting. Locate Deadwood, South Dakota, on a map—or at least point out the Black Hills area of South Dakota. Then, raise these issues with your class:
   - How does this description of the Old West match the picture given in Westerns that you have seen?
   - What skills did a priest need in order to be a competent minister to the people in a small town like Deadwood? If you were trying to write a job description of all of Father O'Brien's duties, what would it look like?
   - Why would sobriety be required as an important trait of a new priest in Deadwood?
   - What role did this story ascribe to sisters?

4) In his letter, Father O'Brien also emphasizes the necessity of establishing a hospital in this settlement. If there is a Catholic hospital in your town, some students might find out about its history: When was it founded? What order of sisters ran it? What did the early buildings look like? In short, Catholic hospitals have made incredibly valuable contributions to the welfare of people. It might be very impressive to document the history of these important institutions and the great women who ran them.

5) Today it is hard to understand how a Catholic bishop could defend slavery. However, considering the time in which he was living, discuss with your class how Bishop Lynch could defend slavery as being consistent with Christianity. Ask them how slavery could be defended biblically, especially if one takes the Bible literally as fundamentalists tend to do. The Catholic Church has been very small in most of the southern states; have the class do some brainstorming as to why the South has such a small Catholic population.

14

Activities for Concept F

The tide of Catholic immigration swelled after 1850, and with it came the establishment of ethnic parishes. Also influencing church order was the democratization of the church institutions. (Pages 277–280 of the student text.)

Review Questions and Exercises from the Student Text

Question 12: What are ethnic parishes and why were they established?

Answer: Ethnic parishes were parishes set up to serve a specific group of immigrants; so there were German parishes, Italian parishes, and so on. In these parishes, religious festivals and practices from the old countries were preserved. In some cases the grammar school classes were taught in German, Polish, or whatever language was spoken in the parish. Ethnic parishes were established to make the transition to the new country easier and to maintain ties to the old country.

Other Questions and Activities for Discussion

1) Many of the larger cities had ethnic parishes: primarily Irish, Polish, German, Italian. Some students may have been assigned earlier to do histories and displays about their grade schools (see concept D, activity 3) and others about Catholic hospitals (see concept E, activity 4). Preparing short histories of local parishes (complete with a display of old photos and other memorabilia) could be not only interesting but also very instructional.

Split the students into teams. Assign one team to each parish in your area or in the town. Have each team compile the following: a written chronology of important events in the parish, a list of pastors, a display of pictures showing scenes from parish life from the beginning to the present, other memorabilia that would be interesting, reports of interviews about parish life from as far back as possible. If the parish had its origins as an ethnic parish, this aspect of its history should be highlighted. These displays and reports could be placed in some public place in the school for other students to see, and they could be made available on parents' nights. Few people really know much about their parishes, and even fewer appreciate their histories.

Conclude by discussing with your students the advantages and disadvantages of ethnic parishes.

2) Here are some topics to discuss in regards to unions today vis-à-vis unions in the days of Cardinal Gibbons:
- Do unions still serve the same functions today that they served when Cardinal Gibbons defended them?
- Would Cardinal Gibbons approve of the role that unions now play in industry, health care services, public services, and education?
- Have unions outlived their usefulness?

Invite a union member to discuss the roles that unions play in protecting workers now. You might also organize a debate over the question, Are unions effectively helping the masses of workers, or are they simply protecting their members?

3) Find a copy of the old Baltimore Catechism. Read parts of it to your students and discuss its methodology with them. What are the advantages and disadvantages of this approach to catechism?

14

235

Activities for Concept G

Ethnic divisions affected the growing Church in Canada too. Particularly numerous were the Irish immigrants who had been driven from their country by the Potato Famine. (Pages 280–282 of the student text.)

Review Questions and Exercises from the Student Text

Question 13: In what ways was the development of the Church in Canada different from its development in the United States? In what ways was it similar?

Answer: The Church in Canada was different from the U.S. Church in that it began with a larger population of Catholics—the French of Quebec Province. Also, French Canadians had been granted freedom of religion earlier than U.S. Catholics, and there was no wall of separation between church and state in Canada. However, in ways similar to the U.S. experience, the ethnic groups that flowed into Canada brought with them ethnic religious practices and ethnic prejudices; and problems arose between Canadian Catholics and Protestants.

Other Questions and Activities for Discussion

1) On a map of Canada, review the location of provinces mentioned in this chapter: Nova Scotia, Quebec, and so on. Remind the students that Canada has a larger area than the United States, and discuss what it must have been like to unite the Church of Canada from Montreal.

Activities for Concept H

In the twentieth century, the Catholic Church became the largest Church in the United States, but it was still looked upon with suspicion and as being foreign. The election of John F. Kennedy as president proved that a Catholic president could lead the country and remain free from a foreign pope. (Pages 282–284 of the student text.)

Review Questions and Exercises from the Student Text

Question 14: How did the two world wars contribute to the unification of the U.S. Catholic Church?

Answer: As a result of their experiences of being threatened by the two world wars, U.S. Catholics became less concerned about their ethnic origins and more concerned about being united as Americans. German Catholics, who had staunchly supported German-language parishes before World War I, became disillusioned with things German and downplayed German in their parishes and schools.

Personal Reflection Exercise

After reading this chapter you have some idea of what life for Catholics was like in North America up until the present. To add to your impressions, try to interview your oldest relative, for example, your great-grandmother or your grandfather. Ask them to describe what it was like to be a Catholic when they were fourteen to seventeen years old. How did the Church fit into their lives when they were growing up? Record the impressions they share with you. Now imagine that, in fifty years, your grandchild comes to you with the same questions. How would you answer them?

14

Other Questions and Activities for Discussion

1) Many of your students' parents will remember the election of John F. Kennedy as president and all the fears on the part of non-Catholics that surrounded his rise to power. Encourage some students to interview their parents about what sort of anti-Catholic myths were used to oppose Kennedy. The students could also interview some Protestants who were adults during the election, asking them to share their opinions about why many Protestants opposed a Catholic for president.

2) Prohibition was a good example of religion influencing public policy. Discuss this with your students.
- Why would many Christians oppose drinking?
- Why would Catholics oppose Prohibition?
- Should public officials make laws based on religious principles?
- How should a person's religion influence his or her decision-making about public policy?
- What are some influential ways in which the Catholic bishops have entered into discussion about public policies? [This might lead into a discussion of the U.S. bishops' pastoral on capitalism.]

3) A student might be instructed to consult the *Catholic Almanac* to find out the current number of Catholics in each state of the United States and other factual information about the status of the U.S. Church. This information could be compiled in a table or on a graph and displayed in the classroom.

Summary Activities for the Chapter

1) As usual, have the students write in their journals about their heralding of the Word, being sacraments of Christ's presence, and serving the People of God. In addition, they might record some reflections about ways in which life in this country has been enriched by the strong presence of the Catholic Church. Finally, ask the students to compose prayers of thanksgiving for the many good aspects of life in North America. These prayers may be used in the prayer service.

2) If you have not already used these questions for daily quizzes, distribute Student Handout 14-A, "Quiz on Chapter 14" (found at the end of this chapter). The answers to the quiz are as follows:

1) c	10) a	19) c	28) b
2) d	11) c	20) b	29) b
3) a	12) a	21) a	30) a
4) d	13) c	22) d	31) b
5) d	14) c	23) a	32) b
6) d	15) a	24) a	33) a
7) c	16) d	25) c	34) d
8) c	17) c	26) a	
9) b	18) d	27) a	

14

3) Student Handout 14–B, "Prayer Service: In Thanksgiving" (found at the end of this chapter), can be used to close the study of this unit. Good songs to use include "Glory and Praise to Our God," by Dan Schutte, in *Glory and Praise,* vol. 1 (Phoenix: North American Liturgy Resources, 1977), and "Amazing Grace," a traditional American hymn. There are many other great North American spirituals that could be either sung by the students or played from a tape or record for meditation.

14

Quiz on Chapter 14

_____ 1) After exploring Georgia, the Carolinas, Mississippi, and Tennessee, this Spanish explorer died while traveling down the Mississippi River to the Gulf of Mexico: **(a)** Magellan **(b)** Columbus **(c)** Hernando de Soto **(d)** Ponce de León.

_____ 2) This Spanish adventurer explored New Mexico, Texas, Arizona, and California in the 1540s: **(a)** Cortés **(b)** Cervantes **(c)** Panza **(d)** Coronado.

_____ 3) One thing that hampered missionary work among the Southwest Indians was that **(a)** the Spaniards sometimes enslaved the Indians **(b)** the priests did not bother to learn Indian languages **(c)** the Indians were almost all nomads **(d)** the Spanish government forbade it.

_____ 4) Which one of the these cities was _not_ first a Spanish mission? **(a)** San Francisco **(b)** Saint Augustine **(c)** Santa Fe **(d)** none of the above

_____ 5) The famous missionary friar in California is **(a)** Ruben Aragon **(b)** Jaime Dalumpines **(c)** Martín de Porres **(d)** Junípero Serra.

_____ 6) This explorer established the first permanent French colony in North America: **(a)** Cartier **(b)** Dufresny **(c)** Leblanc **(d)** Champlain.

_____ 7) _Canada_ means **(a)** many lakes **(b)** land of snow **(c)** community **(d)** home.

_____ 8) The French came to the New World primarily to **(a)** find gold **(b)** cut timber **(c)** trade in beaver pelts **(d)** farm.

_____ 9) The French were enemies of the **(a)** Hurons **(b)** Iroquois League of Five Nations **(c)** Apache **(d)** Seminoles.

_____ 10) This French missionary was killed by Native Americans who opposed the French: **(a)** Isaac Jogues **(b)** Henri de Lubac **(c)** Teilhard de Chardin **(d)** Leonard Le Duc.

_____ 11) The first Native American to be declared blessed in the Church was **(a)** Pocahontas **(b)** Wenonah **(c)** Tekakwitha **(d)** Creek Mary.

_____ 12) This priest explored most of the Great Lakes and the Midwest: **(a)** Marquette **(b)** La Salle **(c)** Lecuyer **(d)** Laval.

_____ 13) The first bishop of a North American diocese was the bishop of **(a)** Nova Scotia **(b)** Ontario **(c)** Quebec **(d)** New Amsterdam.

_____ 14) When the English took Canada from the French, many French Canadians moved from Acadie to **(a)** New Hampshire **(b)** France **(c)** Louisiana **(d)** Minnesota.

_____ 15) The Quebec Act of 1774 **(a)** granted French Catholics freedom of religion **(b)** suppressed Catholicism in Canada **(c)** ended immigration to Quebec **(d)** made French the national language.

_____ 16) In 1619 a Dutch ship off the Virginia colony unloaded **(a)** the Quakers **(b)** the Puritans **(c)** tobacco plants **(d)** slaves.

_____ 17) The Puritans had to leave England in part because **(a)** they plotted to kill the king **(b)** they sided with Catholics **(c)** they thought that the Church of England was too Catholic **(d)** they received a divine revelation to do so.

_____ 18) The first Catholic settlers were granted land in **(a)** Rhode Island **(b)** North Carolina **(c)** Delaware **(d)** Maryland.

_____ 19) This group was most open to people of other denominations living with them: **(a)** Puritans **(b)** Anglicans **(c)** Quakers **(d)** Methodists.

_____ 20) Catholics wanted freedom from England in large part because **(a)** the English forbade the making of altar wine **(b)** Catholicism was illegal in England and the colonies **(c)** the government was Puritan **(d)** England was liberal with Quakers.

_____ 21) Which one of these people was not a Catholic hero of the American Revolution? **(a)** Paquette **(b)** Lafayette **(c)** Pulaski **(d)** Kosciuszko

_____ 22) Who was the first U.S. bishop? **(a)** John Newman **(b)** John Hughes **(c)** John Ireland **(d)** John Carroll

_____ 23) The first U.S. bishop took his office after **(a)** an election by the priests **(b)** an appointment from London **(c)** agreement by the Cardinal of Paris **(d)** nominating himself.

_____ 24) One difficulty that the first bishop did not encounter was **(a)** the illegality of the Church **(b)** lay trusteeship **(c)** a shortage of priests **(d)** little money.

_____ 25) The first diocese west of the Alleghenies in the United States had its diocesan seat at **(a)** Saint Louis **(b)** Saint Genevieve **(c)** Bardstown **(d)** Cincinnati.

_____ 26) The Sisters of Charity were founded by **(a)** Elizabeth Ann Seton **(b)** Mother Cabrini **(c)** Philippine Duchesne **(d)** Kate Chopin.

_____ 27) Catholics in the nineteenth century did not want to send their children to public schools because **(a)** they were virtually Protestant schools **(b)** they did not have football teams **(c)** the discipline was poor **(d)** they could not ride the buses for free.

_____ 28) This political party opposed Catholics and immigrants: **(a)** Bull Moose party **(b)** Know-Nothing party **(c)** Whig party **(d)** Prohibition party.

_____ 29) Catholics during the Civil War were **(a)** unified in opposition to slavery **(b)** fighting on both sides **(c)** left out of the war because they were mostly immigrants **(d)** wondering what to do.

_____ 30) Concerning unions, most American bishops **(a)** supported them **(b)** stayed neutral **(c)** opposed them **(d)** tried to begin unions.

_____ 31) Prior to the two world wars, many German Catholics wanted to **(a)** lose their German identities **(b)** have their own German dioceses **(c)** split from the Catholic Church **(d)** have only English spoken in their schools.

_____ 32) Cincinnati, Saint Louis, and Milwaukee were known as **(a)** the Polish Three **(b)** the German Triangle **(c)** the Beer Capitals **(d)** nothing special.

_____ 33) This document probably had more influence over the faith formation of young people than any other up until Vatican II: **(a)** the Baltimore Catechism **(b)** _Rerum Novarum_ **(c)** the Blue Army Handbook **(d)** the Little Flowers of Saint Francis.

_____ 34) This candidate for the presidency of 1928 was beaten mostly because he was Catholic: **(a)** Calvin Coolidge **(b)** Alf Landon **(c)** Melvil Dewey **(d)** Alfred E. Smith.

Prayer Service: In Thanksgiving

Opening Hymn

Prayer of Thanksgiving: Psalm 138:1–3,7–8

All: I thank you, Yahweh, with all my heart;
            I sing praise to you before the gods.
        I bow down in front of your holy temple and praise your name,
            because of your constant love and faithfulness,
            because you have shown that you and your commands are supreme.
        You answered me when I called you;
            with your strength you strengthened me.
        Even when I am surrounded by troubles,
            you keep me safe;
            you oppose my angry enemies,
            and save me by your power.
        You will do everything you have promised me;
            Yahweh, your love is constant forever.
            Complete the work that you have begun.

Reading of Luke 12:22–32

(Pause for reflection.)

Leader: At this time if any of you would like to express thanks to God for anything the Creator has given us, please do so. We will respond, "Thanks be to God."

Prayer of Praise: Psalm 136:1,4–9,23,25–26

Leader: We give thanks to you, Yahweh, for you are good,

All: your love is everlasting!

Leader: You alone perform great marvels,

All: your love is everlasting!

Leader: Your wisdom made the heavens,

All: your love is everlasting!

Leader: You set the earth on the waters,

All: your love is everlasting!

Leader: You made the great lights,

All: your love is everlasting!

Leader: The sun to govern the day,

All: your love is everlasting!

Leader: Moon and stars to govern the night,

All: your love is everlasting!

Leader: You remembered us when we were down,

All: your love is everlasting!

Leader: You provide for all living creatures,

All: your love is everlasting!

Leader: Give thanks to the God of heaven,

All: your love is everlasting!

Closing Hymn

CHAPTER 15

War, Fascism, and Communism

Major Concepts

A. At the beginning of the twentieth century, the Church was faced with World War I—a total, global war in which millions of lives were lost, boundaries were shifted, and the balance of power changed irrevocably. The Church tried to make peace but was left trying to aid the victims of a war it could not stop; it warned the victors not to plant the seed of another war by humiliating the vanquished.

B. Another result of World War I was disillusionment with old answers to human problems. Casting around for new sources of meaning, people found a variety of answers: capitalism, justified by social Darwinism; psychology; and totalitarianism in its two forms—Communism and Fascism.

C. Fascists took control of two primarily Catholic countries: Italy and Spain. The Church maintained an uneasy peace with the Fascists in these two countries. Hitler and the Fascists' rise to power in Germany led to World War II and the genocide of millions of people. The Church condemned Nazism, aided refugees, tried to mediate, and came under attack by this political party that was determined to eradicate every resistance.

D. In the war with Japan, the Asian countries were devastated. Missionary efforts were put to an end when priests, nuns, brothers, and lay missionaries were either put in internment camps or executed.

E. The aftermath of World War II was far worse than that of World War I: the arsenal of war was made immeasurably worse with the addition of the atomic bomb; millions of people had been slaughtered and millions were left starving and homeless; the Soviet Union placed eastern Europe under its domination. In addition, the victors again changed the boundaries of the world, and colonies demanded freedom. Amidst the tragedies and changes, the Church did what it could to serve the needy, make peace, and protect freedom of religion.

Activities for Concept A

At the beginning of the twentieth century, the Church was faced with World War I—a total, global war in which millions of lives were lost, boundaries were shifted, and the balance of power changed irrevocably. The Church tried to make peace but was left trying to aid the victims of a war it could not stop; it warned the victors not to plant the seed of another war by humiliating the vanquished. (Pages 288–290 of the student text.)

Review Questions and Exercises from the Student Text

Question 1: What tremendous problems did World War I create for the Church? How did the Church deal with these problems?

Answer: As a Servant, the Church aided the millions of needy people who were victims of the war (and in doing so, almost completely depleted the Vatican resources). Hundreds of religious and priests had been killed in the war. Churches were destroyed.

Antagonisms between countries meant antagonism between fellow Christians. The popes tried to be peacemakers.

Question 2: How were the seeds of World War II planted at the Treaty of Versailles?

Answer: The reparations demanded of Germany and its allies were so harsh that they humiliated these once proud peoples by forcing them into destitution. Out of the bitterness of this humiliation would come the demand for national pride and for revenge.

Question 3: How did the First and Second World Wars influence the colonies of the European powers? And, how did they influence the Church in these colonies?

Answer: During the world wars, the control of countries like Britain and France over their colonies slipped. Nationalism within the colonies grew, and European colonialism was threatened. Missionaries, most of whom came from the colonizing country, were identified with the colonizers. Nationalism in the colonies placed the Church in a precarious position.

Other Questions and Activities for Discussion

1) Many Catholic Action organizations existed before the pontificate of Pope Pius X, but lay Catholics began many more service organizations after Pius's papacy. Students might be assigned to do short reports on each of the following Catholic Action groups; the years of their respective foundings are given.

> The Confraternity of Christian Doctrine (1905)
> National Council of Catholic Women (1920)
> The Grail (1921)
> Legion of Mary (1921)
> National Catholic Rural Life Conference (1923)
> Catholic Near East Welfare Association (1926)
> Catholic Medical Mission Board (1928)
> Association of Catholic Trade Unionists (1937)
> Catholic Relief Services (1943)
> Christian Family Movement (1947)
> Pax Christi (1948)
> Movement for a Better World (1952)
> Edith Stein Guild, Inc. (1955)
> Jesuit Volunteer Corps (1956)
> Center for Applied Research in the Apostolate (CARA) (1964)
> Center of Concern (1971)
> Group Seven (1971)
> National Council of Catholic Laity (1971)
> NETWORK (1971)

The addresses of the groups listed above and of many other lay apostolates are given in the *Catholic Almanac*. A speaker from one (or several) of these groups might be invited to talk to your class about Catholic Action and about his or her particular group.

2) The Church was ineffective in preventing World War I. Examine with your students why the Church has a difficult time being a peacemaker—even between mostly Catholic countries.

3) On a map, point out the countries who were fighting each other in World War I. If any of the colonial powers lost this war, they risked losing their territorial possessions. Indicate to your students some of the colonies that were at stake in the war.

> a) Britain's colonies: India, Malaysia, Hong Kong, Burma, Somalia, Kenya, Uganda, Rhodesia, South Africa, British Guiana, British Honduras (Belize)

15

b) France's colonies: Indochina (Vietnam, Cambodia, Laos), French West Africa (Mali, Niger, Nigeria, Upper Volta, Cameroon, Chad, Ivory Coast), Algeria, Morocco, Tunisia

c) Germany's colonies: Tanzania, German South-West Africa (Namibia)

d) Holland's colonies: Indonesia, Dutch Guiana

e) the United States' colony: the Philippines

f) Turkey's colonies: Egypt, much of Saudi Arabia, Lebanon, Syria, Kuwait, Palestine (Israel), Sudan

g) Belgium's colony: Congo (Zaire)

This is not a complete list, but it shows how much of the world was at stake when the colonial powers fought in World War I.

4) For hundreds of years the Irish tried to throw off British rule of Ireland. Finally, in 1921, the Irish Free State was formed, but Ulster, or Northern Ireland, remained part of Britain. This is a classic case of the problems of colonization that live on and on. Have your students bring in newspaper or magazine articles from the last month or two about incidents of the ongoing hatred in Northern Ireland. What has been the Church's role in the conflict between Catholics and Protestants in Northern Ireland?

5) Many chaplains died in World War I, just as they have in other wars before and since. If possible, invite an active or retired military chaplain to talk to your students about the role of a military chaplain. What is a chaplain's job? Are there tensions between being a military chaplain and being a priest? Are there tensions between preaching peace through love and working for the military?

6) Have a few students report on some of the particularly harsh terms of the Versailles treaty.

7) Ask the students to reflect on and then write in their journals about the following situation and questions:

Think about the most humiliating thing that has ever happened to you. In your journal, write down the following: who was there; when it took place; and what, why, and where it happened. Be as complete in your description as possible. No one will read this journal entry without your permission.

- Now, write down a description of how you felt when this event was going on and how you felt afterward. What were you thinking about immediately afterward?
- How did you feel toward the *source* of the humiliation? What thoughts were running through your mind about it (or him or her or them)?
- Do you often remember this incident even now? Why, or why not?
- Have you ever been with a group of people—like a team—who have been humiliated? Describe briefly what happened.
- What feelings and thoughts were expressed by the group after the humiliation?

After the students have finished their writing, invite volunteers to share parts of their stories with the class. (Warn them, however, to say only those things that they want the class to know and about which they will feel comfortable afterward.) When the students have finished, discuss these questions:

- Does your experience of humiliation relate to what the German people must have felt after the Versailles treaty? If so, how? If not, why not?
- How big a factor can revenge become in regaining one's sense of self-worth?
- Why would the Allies ignore Pope Benedict's advice about not humiliating the Germans after World War I?

15

Activities for Concept B
Another result of World War I was disillusionment with old answers to human problems. Casting around for new sources of meaning, people found a variety of answers: capitalism, justified by social Darwinism; psychology; and totalitarianism in its two forms—Communism and Fascism. (Pages 290–294 of the student text.)

Review Questions and Exercises from the Student Text

Question 4: Why did the First World War cause a search for meaning among people? Why was religion unsatisfactory for some people? To what did people turn for their sense of meaning?

Answer: After World War I, people were overcome with a sense of disillusionment, and many felt that another war was imminent. Some people felt let down by religion—it had not prevented the war. People wanted better solutions to their problems. Thus, many people looked for answers in new areas: unbridled capitalism, Fascism, Communism, or the new psychology. During the Roaring Twenties, others just wanted to have a good time and forget the war.

Personal Reflection Exercise

> Pointing out ways in which Communism and Fascism oppress religion is quite easy. Perhaps it would be useful for us to consider ways in which capitalism can be oppressive to religion as well. Take some time to think about ways in which capitalism influences people's morals. If a person were really committed to capitalism, how would this commitment influence his or her relationship to the parish community? Capitalism is based on there being corporate winners and losers. Pushed to an extreme, what effect would capitalism have on the Church's being the People of God?

Other Questions and Activities for Discussion

1) The students would profit from interviewing someone who lived through the Roaring Twenties and the aftermath of World War I. Here are some questions they might ask their grandparents or other older people who remember those times:
- How did the war affect your life? What do you remember most about the war and its aftereffects?
- Were the Roaring Twenties really all that wild? Why, or why not?
- How did people feel about the future after the First World War? Were they generally optimistic or pessimistic?
- Did people really believe that this would be the war to end all wars?
- How did the war change the United States?
- Did some people, at the time, recognize that the Versailles treaty would lead the Germans to react as they did (choosing the Nazis and Hitler to lead them back to national pride)?

2) In the same interview with an older person who remembers the 1920s and 1930s, these or similar questions might be asked about capitalism:
- Were U.S. workers protected from harmful working conditions and unfair labor practices during that period?
- How would you describe the situation of the worker during those years?
- Looking at unions then and unions now, how would you describe the changes in their power or influence?

15

- Is capitalism as free of restraints now as it was in the twenties and thirties? What do you think of the situation today?
- Do you think that religion had much influence on the leaders who started World War I and/or on capitalists?
- What should be the Church's role in preventing wars and protecting workers' rights?

The students should give oral reports about their interviews.

3) Perhaps a discussion of the effects of uncontrolled capitalism would be appropriate at this stage. Here are some additional questions to pursue after the students have responded to the personal reflection exercise (see p. 305 in the student text):
- What are some of the problems of uncontrolled capitalism?
- What are some advantages of capitalism over Communism?
- We like to think of ourselves as a democratic country, a country run by the people for the people. Do you think that most U.S. citizens are more committed to democracy or to capitalism?
- What are some situations in which the common good comes into conflict with capitalism?
- What are some situations in which the common good, as decided democratically, is circumvented or overridden by capitalistic concerns?
- Do you think that religious values frequently enter into business decisions?
- Would some of the corporate activities that go on today happen if religious values were taken more into account?

The students could be asked to find some newspaper or magazine articles about business deals that have put employees out of jobs or that have put someone else out of business or about a corporation charged with ripping off someone.

4) Freud rightly condemned unhealthy guilt, but there can be a healthy sense of guilt as well. Guilt is something worth talking about with your students:
- When can guilt, as Freud described it, be unhealthy? be harmful?
- What would people be like if they never felt guilt for their harmful actions?
- When is it a good thing to feel guilty?
- Freud seemed to think that there were far too many laws and rules that oppressed people. But how can laws and rules be helpful in our developing our identities and in keeping society a worthwhile place to live?

5) Here are some issues to raise about totalitarianism:
- What kind of people do you think would be most attracted to a totalitarian political philosophy?
- What are some countries that have set up Communist governments through revolutions by the common people?
- Why did they select Communism and not capitalism as their system of economics and government?
- Why is capitalism less attractive to the poor?

15

Activities for Concept C

Fascists took control of two primarily Catholic countries: Italy and Spain. The Church maintained an uneasy peace with the Fascists in these two countries. Hitler and the Fascists' rise to power in Germany led to World War II and the genocide of millions of people. The Church condemned Nazism, aided refugees, tried to mediate, and came under attack by this political party that was determined to eradicate every resistance. (Pages 294–299 of the student text.)

Review Questions and Exercises from the Student Text

Question 5: Describe the differences between Fascism and Communism. How are they both considered totalitarian systems? What is the place of religion in both of these types of totalitarianism?

Answer: Communism called for a workers' revolution that would set up a state where all workers were treated equally; there would be no classes. A centralized party would rule in the name of the people. Fascists wanted to set up a state that was dominated by one group. Under Hitler's Fascist government, the controlling group were the Aryans, or pure Germans. National unity in Germany was rooted in racial supremacy. Both Fascism and Communism are totalitarian because a small group dedicated to a single ideology controls all aspects of life for the people. Religion is suppressed, even if not directly, because it offers an alternative worldview and because it sometimes actively challenges totalitarian ideology.

Question 6: Why did Fascism appeal to the Italian and German peoples?

Answer: Italian Fascists promised a return of the Italian empire; once again Italy would become a world power or at least a country with pride in its heritage. For centuries Italy had been divided into small, warring city-states, and on and off it had been under foreign domination. Likewise, in Germany, Hitler and the Fascists promised a return of pride in the German people and in their history. The Nazis wanted to lead Germany to greatness after the humiliation of World War I. This was a popular appeal to Germans.

Question 7: How did Mussolini and Hitler treat religion—especially the Catholic Church?

Answer: Mussolini had to be especially careful in his dealings with the Church because it was a powerful force in Italian life. However, he thought that the Church should be subordinate to the Fascist government. In 1929, he signed the Lateran Agreement with the Vatican. The Vatican recognized the king and the independence of Italy. The pope agreed to stay out of Italian politics. On his side of the agreement, Mussolini recognized the independence of Vatican City and its neutrality. Some compensation was paid to the Vatican for the loss of Rome and the Papal States. In addition, religious orders gained legal status, Catholicism could be taught in all secondary schools, and Italian marriages would abide by church law.

Hitler, especially after *Mit Brennender Sorge* was read from church pulpits, tried to drive the Church into complete submission. Catholic organizations and newspapers were suppressed. Lay leaders and priests who were even slightly critical of the Nazis were imprisoned and sometimes executed. Usually bishops were left alone; Hitler intimidated them through his harassment of priests, religious, and laypeople.

15

Question 8: Under what difficult circumstances did the Church in Spain work? Why did the Church side with Franco and the Nationalists?

Answer: During the 1920s, Spain had a republican government dominated by anticlerical Communists. The government condoned anti-Church activity. Church property was seized, religious orders were suppressed, education was secularized, and many priests, religious, and lay leaders were murdered. In short, the Church was persecuted. When Franco and the Nationalists tried to overthrow the republican government, the Church supported Franco because it was thought that Catholics would have more freedom of action under him.

Question 9: Why did Pius XI condemn the Nazi practices in Germany?

Answer: Not only were the Nazis harassing the Church, but they also staged pagan rituals, committed brutal persecutions, and sought revenge for the Germans' humiliation.

Question 10: How did Hitler use the Jews as scapegoats? What was the Church's response? Why did the Church respond as it did?

Answer: The Jews were blamed for Germany's defeat in World War I and for conspiring to take over Germany's economy. [*Teacher's note:* Hitler claimed that the Jews had weakened the German racial purity, thus weakening the country. Having one scapegoat united the German people.] The Church objected to Hitler's actions but to no avail; the more it objected, the more reprisals were committed against the Church in Germany. [*Teacher's note:* First, the Church tried diplomacy to stop Hitler, but when this failed, the Church sheltered Jews and other refugees. The Church felt that a direct attack on Hitler was useless and would only cause Catholics to suffer more. The Vatican thought it better to appear neutral and do what it could.]

Other Questions and Activities for Discussion

1) You might wish to discuss the Germans' acceptance of the Nazi party and Pope Benedict's warning that the Versailles treaty would cause the Germans to seek revenge. Ask some students to research the political and economic condition of Germany right before Hitler came to power. Highlight for the class these conditions: Germany was experiencing a terrible depression; they had to pay enormous reparations to the victorious countries of World War I; they had no armed forces of their own.

2) Starting with Pope Pius XI's condemnation of Nazism, discuss the pope's role in criticizing governments.

- Why did Pope Pius XI send his letter *Mit Brennender Sorge* when he knew that the Nazis would retaliate?
- Should the popes condemn political parties, especially when that condemnation will cause problems for loyal Catholics?
- Why do you think most Catholics continued to cooperate with the Nazi party even though the pope had condemned it?
- What would happen to the role of the Church in the world if the pope did not take stands against governments like that of Hitler?
- Are there any governments in the world that you think the pope should condemn as being inhuman, savage, or destructive to their citizenry? Why?
- Would the pope's criticisms of an inhumane government do any good for its people? Or, would Catholics in that country become even more oppressed?
- Under what conditions do you think a pope should do what Pope Pius XI did when he sent *Mit Brennender Sorge* to the German people?

15

250

3) You might wish to talk with your students about racism, using the case of the Nazis as a starting point:

- The Nazis appealed to the German people's sense of racial superiority. They committed mass genocide against the Jews, gypsies, and other minorities—all under the reason of purifying the German people. Does such an attitude persist today among races of people? Where do you see racism today?
- Are there any groups with which you are familiar that would systematically exterminate another race of people that they feel are inferior? [A few students might do research in recent magazines about the neo-Nazi parties that are flourishing in some places in this country; if you have not yet discussed the Ku Klux Klan, you might do so at this time.]
- Could someone be a good Catholic and belong to one of these groups?
- Can you cite any examples from the newspapers that illustrate that racism and anti-Semitism still exist? [Some students might have been previously assigned to look for recent examples.]
- Does prejudice against Jews exist in this country? Can you give some examples?
- How would you trace the development of this anti-Jewish prejudice throughout Western history? We have certainly seen many examples of it in the stories in the textbook.
- Why do prejudices against racial or ethnic groups seem to persist for so long?
- How can people overcome prejudices with which they grow up?
- Can anyone who is prejudiced toward other racial groups or religions claim to be morally superior to the Nazis?

4) An issue related to the genocide committed by the Nazis is the silence on the part of most Germans (and indeed of many intelligence agencies of the Allies) who knew of the atrocities being perpetrated. Tacit permission given to evildoers is a dilemma worth discussing here.

- Why were the German people, many of whom did not approve of the genocide being carried out by the Nazis, so silent about what was happening to the Jews, gypsies, and people who opposed Hitler?
- Have large corporations or our government commonly perpetrated or permitted social evils against minorities or other groups? Have people remained silent about such injustices? Can you think of some examples?
- According to law, if you give money, food, clothing, and shelter to a criminal, you become an accessory to the crime itself and, therefore, subject to prosecution. Does this same principle apply to people who pay taxes to support a government that does evil? Should this principle apply?

To further explore this dilemma, describe to your students the following case, "Sarah's Silence?":

Sarah is an account executive for a large food-processing corporation. Her company has recently begun selling pineapple that is raised in the Philippines on huge plantations. Sarah's corporation purchased these plantations from a holding company owned by a Philippine named General X. The enterprise is extremely profitable for her company because growing, harvesting, and canning the pineapples in the Philippines is far cheaper than doing so in Hawaii.

As Sarah is reviewing the accounts for the Philippine operation for her year-end report to the corporation board, she notices odd payments made to General, X and especially unusual payments to military subordinates of General X. Because she is responsible for outlays, Sarah does some digging into the way in which the company purchased the land and got the operation under way.

What Sarah finds out shocks and disturbs her. The company did indeed buy the land, but they paid huge amounts of money to General X and other Philippine government officials who did not own the land, but who shoved poor farmers off the land that their families had farmed for generations. These farmers did not hold legal deeds to the land; the general and his cronies filed claim to the land

15

251

and then, because of bribes, got deeds. Sarah's company then bought the land and paid the cost of removing the poor farmers. The farmers were left homeless, and some had actually been killed or imprisoned by the army because they refused to be evicted. In finding out all of this, Sarah is confused; her conscience is deeply disturbed.

- If you were Sarah, what would you do?

Split the class into groups to discuss what they would do. Then discuss the solutions with the total class. Finally, ask these questions:

- How is Sarah's dilemma like that of the German people during the Nazi persecution of the Jews?
- How are her options similar to and different from the options facing the Germans?
- Does this sort of situation confront people regularly?
- Do we place as much blame on corporations who do the sort of thing Sarah's company did as we do on the German people who allowed the Nazis to do what they did?

The case of Sarah is based on an actual event. Poor farmers in Mindanao were evicted from their land by the Philippine Army, who were under an avaricious general being paid by an American pineapple canning company. At present, most of the pineapple eaten in North America comes from the Philippines.

5) There are many excellent films on the holocaust. Showing a film on this subject would be useful at this point in the course, especially if racism, prejudice, and the holocaust are not covered in a separate course on faith and justice.

6) One of the first actions taken by totalitarian governments like the Nazis is to control the press. A free press is important to ensure other freedoms, like freedom of religious practice. This is a topic worth considering with your students.

- Why would Hitler close down the Catholic newspapers after the public reading of *Mit Brennender Sorge?* What did he hope to accomplish by this?
- Are newspapers really all that important?
- How is freedom of the press closely related to freedom of worship?
- What happens if the flow of information is tampered with by a government?
- What are some contemporary examples of press censorship?
- Were any of these examples of censorship really justified?
- Does the press sometimes publish material that can be terribly damaging to people or to the security of the government? What are some examples?
- Which does the greater harm—a free press that makes mistakes and reports some events that might be best left unreported or a press that can be censored?

7) If possible, have a survivor of the holocaust talk to your class. The Anti-Defamation League of B'nai B'rith (823 United Nations Plaza, New York, NY 10017) and the Secretariat for Catholic-Jewish Relations, National Conference of Catholic Bishops (1312 Massachusetts Avenue NW, Washington, DC 20005) sometimes have lists of speakers.

8) Again, many interview topics suggest themselves. The students could interview people who were adolescents or adults during World War II about one or several of the following subjects:

- a) How did the war affect parish life? Did priests talk about the war from the pulpit?
- b) How did people talk about the Germans and Hitler? Why did we only enter the war after Japan bombed Pearl Harbor?

15

c) There were many groups who resisted the U.S. entrance into the war; what were their motives?

d) How aware of the genocide were most Americans? If they were aware, what were their reactions; if not, why weren't they aware?

e) What was the popular image that Americans had of the papal reaction to Fascism? Did they think that the popes approved or disapproved of Franco, Mussolini, and Hitler?

f) Should the bishops, pope, and Church have done more to prevent the rise of Fascist governments in Spain, Italy, and Germany?

9) There was a resistance movement in Germany, and, as noted in the student text, members of the resistance tried to assassinate Hitler. Several of the plotters were Catholic. You may have talked with your students about forms of resistance to oppression before, but the attempt on Hitler's life raises some hard questions:

• Hitler was clearly committing horrible acts of barbarity, but if someone took Hitler's life, would he or she be doing something just as barbarous?

• If you were a member of the resistance, would you vote for the assassination attempt on Hitler? Why, or why not?

Actually, you might want to stage a debate on this issue. The class should play the role of members of the German resistance movement; they have come together to decide whether or not to kill Hitler. One side wants to kill him; the other side does not. A team of students can argue each side, and the class can vote on their course of action.

10) A variation of or addition to activity 9 would be to split the class into groups of four or five students. Each group must come up with a plan of action for resisting Hitler. They should pretend to be German resistance members who are determined to overthrow Hitler and his Nazis. They know that they cannot end Fascism completely, but their goal is to cripple Hitler and the Nazis so badly that the war will have to end and that genocide will cease. Obviously, their plans cannot be too detailed, but an outline of actions should emerge. Then, they must be able to justify their actions as being morally consistent with Christianity. After all the groups have finished work, each group should present its plan as if to a resistance meeting. Each plan can be critiqued by the other students.

11) Two Catholics who did resist Hitler were Franz Jägerstätter and Friar Maximilian Kolbe. Students could report on these two people. (For information on Jägerstätter, see Thomas Merton, *Faith and Violence* [Notre Dame, IN: University of Notre Dame Press, 1968].)

Activities for Concept D

In the war with Japan, the Asian countries were devastated. Missionary efforts were put to an end when priests, nuns, brothers, and lay missionaries were either put in internment camps or executed. (Pages 299–300 of the student text.)

Review Questions and Exercises from the Student Text

Question 11: How did Japan's conquest of most of Asia influence the Church?

Answer: Most of the missionaries in Asia were French, British, Dutch, or American—all enemies of Japan. Consequently, they were either executed or imprisoned by the Japanese. After the war and their release, some missionaries were too ill to continue, and some were too old. The war was a serious setback to missionary efforts in Asia.

15

Other Questions and Activities for Discussion

1) Japan's responsibility for the war in the Pacific is undeniable, but the West, especially the United States, contributed to the situation in Japan that propelled the Japanese toward this confrontation. When the U.S. Navy forced Japan to trade with the West, it ended three hundred years of isolation. The Japanese entered into modernizations with all the fervor and discipline that is part of their culture. Soon bright Japanese students were studying armies in Germany, naval strategy in Britain, commerce in the United States, science in France. In short, Japan decided to learn what it could from the "modern" West. Quickly Japan became a mercantile, industrial nation; the standard of living rose; the population figures rose too. Since Japan had few raw materials to feed its industrial growth, it needed to find resources. Japan had to import food too. Subsequently, Japan realized that it would inevitably confront the European colonizers in Asia—especially the British.

Another lesson that Japan learned from the Europeans and Americans was this: if you need land, take it from weaker nations. They saw what France, Britain, Holland, and the United States had done. Having built sophisticated armed forces, Japan was victorious over the Russians, and they took Korea. In addition, Japan believed that it was their destiny to drive the Europeans out of Asia. A group of Japanese politicians believed that colonized Asians would welcome the Japanese if they drove out the European colonizers. Thus, when conditions seemed right—when Britain's presence was weakened in Asia by the war in Europe, France was conquered by Germany, and the United States was still poorly prepared for war—the Japanese put their plan into action. What is important to remember is that while the atrocities of the Japanese forces cannot be overlooked, the policies of colonization and the avaricious way in which European countries and the United States approached Asia contributed to the disasters of the Pacific war.

After an introductory explanation like the comments above, continue by asking these questions:

- Do you see any recent signs of the United States' trying to impose its will on smaller, weaker countries?
- What has ultimately happened historically when a powerful country colonizes or dominates a weaker nation?
- What kind of relationships should countries try to have with one another, especially powerful, developed countries and smaller, poorer countries?
- What Christian principles would help politicians when they consider their relationships with other countries?

2) A good deal of racism was involved in the war with Japan. Many people in the West considered Orientals to be vastly inferior to them; in turn, the Japanese tended to consider westerners to be barbarians, and the Chinese used expressions like Brown Dwarfs to caricature the Japanese. Inevitably this racism manifested itself in the way propaganda was used to denigrate the other side.

Assign a few students to research the anti-Japanese propaganda used during the war; there should be a mass of material on this subject. The students can present a report showing samples of anti-Japanese propaganda. Then ask your students to interview someone who was an adult during World War II about the anti-Japanese feeling. Here are some possible questions for the interviews and for discussion in class:

- Why were people so surprised by the Japanese attack on Pearl Harbor?
- Where were you when you heard the news on the radio?
- Before and during the war, what popular opinions existed about the Japanese as a people?
- Do you think that the United States took Japan seriously enough before the war?
- Did people react as strongly to the Germans as they did to the Japanese?

15

- Were Americans aware that thousands of Japanese-Americans were put into concentration camps for the duration of the war?
- Were there racial overtones to the anti-Japanese propaganda that were not present in anti-Nazi propaganda?
- Did the fact that Japan was a non-Christian nation affect the West's reaction to the Japanese?

3) On a map, point out the extent of the territory that Japan controlled in Asia. Indicate the countries that were heavily Christian and specifically those that were Catholic.

Activities for Concept E

The aftermath of World War II was far worse than that of World War I: the arsenal of war was made immeasurably worse with the addition of the atomic bomb; millions of people had been slaughtered and millions were left starving and homeless; the Soviet Union placed eastern Europe under its domination. In addition, the victors again changed the boundaries of the world, and colonies demanded freedom. Amidst the tragedies and changes, the Church did what it could to serve the needy, make peace, and protect freedom of religion. (Pages 300–304 of the student text.)

Review Questions and Exercises from the Student Text

Question 12: What new problems faced humankind and the Church after World War II?

Answer: After World War II, just the enormity of destruction was a new experience; tens of millions of people had been killed. In this sort of war there were no noncombatants; bombs do not distinguish the innocent from the soldiers. All sorts of new weapons were employed in World War II, but the ultimate destructive instrument was the atomic bomb. A close relationship developed between the military and industry. The Soviet Union now exerted itself as a world power, placing most of eastern Europe under Communist regimes. Boundaries were changed in much of the world once again.

Question 13: What attitudes did Pope Pius XI and Pope Pius XII have about Communism? What did they say to Catholics about Communism?

Answer: Both popes condemned the antireligious thrust of Communism. As the Communists repressed the Church more and more, Pope Pius XII excommunicated any Catholics involved in Communist activities and encouraged anti-Communist resistance.

Question 14: Describe the relationship that has existed between Communism and the Church since World War II. Have there been any signs of change in this relationship?

Answer: The Church has continually condemned the antireligious activities of Communist regimes; the Communists have in turn persecuted Catholics and members of other religions. Only in Poland has the Catholic Church been able to maintain its strength. There are few signs of a change in this tension.

Other Questions and Activities for Discussion

1) One of the results of World War II that still confronts us is the atomic bomb. Perhaps, in the context of this chapter, you could raise these issues with your class:
- Why did the United States drop the atomic bombs on Hiroshima and Nagasaki?
- What effects is this action still having on the world?
- Do you think that those who developed and dropped the bomb knew or thought about all the long-range effects?
- How has the atomic bomb and nuclear warfare influenced the Church?
- What is the position of the Church on nuclear arms?

15

2) Ask your students to compare the treatment of Germany and Japan after World War II to the treatment of Germany after World War I.
- How was the treatment different?
- Which way of treating an enemy seemed to work better?
- Why was the treatment different? Was it more Christian?

3) Students could prepare reports about Cardinal Mindszenty and Archbishop Grosz of Hungary, and Cardinal Stepinac of Yugoslavia: all who suffered at the hands of the Communists. After brief oral reports on these efforts to suppress the Church have been given to the class, discuss this topic with the students:
- Considering what we have been discussing about totalitarian governments, why were the Communists so determined to wipe out the Church in Hungary, Yugoslavia, Czechoslovakia, and other Communist countries?

4) The film *Total War* (National Film Board of Canada, 26 min., black and white) brings an excellent focus on the long-range effects of World War II. In the producer's typically excellent fashion, this film shows how war influences all aspects of life. "Starting with the solemn memories of Flanders Field, it recalls the Europe of the 1930s, the German acceptance of Hitler, the rape of Austria, the capitulation of the French, the struggles of the English, and the suffering of civilians during Hitler's 'War of Terror.'" Also included are some of the questions raised by the use of the atomic bomb. This is an excellent summary of what war does to us. A study guide accompanies the film and is quite helpful. *Total War* is available from the Learning Corporation of America.

Summary Activities for the Chapter

1) As usual, the students should reflect on how they live the models of the Church. In addition, ask them to recall and then record in their journals how they have sought revenge (describing one or two examples), how they felt about doing it, whether it solved anything, what it did to their relationships with others and with God, and how they felt about themselves afterward.

2) If you have not already used these questions for daily quizzes, distribute to the class Student Handout 15–A, "Quiz on Chapter 15" (found at the end of this chapter). The answers for the quiz are as follows:

1) d	10) c	19) a	28) b
2) b	11) c	20) d	29) c
3) d	12) d	21) b	30) c
4) c	13) a	22) a	31) a
5) a	14) d	23) a	32) a
6) d	15) b	24) b	33) a
7) b	16) a	25) a	
8) c	17) b	26) d	
9) b	18) b	27) c	

15

3) Student Handout 15-B, "Prayer Service: For Strength in the Face of Evil" (found at the end of this chapter), can be used to close the study of this unit. The two readings on the handout are by Rev. Dietrich Bonhoeffer and Fr. Alfred Delp, SJ—both of whom were executed by the Nazis in 1945 for their resistance activities. These selections are taken from the meditations they wrote while awaiting execution. Bonhoeffer and Delp were both persons of hope, faith, and love.

Songs that might be used in this prayer service include "If God Is for Us" by John Foley, in *Glory and Praise,* vol. 1 (Phoenix: North American Liturgy Resources, 1977), and "Let There Be Peace on Earth" by Sy Miller and Jill Jackson.

15

Quiz on Chapter 15

_____ 1) Which one of these was not newly used in World War I? **(a)** airplanes **(b)** submarines **(c)** poisonous gas **(d)** repeating rifles

_____ 2) Which of these countries was not involved in World War I? **(a)** Japan **(b)** Thailand **(c)** Turkey **(d)** Italy

_____ 3) Pope Benedict XV took a position **(a)** against Germany **(b)** against Britain **(c)** for the Allies **(d)** that the war was unjustified.

_____ 4) The United States entered the First World War when **(a)** Russia took sides with Germany **(b)** Japan attacked Russia **(c)** a German submarine sank the _Lusitania_ **(d)** Britain entered the war.

_____ 5) While World War I was raging, Russia **(a)** was having a civil war **(b)** suffered a famine **(c)** remained neutral **(d)** sent troops to take Finland.

_____ 6) The treaty to end World War I was called the Treaty of **(a)** Berlin **(b)** Brussels **(c)** Yalta **(d)** Versailles.

_____ 7) After the treaty, Pope Benedict warned the Allies that **(a)** Germany should be further humbled **(b)** the treaty would cause the Germans to seek revenge **(c)** the Vatican did not receive enough reparations **(d)** Ireland would be a German ally.

_____ 8) This country emerged as a power to be reckoned with after World War I: **(a)** Turkey **(b)** China **(c)** Japan **(d)** Sweden.

_____ 9) One result of the First World War was that Britain and France **(a)** renewed the tension between each other **(b)** slipped in their control over their colonies **(c)** became even stronger **(d)** gained trading partners.

_____ 10) The 1920s were called the **(a)** Anxious Twenties **(b)** Silly Twenties **(c)** Roaring Twenties **(d)** Rowdy Twenties.

_____ 11) Darwin's theory of "survival of the fittest" was used to justify **(a)** Communism **(b)** Fascism **(c)** capitalism **(d)** socialism.

_____ 12) The father of psychology is considered to be **(a)** Jung **(b)** Fromm **(c)** Frankl **(d)** Freud.

_____ 13) Some early psychologists taught that religion was unhealthy because **(a)** guilt led to anxiety **(b)** it was the opiate of the masses **(c)** it required faith **(d)** it was old-fashioned.

_____ 14) When a country is controlled by a single party that is dedicated to one ideology and that dominates all aspects of life it lives under a government ruled by **(a)** capitalism **(b)** pluralism **(c)** oligarchy **(d)** totalitarianism.

_____ 15) Communism calls for the establishment of **(a)** a dictatorship by a small group of managers **(b)** a workers' revolution that would set up a workers' state **(c)** free elections **(d)** a clear class structure.

_____ 16) In the Soviet Union, Christians were **(a)** denied jobs because of their religion **(b)** free to worship without harm **(c)** executed on sight **(d)** allowed to migrate.

_____ 17) Fascism stresses **(a)** rule by the masses of workers **(b)** rule by a special class or race **(c)** free trade **(d)** freedom for the oppressed.

_____ 18) Mussolini made an uneasy peace with the Church when he signed the **(a)** Vatican Accord **(b)** Lateran Agreement **(c)** Treaty of Rome **(d)** Geneva Convention.

_____ 19) Pope Pius XI publicly criticized absolutist states that controlled all aspects of life in his encyclical **(a)** _Quadragesimo Anno_ **(b)** _Rerum Novarum_ **(c)** _Pacem in Terris_ **(d)** _Urbi et Orbi._

_____ 20) Italians invaded this country despite the pope's criticisms: **(a)** Dalmatia **(b)** Morocco **(c)** Bulgaria **(d)** Ethiopia.

_____ 21) Francisco Franco's Nationalists were actually **(a)** Communists **(b)** Fascists **(c)** Theists **(d)** Republicans.

_____ 22) During the Spanish Civil War, many priests and religious were killed by the **(a)** Communists **(b)** Nationalists **(c)** Fascists **(d)** Misogynists.

_____ 23) In regard to the German Nazis, Pope Pius XI **(a)** condemned them in _Mit Brennender Sorge_ **(b)** excommunicated them all **(c)** wanted an alliance **(d)** was scared into inaction.

_____ 24) Hitler gained power in Germany by promising the German people **(a)** free speech **(b)** a return of national pride **(c)** colonies in Asia **(d)** no taxation on staple goods.

_____ 25) The Jews were used by Hitler as scapegoats because **(a)** they were non-Aryan **(b)** no one would care **(c)** they were economically weak **(d)** they were Communists.

_____ 26) Hitler suppressed the Church by **(a)** jailing all the bishops **(b)** excluding Catholics from the army **(c)** forming Catholic trade unions **(d)** closing all Catholic presses.

_____ 27) Edith Stein was sent to a concentration camp because **(a)** she was a nun **(b)** she was in the underground **(c)** she was Jewish by birth **(d)** she was a gypsy.

_____ 28) The Kreisau Circle was a group who **(a)** provided secret information to Hitler from within the United States **(b)** planned to end Hitler's rule **(c)** played chess with the popes **(d)** led anti-Jewish rallies in Germany.

_____ 29) Japan opened up to the rest of the world because **(a)** the emperor wanted more land **(b)** the Chinese signed a trade treaty with them **(c)** U.S. warships forced them to **(d)** Teddy Roosevelt made a special deal with them.

_____ 30) The war with Japan was brought to a close when **(a)** the emperor was killed **(b)** the United States took Okinawa **(c)** atomic bombs were dropped on Hiroshima and Nagasaki **(d)** Tojo was deposed.

_____ 31) Pope Pius XII was recognized as a hero, in part because **(a)** his efforts saved four hundred thousand Jews **(b)** he stayed neutral **(c)** he supported Mussolini **(d)** he fought in the underground resistance.

_____ 32) Which of these countries was not placed under the power of the Soviet Union after World War II? **(a)** Austria **(b)** Hungary **(c)** Poland **(d)** Czechoslovakia

_____ 33) The Soviet Union opposed Catholicism because it **(a)** was a rival ideology **(b)** owned lots of land **(c)** supported capitalism **(d)** opposed Orthodoxy.

Prayer Service:
For Strength in the Face of Evil

Opening Hymn

Leader: We are frequently confronted with evil. How do we find strength in evil times? This question has perplexed all serious Christians from the beginning. We will listen to two readings today, one by a Lutheran pastor and the other by a Jesuit priest—both were Germans executed by the Nazis in 1945 for their nonviolent resistance activities. These meditations were written in prison right before their executions. Let us remember that we are in God's presence and ask for openness to the will of God.

Reading from Rev. Dietrich Bonhoeffer's *Letters and Papers from Prison:*

Reader: . . . I discovered and am still discovering up to this very moment that it is only by living completely in this world that one learns to believe. . . . This is what I mean by worldliness—taking life in one's stride, with all its duties and problems, its successes and failures, its experiences and helplessness. It is in such a life that we throw ourselves utterly in the arms of God and participate in his sufferings in the world and watch with Christ in Gethsemane. That is faith, . . . and that is what makes a man and a Christian (cf. Jeremiah 45). How can success make us arrogant or failure lead us astray, when we participate in the sufferings of God by living in this world?

(Pause for reflection.)

Reading from Fr. Alfred Delp's *Prison Meditations:*

Reader: But one thing is gradually becoming clear—I must surrender myself completely. This is seed-time, not harvest. God sows the seed and some time or other he will do the reaping. The one thing I must do is to make sure the seed falls on fertile ground. And I must arm myself against the pain and depression that sometimes almost defeat me. If this is the way God has chosen—and everything indicates that it is—then I must willingly and without rancour make it my way. May others at some future time find it possible to have a better and happier life because we died in this hour of trial.

I ask my friends not to mourn, but to pray for me and help me as long as I have need of help. And to be quite clear in their own minds that I was sacrificed, not conquered. It never occurred to me that my life would end like this. I had spread my sails to the wind and set my course for a great voyage, flags flying, ready to brave every storm that blew. But it could be they were false flags or my course wrongly set or the ship a pirate and its cargo contraband. I don't know. And I will not sink to cheap jibes at the world in order to raise my spirits. To be quite honest I don't want to die, particularly now that I feel I could do more important work and deliver a new message about values I have only just discovered and understood. But it has turned out otherwise. God keep me in his providence and give me strength to meet what is before me.

"Prayers in Time of Distress" by Rev. Dietrich Bonhoeffer

All:

O Lord God,
Great is the misery that has come upon me;
My cares would overwhelm me,
I know not what to do.
O God, be gracious unto me and help me.
Grant me strength to bear what thou dost send,
and let not fear rule over me.
As a loving Father, take care of my loved ones. . . .

O merciful God, forgive me all
the sins I have committed against thee,
and against my fellowmen.
I trust in thy grace, and commit my
life wholly into thy hands,
Do with me as seemeth best to thee, and as
is best for me.
Whether I live or die, I am with thee,
and thou art with me, my God.
Lord, I wait for thy salvation,
and for thy Kingdom.
Amen.

Closing Hymn

CHAPTER 16

The Church Now and in the Future

Major Concepts

A. Despite many obstacles, the Church has grown vigorously in Asia, Africa, and South America. All these areas suffer from a shortage of priests, various levels of oppression from governments, and some conflict between Catholics who fight for the poor and those who maintain the status quo.

B. Vatican Council II, initiated by Pope John XXIII, moved the Church to respond to the times through liturgical renewal, the Church's reaching a new understanding of itself, ecumenism, a new historical perspective, and dialogue with the world.

C. The future of the Church will be created by us, inspired by true Christians like Dorothy Day and Mother Teresa. The Church will continue to be Herald, Servant, Institution, Sacrament, and People of God.

Activities for Concept A

Despite many obstacles, the Church has grown vigorously in Asia, Africa, and South America. All these areas suffer from a shortage of priests, various levels of oppression from governments, and some conflict between Catholics who fight for the poor and those who maintain the status quo. (Pages 308–314 of the student text.)

Review Questions and Exercises from the Student Text

Question 1: What problems affected the missionary work in the young churches? Why is the term *young churches* used?

Answer: When colonies became independent from European countries, in some cases, there was a strong rejection of foreigners and foreign influences. Since missionaries were mostly foreigners, in some places they were expelled from newly independent nations. Thus, shortages in liturgical ministers became a problem. With the terrible examples of genocide and total war following World Wars I and II, the credibility of Christianity as a peacemaking religion was undermined: how could Christians be so brutal and barbarous to one another? The scandalous scene of Christian sects arguing among themselves left many people confused. Finally, the stress on individualism in the West seemed to run counter to the need for social change in many developing countries.

The churches in Asia, Africa, and South America are called "young churches" because they have only recently been established by local clergy and bishops, with their own unique styles replacing the forms instituted by the foreign missionaries.

Question 2: The missionary effort in Asia has been hampered by certain factors unique to Asia. What are some of those factors?

Answer: In Burma, China, Vietnam, Laos, and Cambodia, Communist governments have hampered the work of the Church. Islamic countries like Indonesia, Malaysia, and Pakistan have placed restrictions on Christian activities. Moreover, many

Asians think that Christianity is a "Western" religion and that becoming westernized is tantamount to accepting something foreign and inferior.

Question 3: The conversions in Africa have been very encouraging. Why have the missionaries had such success there? What problems are unique to Africa?

Answer: The African culture has always nurtured a deeply religious spirit among its people. Many Africans were evangelized while attending Christian mission schools. However, during independence movements in some African countries, missionaries were expelled from the former colonies along with representatives of the colonial governments. Illiteracy is a large problem, as are polygamy and unstable governments; these difficulties hamper the work of the Church in Africa.

Question 4: South and Central America are the most Catholic regions in the world. However, significant difficulties plague the Church in these regions. What are some of these? How has the Church's role in South and Central America changed over the years?

Answer: After the colonies' independence in the 1800s, there were few priests to serve the people. Spanish missionaries were then replaced with missionaries from other European or North American countries. Oppressive regimes have succeeded each other in many countries; the common people are all too often kept illiterate, poor, and powerless. Even though the Church has come, more and more, to the aid of the poor, in doing so, church leaders have become targets of attacks by those wishing to protect the status quo. Basic Christian Communities have been established in many dioceses all over South and Central America; these provide spiritual, emotional, and practical aid to their members.

Other Questions and Activities for Discussion

1) Most dioceses in North America have missions somewhere in the world where laypersons, religious, and priests work. Find out where the mission is for your diocese. Through contacts with someone in the mission or with someone in the diocesan office, have a student gather information about what sort of work the diocese sponsors there, what needs the mission has, and so on. Then your class might sponsor a drive to help the mission.

2) If your school is administered by a religious order, ask someone from the order to talk with your class about the order's missions. And again, your class could mount a campaign to help these missions.

3) Assign one country in Africa, Asia, South, or Central America to each student, who should prepare a very brief (about two-minute) report on Catholicism in that country. Each report should provide an overview of the following information: numbers of Catholics, priests, religious, lay workers; church-sponsored institutions serving the people; problems facing the Church. Be sure each student points out his or her country on the map before the report. The *Catholic Almanac* is the most current source of this information, but the *Catholic Encyclopedia* is also useful.

4) Send for some information from the Jesuit Volunteer Corps, the Maryknoll program, or the Catholic Extension office. Each of these groups has excellent programs for lay, religious, or clerical volunteers who work in the young churches for a short period of time. While these agencies only want college graduates, you might be planting seeds in the minds of your students.

5) The film *The Empty Cup* (TeleKETICS, 17 min., color), examines the role of the missionary today. In a mountain town in the Andes, a U.S. priest arrives full of ideas and energy and with the conviction that he can make a lot of improvements. When everything that he wants to do seems to meet with slowdowns and even resistance, he becomes frustrated. Through his contact with a dying man, he learns to listen patiently to the poor people he is trying to serve and to accept the wisdom they have. With his newfound appreciation, he is finally able to serve effectively. This well-photographed film comes with a useful study guide.

6) Another movie worth showing is *The Eye of the Camel,* an Insight film from Paulist Productions, available through Audience Planners (28 min., color or black and white). Father Luis helps parishioners organize a strike against a factory owner who is exploiting the workers. Meanwhile, the factory owner makes a donation to the bishop to set up a barrio clinic. The bishop is asked to calm Father Luis and remind him that his business is the souls of his people. The bishop is committed to helping the barrio, but also to maintaining the status quo. While breaking the strike, the police kill Father Luis and three workers. The bishop sees that he must act; he sells his residence, moves into the barrio, and joins the strikers. The film, even if somewhat dated, rather effectively points out the dilemmas facing the Church, especially in South and Central America. It could help students understand the stance of religious people in countries like Guatemala, El Salvador, and the Philippines. The film has a study guide with helpful questions for discussion.

7) Instruct the students to search newspapers and magazines from the last few weeks for articles and pictures about persecution of Christians or conflict between church and state—especially in Asia, Africa, and South America. In places like South Africa, El Salvador, and Chile, the Church is struggling on the side of the poor who are frequently oppressed not only by their own dictatorships but also by the U.S. government that supports these dictatorships. Students need to be aware of the role that developed countries play in the suppression of people in Third World countries.

Activities for Concept B
Vatican Council II, initiated by Pope John XXIII, moved the Church to respond to the times through liturgical renewal, the Church's reaching a new understanding of itself, ecumenism, a new historical perspective, and dialogue with the world. (Pages 314–317 of the student text.)

Review Questions and Exercises from the Student Text

Question 5: Explain the major areas of renewal promoted by the Second Vatican Council. Think of some examples of how the council has influenced members of your family. Perhaps interview your parents or some adult friends and relatives. Ask them how Vatican II changed many of the practices of Catholicism. Try to gather as many opinions and feelings as you can about the effects of the council.

Answer: Vatican Council II focused on five main areas of renewal: (*a*) liturgical worship underwent many changes; (*b*) the Church placed new emphasis on the Church as the People of God instead of on its institutional role; (*c*) the ecumenical movement initiated dialogue with other Christian groups and with non-Christians in order to achieve better understanding and establish better mutual cooperation; (*d*) a sense of history informed many of the deliberations of the council; and, (*e*) the council opened up avenues of discussion with all sectors of the modern world.

Other Questions and Activities for Discussion

1) To demonstrate the continuity in church tradition, have your students reread Pope John's words (on p. 59 of the student text) with which he convened Vatican Council II. Remind them that councils have always been used to settle problems in the Church, to renew the spirit of the people, and to respond to new developments or challenges in the world. You might also review some decisions from other councils that have shaped the Church.

2) Guest speakers would be appropriate to discuss Vatican II. For example: the diocesan director of liturgy could explain many of the renewed practices in worship; the diocesan director of ecumenism could outline what is being done to bring more harmony between Christian groups.

3) Perhaps one of the most obvious ways in which the Church is in dialogue with the modern world is the travels of Pope John Paul II and indeed those of Pope Paul VI too. Ask some students to bring in clippings or photocopies of articles about the pope's recent journeys. Then discuss these questions:
- What seems to be the purpose of the pope's trips?
- Is it more important for the pope to stay at the Vatican and administer the Church or to be out on these trips?
- What good seems to come from his trips?
- Do you think that the pope is able to really meet the common people and find out what they are feeling and thinking? Is it possible at all for him to do this?
- If you had five minutes alone with the pope, what would you tell him or ask him? Why?
- If the Church is to dialogue with the modern world, is it important that the Church stay aware of developments in science, technology, sociology, and psychology? Why, or why not? Give some examples to support your conclusions.

4) Here is an activity that should help reveal some concerns that your students have about the Church and the world. Tell your students to write down in their journals an agenda of at least five points for Vatican Council III. They are to imagine themselves to be representatives to this council (maybe at the next council there will be a significant lay representation). The agenda items can be in the form of questions or statements, but they must represent the most pressing issues facing the Church at this time.

After each student has written his or her list, form the class into groups of four or five students. Each group is to decide on an agenda for Vatican Council III, ranking the issues from 1 (the most important issue) to 5 (the least important issue). One member from each group should write their agenda on the chalkboard and explain why the group chose the items they did and ranked them in the order they did. When all have finished, point out common concerns between the groups and compose one class agenda. Discuss the implications of each point.

Activities for Concept C

The future of the Church will be created by us, inspired by true Christians like Dorothy Day and Mother Teresa. The Church will continue to be Herald, Servant, Institution, Sacrament, and People of God. (Pages 317–323 of the student text.)

Review Questions and Exercises from the Student Text

Question 6: In many ways, the Church reflects the models of Herald, Servant, Institution, People of God, and Sacrament as well today as it ever did. How so? List some examples of how the Church models itself in the world today.

Answer: As Herald, the Church is spreading the Word all over the globe through preaching, printing presses, translations of the Bible and other religious materials, and radio and television programs. The Servant Church has never been more obvious; through religious orders and lay associations and groups like the Catholic Worker, people are being served as Christ would serve them. The Institutional Church has reformed itself from being a bureaucracy tied to preserving itself to being much more a source of help for the mission of the Church. As communities of Christians are being built through ecumenism, Basic Christian Communities, and other activities, the Church is becoming more clearly the People of God and Sacrament.

Personal Reflection Exercise

Reflect back over the whole history of the Church as presented in this book. What images, events, and people did you find most inspiring, most worthy of imitation? In what ways has the Church remained the same throughout history? Has the Church played a vital role in the development of humankind? Will the Church play an important part in the future? List ways in which you see yourself being part of the Church in the future.

Other Questions and Activities for Discussion

1) Bring to class some copies of *The Catholic Worker* or just clippings and artwork from it. Distribute these among the class members. Tell the students to read through or study the materials and to be able to summarize what the messages of the articles or pictures are. Ask the students to report on what they learned from their portions of *The Catholic Worker*. Then ask these questions:
- Given the ideas that we have discussed from this newspaper started by Dorothy Day, what sort of issues was she most concerned about?
- If you lived the way these articles indicate, what sort of life would you have? What sort of world would we build?

2) If there is a Catholic Worker house in your city or town, ask a member of the community there to tell your class about life in a Catholic Worker house. Even better, plan a field trip to a Catholic Worker house.

3) The film *Everyone, Everywhere* (TeleKETICS, 11 min., color) is highly recommended. This very effective movie juxtaposes pictures of the Missionaries of Charity working in India, England, and the United States with film of Mother Teresa speaking about the challenges of seeing the poor in all persons who are alienated, lonely, suffering, or abandoned. She reminds us that we are all called to be missionaries—no

matter where we work or live. This would be a very useful film to accompany the discussions of the student text material on Mother Teresa (see pp. 320–322), or it could be worked into the final prayer service.

4) Have your students write down their prayers for the Church. Each prayer should be three sentences long. The first sentence should be a petition asking God to do something for the Church. The second sentence should praise God for some aspect of the Church. The final sentence should be a prayer of personal thanksgiving for some blessing God has granted the individual. Each student can be asked to share his or her prayer during the final prayer service.

Summary Activities for the Chapter

1) The students might complete the personal reflection exercise on page 324 of the student text as a summary activity to be recorded in their journals.

2) If you have not already used these questions for daily quizzes, distribute to the class Student Handout 16-A, "Quiz on Chapter 16" (found at the end of this chapter). The answers to the quiz are as follows:

1) c	5) c	9) a	13) a
2) b	6) a	10) d	14) a
3) a	7) c	11) c	
4) d	8) b	12) c	

3) The final, class prayer service is a chance to meditate on our role in the Church and to pray for the Church. There is no student handout for this service. Instead, students should have their journals opened to their responses to the personal reflection exercise for this chapter and to the prayers they wrote for the Church (see concept C, activity 4).

You might wish to open and close the prayer service with one of these hymns: "If God Is for Us" by John Foley, and "Play Before the Lord" by Bob Dufford, in vol. 1; or "City of God" and "Here I Am, Lord" by Daniel Schutte, in vol. 3 of *Glory and Praise* (Phoenix: North American Liturgy Resources, 1977, 1982).

After opening with a song, remind the class that God is present in their midst. Then ask the students to share their reflections about the following topics:
- What images, events, and people have you found most inspiring, most worthy of imitation?
- What role has the Church played in humankind's development?
- What roles will the Church play in the future?

Give the students time to meditate on this question:
- In what ways do you see yourself being a part of the Church in the future?

Then ask them to share their prayers for the Church, and close with a song.

Quiz on Chapter 16

_____ 1) In places where the Church is newly independent of foreign church leaders, it is called **(a)** an independent church **(b)** a free church **(c)** a young church **(d)** a Third World church.

_____ 2) Many former colonies lost their respect for and awe of their colonizers' moral or cultural superiority because of **(a)** the colonizers' religious policies **(b)** World Wars I and II **(c)** Communism **(d)** capitalism.

_____ 3) One source of confusion about missionaries among non-Christians was **(a)** the infighting among various Christian sects **(b)** the clothing they wore **(c)** different languages **(d)** musical tastes.

_____ 4) Most of Asia's Christians live in **(a)** Malaysia **(b)** Indonesia **(c)** Korea **(d)** the Philippines.

_____ 5) The unification of this country under a Communist government has hampered church activities: **(a)** Thailand **(b)** Korea **(c)** Vietnam **(d)** Taiwan.

_____ 6) People who converted to Christianity because missionaries gave them food were called **(a)** rice Christians **(b)** the fallen **(c)** apostates **(d)** traitor Christians.

_____ 7) This Communist leader unified the peasants to overthrow the government of China: **(a)** Yuan Shih **(b)** Moo Goo Gai Pan **(c)** Mao Tse-tung **(d)** Wylie Chua.

_____ 8) One difficulty facing the African Church is **(a)** polysynchronicity **(b)** polygamy **(c)** philandering **(d)** philanthropy.

_____ 9) One reason there are so few native clergy in South America is that **(a)** for centuries the Spanish king forbade the ordination of native clergy **(b)** there was little desire on the part of local people to become priests **(c)** most people refused Catholicism **(d)** the popes did not want local clerics.

_____ 10) One source of great aid to the poor Catholics of South America is the **(a)** hacienderos **(b)** totalitarian governments of people like Pinochet **(c)** U.S. support of oppressive regimes **(d)** Basic Christian Communities.

_____ 11) By the year 2000, it is estimated that roughly this percentage of Catholics will live in Third World countries: **(a)** 30 percent **(b)** 50 percent **(c)** 70 percent **(d)** 90 percent.

_____ 12) This pope convened Vatican Council II: **(a)** Pius XII **(b)** Paul VI **(c)** John XXIII **(d)** John Paul I.

_____ 13) Attempts to reach a better understanding between different faiths is called **(a)** ecumenism **(b)** ecclesialism **(c)** euphonianism **(d)** cacophony.

_____ 14) One decision that helped open the Church to the world was when Vatican Council II **(a)** eliminated the Index of Forbidden Books **(b)** allowed audiences with the pope **(c)** opened its own post office **(d)** installed telephones in the Vatican.

Acknowledgments (*continued*)

The scriptural excerpts on pages 40, 51, and 148 are from The Jerusalem Bible, published and copyright © 1966, 1967, and 1968 by Darton, Longman & Todd, Ltd., London, and Doubleday & Company, Inc., New York. Reprinted by permission of the publishers.

The prayer on page 61 and the two prayers on page 99 are from *Early Christian Prayers*, edited by A. Hamman (Chicago: Henry Regnery Co., 1961). Used with permission.

The excerpts by Saint Basil and by Saint Ambrose on page 111 are from *The Faith of the Early Fathers*, vol. 2, translated by W. A. Jurgens (Collegeville, MN: The Liturgical Press, 1970). Used with permission.

The excerpts by Saint Jerome on pages 111–112 are from *Selections from St. Jerome: The Satirical Letters of St. Jerome*, translated by Paul Carroll (Chicago: Gateway Editions, 1956). Used with permission of Regnery Gateway Inc.

The excerpt by Saint Augustine on page 113 is from *Saint Augustine: Letters*, vol. 5, translated by Sister Wilfrid Parsons, SND (New York: Fathers of the Church, 1956). Used with permission.

The excerpts by Saint Ambrose and by Saint Patrick on page 116 are from *A Treasury of Early Christianity*, edited by Anne Fremantle (New York: The New American Library, 1960).

The excerpt by Saint Augustine on page 116 is from *St. Augustine: Sermons for Christmas and Epiphany*, translated by Thomas Comerford Lawler (Westminster, MD: The Newman Press, 1952). Used with permission.

The passages on pages 127–128 are from *History of the Franks* by Gregory, Bishop of Tours, translated by Ernest Brehaut (New York: Octagon Books, 1965). © 1916, Columbia University Press. By permission.

The text of the English canons on page 129 is from *Code of Canon Law, Latin-English Edition*, © copyright 1983 by Canon Law Society of America. Used with permission.

The selections on page 130 are from *The Koran*, translated from the Arabic by J. M. Rodwell (New York: Dutton, 1963). Used with permission.

The psalms on pages 133, 148–149, and 242–243 are from *Psalms Anew: A Non-Sexist Edition* by Maureen Leach, OSF, and Nancy Schreck, OSF (Dubuque: The Sisters of Saint Francis, 1984).

The excerpts on page 139 are reprinted with permission from *A New Look at the Sacraments*, original edition copyright 1977, in revised and expanded edition copyright 1983 by William J. Bausch (paper, 288 pages, $5.95) and published by Twenty-Third Publications, Mystic, CT 06355.

The selections on page 143 are from *Early Lives of Charlemagne* by Eginhard and the Monk of St. Gall, translated by A. J. Grant (New York: Cooper Square Publishers, 1966).

The scene on pages 144–145 is adapted from *Charlemagne: The Legend and the Man* by Harold Lamb (New York: Bantam Books, 1954). Copyright © 1954 by Harold Lamb. Reprinted by permission of Doubleday & Company, Inc.

The scene on pages 160–161 is from *Seven Miracle Plays* by Alexander Franklin (Oxford: Oxford University Press, 1963). Used with permission.

The scene on pages 162–163 is reprinted by permission of the Putnam Publishing Group from *Becket; Or, the Honour of God* by Jean Anouilh, translated by Lucienne Hill. Copyright © 1960 by Jean Anouilh and Lucienne Hill. Reprinted also by permission of Michael Imison Playwrights Limited.

The dialogue on pages 164–165 is reprinted with the permission of Macmillan Publishing Company from *Characters of the Inquisition* by William T. Walsh. Copyright 1940 by Macmillan Publishing Company.

The description on page 180 is from *A Distant Mirror: The Calamitous 14th Century* by Barbara W. Tuchman (New York: Alfred A. Knopf, 1978). Used with permission.

The eyewitness account on page 180, the three tales on page 185, and the two passages on page 201 are from *Translations and Reprints from the Original Sources of European History*, vol. 2 (Philadelphia: University of Pennsylvania Press, n.d.). Used with permission.

The lyrics on page 181 are from *Carmina Burana* by Carl Orff. Copyright 1953 by Associated Music Publishers, Inc., New York.

The scenes on pages 183–184 are from *Savonarola* by Urban Nagle, in *Theatre for Tomorrow: Three New Plays* (London: Longmans, Green and Co., 1940).

The passage on page 186 is from *The Canterbury Tales of Geoffrey Chaucer*, translated by R. M. Lumiansky. Copyright © 1948, 1975 by Simon & Schuster, Inc. Reprinted by permission of Simon & Schuster, Inc.

The letter on pages 192–193 is from *Martin Luther: Selections from His Writings*, edited by John Dillenberger (Garden City, NY: Doubleday & Company, 1961). Copyright © 1957 by Muhlenburg Press. Used by permission of Fortress Press.

The scenes on pages 202–203 are from *Luther* by John Osborne, in *The Best Plays of 1963–1964*, edited by Henry Hewes (New York: Dodd, Mead & C 1964). Used with permission.